A NEW SCIENCE OF INTERNATIONAL RELATIONS

For Amelia and Leticia Monteiro Popolo,
Os Meus Olhos Enormes

A New Science of International Relations

Modernity, Complexity and the Kosovo Conflict

DAMIAN POPOLO
Lancaster University, UK

Routledge
Taylor & Francis Group
LONDON AND NEW YORK

First published 2011 by Ashgate Publishing

2 Park Square, Milton Park, Abingdon, Oxfordshire OX14 4RN
711 Third Avenue, New York, NY 10017

Routledge is an imprint of the Taylor & Francis Group, an informa business

First issued in paperback 2018

British Library Cataloguing in Publication Data
Popolo, Damian.
A new science of international relations : modernity, complexity and the Kosovo conflict.
1. International relations--Philosophy. 2. Complexity (Philosophy) 3. Epistemics. 4. Kosovo War, 1998-1999. 5. Intervention (International law) 6. Operation Allied Force, 1999. 7. Foucault, Michel, 1926-1984.
I. Title
327.1'01-dc22

Library of Congress Cataloging-in-Publication Data
Popolo, Damian.
A new science of international relations : modernity, complexity and the Kosovo conflict / Damian Popolo.
p. cm.
Includes bibliographical references and index.
ISBN 978-1-4094-1226-7 (hardback)
1. International relations--Decision making 2. Complexity (Philosophy) 3. Foucault, Michel, 1926-1984--Political and social views. 4. Kosovo War, 1998-1999--Diplomatic history. 5. Kosovo (Republic)--Politics and government--1980-2008.
I. Title.
JZ1253.P67 2010
327.101--dc22

2010043187

ISBN 978-1-4094-1226-7 (hbk)
ISBN 978-1-138-37969-5 (pbk)

Contents

List of Figures and Tables

Figures

Table

PART 1
Complexity, Modernity and International Relations Theory

Introduction

> Here one is reminded of a somewhat modified expression of Proudhon's: whoever invokes humanity is trying to cheat. To confiscate the word humanity, to invoke and monopolize such a term probably has certain incalculable effects, such as denying the enemy the quality of being human and declaring him to be an outlaw of humanity.
>
> Carl Schmitt, *The Concept of the Political*[1]

> Once, after the father of metaphysics had expounded his theory of forms using neologisms such as 'tablehood' and 'cuphood', Diogenes responded: "Plato, table and cup I see, but your 'tablehood' and 'cuphood' – no way". This story resembles the occasion when Plato deployed his vaunted method of collection and division to define man as a 'featherless biped', and Diogenes produced a plucked chicken as a counterexample saying, "Here is Plato's man!"
>
> Robert Bracht Branham, "Defacing the Currency: Diogenes' Rhetoric and the Invention of Cynicism"[2]

This book is primarily about substantiating a number of interrelated claims, which, taken together, can provide the basis for the establishment of new approaches in the study of International Relations (IR). The main claims, or hypotheses, are summarised below.

First, IR as a discipline was constituted according to the rules of what Foucault described as the modern episteme. In this intellectual framework, metaphysics and transcendentalism characterise ways in which knowledge on any particular issue is generated and deployed. Second, IR, as with many other disciplines in the social sciences, based its claims to scientific knowledge on methods and epistemologies derived from the natural sciences. These epistemologies have been rendered obsolete following the emergence of Complexity science. Third, the metaphysics inherent within IR theory can be detected in the practice of IR, and these broadly underpin the ways in which conflict – in this case the Kosovo conflict – is understood and acted upon. The metaphysics in the theory and practice of IR

1 Carl Schmitt, *The Concept of the Political* (Chicago: Chicago University Press, 1996), 54.

2 Robert Bracht Branham, "Defacing the Currency: Diogenes' Rhetoric and the Invention of Cynicism", in *The Cynics: The Cynic Movement in Antiquity and its Legacy*, eds, Robert Bracht Branham and Marie-Odile Goulet-Cazé (Berkeley: University of California Press, 1997), 88.

are mutually constituted. Fourth, the importance of Complexity as an approach to knowledge that supersedes the rules of the modern episteme needs to be fully outlined before new approaches to knowledge based on Complexity-inspired ideas can be established.

Complexity can indeed provide alternative paths to the understanding of IR theory, practice and of conflict, but it needs to be given a solid theoretical basis first, and this is what Foucault's description of epistemes provides. Foucault's analysis is particularly relevant, as it is in itself the extension of a long French tradition in the philosophy of science, which focuses largely on the construction of European scientific thought. Foucault's background in the philosophy of science and the relevance of French, and more broadly Continental, philosophical traditions for an understanding of Complexity's origins will be outlined throughout the book. In particular, Chapter 1 will demonstrate that key Complexity theorists were inspired by the likes of Bergson and Goethe: this has serious implications for how we understand Complexity in the context of Western philosophy, and for contemporary debates on the nature of Complexity.

A very relevant example of transcendental thinking relates to the idea of 'humankind' as an abstract essence, which is, in turn, essential for the formulation of concepts such as 'Humanitarian Intervention'. Events surrounding the Kosovo conflict have often been characterised as a (welcome) example of just such type of intervention. Yet, as the introductory quotes above suggest, notions such as 'humanity' and 'humankind' are not uncontroversial. Whilst Carl Schmitt worried about the political consequences of deploying these terms, Diogenes of Sinope – the founder of Greek Cynicism – denied that notions such as 'tablehood', 'cuphood' and, by extension, 'humankind', make any sense at all. In reality, the crux of any argument regarding the possibility of analysing the political can be discerned in this very early opposition between the father of (transcendental) political philosophy and the father of cynicism: can we think beyond the immanent reality of the human condition, into the realm of the transcendental, and if we can, what are the consequences of doing so?[3]

In this context this study is also an attempt at exploring what makes such transcendental understandings of 'humankind' possible, how these understandings come about, what role they play in the generation and deployment of knowledge, what the consequences of adopting such terms in political reasoning are and, finally, how these notions can be challenged through a critical understanding of Complexity science. The research is based on three pillars that allow the issues above to be addressed. The first pillar is provided by Michel Foucault's analysis of epistemic fluctuations, which reveal – amongst other things – the conceptual and

---

3 Indeed, Alfred North Whitehead famously suggested that the entire Western philosophical tradition is but a footnote to Plato. Since Plato is also referred to as the father of metaphysics, it is relatively simple to discern in the origin of this metaphysical tradition – and in the opposition to such tradition – the fundamental questions for all political philosophy.

historical roots of a very modern approach to metaphysical knowledge, that is, the sort of knowledge that allows for notions such as 'humankind' and, by extension, of 'humanitarian intervention' to make sense. The second pillar is an epistemic understanding of how modern IR theory (and practice) was constructed. The third pillar is constituted by a Foucauldian analysis of Complexity science as an approach to knowledge that fundamentally undermines any modern, metaphysical analysis of human relations: this will allow the crucial differences between Complexity and current metaphysical approaches in IR (the second pillar) to be fully visible. Finally, the Kosovo conflict will be presented as a case study which will outline the practical implications and consequences of, for example, classifying humans through the metaphysical notions of 'humanity', 'ethnicity', or, as it happens, 'featherless bipedalism'. Such a case study will also present the ways in which IR theory and practice approached the conflict from an essentially metaphysical perspective.

The present work thus emerges out of three questions.

Three Research Questions

1. In what way can the emergence of what we loosely refer to as 'Complexity Theory' enhance our understanding of social affairs generally, and of IR in particular?
2. Why is the Kosovo conflict a particularly good example of illustrating the role that Complexity can have in enhancing such understanding? To what extent can we speak of a new Complexity-based *episteme* as a break from the current configuration of knowledge?
3. What epistemic constraints led to a particular understanding of the Kosovo conflict which resulted in a particular response? And how would a Complexity-based approach produce different understandings, and different solutions?

A number of studies that rely on Michel Foucault's analysis of epistemes show that there are epistemic constraints to what can actually be thought in specific contexts. For example, Ian Hacking's work on the emergence of probability shows that some epistemic constraints have to be in place before probability can be conceived.[4] Those constraints, however, transcend the specific field of mathematics as such – they operate at the meta-level, and impose conditionality on all forms of knowledge. Similarly, the quote above points to an interesting question: why can Plato think of 'tablehood', 'cuphood' and 'humankind' when Diogenes only sees cups, tables and humans (or plucked chickens, as it may be the case)?

4 Ian Hacking, *The Emergence of Probability: A Philosophical study of Early Ideas about Probability, Induction and Statistical Inference* (Cambridge: Cambridge University Press, 2006).

These epistemic constraints characterise the way in which we generate and deploy knowledge. Such constraints also characterise the way in which we frame, understand and consequently seek to resolve, conflict. The task of the epistemic approach, in this context, is to ask the following questions: what elements conditioned the way in which a conflict was framed, understood, and acted upon? More importantly – in our case – are those elements, those epistemic constraints, being *challenged*? Here is where Complexity becomes of relevance, for Complexity will be presented as a challenge to the modern episteme and to all related epistemic constraints on the production and deployment of knowledge. In other words, Complexity is, here, presented not as a 'scientific revolution' in a Kuhnian sense, or as an example of epistemological progress *à la* Lakatos, but as genuine Epistemic Revolution in the Foucauldian sense: a revolution whose ramifications impact on all fields of knowledge, including knowledge related to conflict understanding and resolution.

This is broadly the answer to question one: Complexity provides a framework of thought whereby the current epistemic rules that govern the production of knowledge can be effectively understood and challenged. Here, one should be reminded of Nietzsche's fundamental insight according to which all things are subject to interpretation, and whichever interpretation prevails at a given time is a function of power and not truth. Complexity, consequently, provides a framework to challenge not only means of knowledge generation, but also of any power practice associated with it.

Why Kosovo then? Kosovo represented a first in many respects. It was the first time that the North Atlantic Treaty Organisation (NATO) – a defensive alliance – initiated a war; this in itself entailed a number of important novelties. It was the first time that NATO broke its own constitution – which stipulates that NATO can only act in the context of defensive operations. It was the first time that a NATO Supreme Allied Commander (Clark) gave a direct order to an officer in the field authorising the use of force against Russian troops (Priština airfield incident). It was also the first time that an officer in the field (Jackson) disobeyed an order from the Supreme Allied Commander, or had it overridden by a single Government belonging to the NATO alliance, rather than by NATO itself. More importantly, however, it was the first time that a number of Governments were involved in an act that was legally dubious under the Charter of the United Nations (UN) in the post cold war period. It was the first time that humanitarian concerns were invoked as legitimate justifications for intervening in the affairs of a sovereign nation state and a member of the UN. It was the first time that air power alone was used to attain decisive military victory in the context of humanitarian intervention, which in itself entailed other interesting novelties: for example, it was the first time that industrial and media facilities in provinces other than those of immediate concern (Serbia) were targeted in order to prevent humanitarian disasters and ethnic conflict elsewhere (Kosovo). The other first, of course, was the introduction in post war Europe of ethnic cleansing practices. Finally, Kosovo represents an important 'first' in the European context, which has important consequences for the way in which Europeans approach conflict, produce knowledge, use such knowledge to interpret crises and to act upon it. As Medvedev and van Ham put it: "In 'Kosovo', Europe has for the first time faced the increased independent agency – some would say the dominant role – of technology and the media in security matters, turning the war into a form of symbolic exchange and 'European security' into a simulacrum."[5]

Overall, it was the first major confrontation in the post cold war period, which established the rules and principles of a new international order:[6] it is in this context that it is particularly important to examine what allowed these new 'firsts' in knowledge practices and actions to be thought and implemented. Again, it is also in this context that it becomes particularly important to understand whether such constraints can be located within the development of the modern episteme – and whether Complexity represents an epistemic challenge to such constraints.

All of these novelties lead to a refining of the questions posed above: what epistemic constraints led to a particular understanding of the Kosovo conflict which resulted in a particular response? What constraints led to the framing of peoples, first as 'Yugoslavs', then as 'Kosovars', or 'Serbs', and so on? And again – are those constraints being challenged? Before proceeding to present the way in which answers to the three research questions presented above will be answered throughout this work, it may be useful to present a number of concrete examples (not necessarily all from Kosovo) of discourse formation practices that would benefit from a Complexity-informed epistemic approach.

Three Balkan Stories

On 24 April 1999, a generation of young Europeans woke up to the headline "Once you kill people because you don't like what they say, you change the rules of war".[7] Early that morning, the building housing Radio-Television Serbia (RTS) was struck by NATO cruise missiles. 16 employees, mostly technicians and support staff were killed, whilst 16 other civilians were injured. *The Guardian* reported that some victims "had to be identified by a single personal effect: part

---

5 Peter Van Ham and Sergei Medvedev eds, *Mapping European Security After Kosovo* (Manchester: Manchester University Press, 2002), 4.

6 It is worth noting that the first Gulf War cannot be understood in such a way, as it was carried out on the basis of a legitimate UN mandate and was therefore the subject of widespread consensus. For the other consequences of Kosovo in the context of the new security regimes, see Martin Smith and Graham Timmins, *Uncertain Europe: Building a New Security Order?* (London: Routledge, 2001), and Martin Smith, *The Kosovo Crisis and the Evolution of Post Cold War European Security* (Manchester: Manchester University Press, 2003).

7 Robert Fisk, "Once you kill people because you don't like what they say, you change the rules of war", *The Independent* (London), 24 April 1999.

of a sock, a ring. Mirjana Stoimenovski, mother of one of the victims, waited four days in front of the RTS building for news of her son's death."[8] The BBC explained that "reporters at the scene said they saw the almost decapitated body of one man dangling from the rubble, and the body of a make-up artist. Another man was trapped between two concrete blocks. Doctors amputated his legs at the site but he later died."[9] The state-run news agency *Tanjug* confirmed that about 150 people were inside the building at the time of the attack.[10]

The British Prime Minister, Tony Blair, later explained that bombing television stations was "entirely justified" since they were part of the "apparatus of dictatorship and power of Milošević." He added: "The responsibility for every single part of this action lies with the man who has engaged in this policy of ethnic cleansing and must be stopped." The Prime Minister insisted that it was "very, very important people realise this."[11] The insistence may have been aimed at the confusion created in previous weeks regarding the exact definitions of 'TV station', 'military target', and the relationship between the two. The British Development Secretary, Claire Short, stated: "this is a war, this is a serious conflict, untold horrors are being done. The propaganda machine is prolonging the war and it's a legitimate target."[12] The view seemed to be shared by the entire British Government. This is what Sir Ian Garnett, the Chief of Joint Operations at the Ministry of Defence, had to say: "Milošević's propaganda machine consists of transmitters but also the studios from which the information is transmitted. That makes it part of the overall military structure. Both elements have to be attacked."[13] And this is NATO's Air Commodore David Wilby: "RTS was a legitimate target which filled the airways with hate and lies over the years."[14]

But things were not so simple. Jamie Shea, the NATO Council spokesman, had previously stated that RTS was not a target, distinguishing between transmitters "integrated into military command and control communications and normal broadcasting facilities."[15] What was all of this fuss as to transmitters about? Under the Geneva Convention 'television channels and equipment' can be legitimate targets only if they are 'an integral part of the military apparatus'.[16] On 12 April, Shea confirmed that "there is no policy to strike television and radio *transmitters as such.* Allied air missions are planned to avoid civilian casualties, including of

---

8 Natasha Joffe, "At War with NATO", *The Guardian* (Manchester), 23 October 2001.

9 Richard Norton-Taylor, "Serb TV Station was Legitimate Target, says Blair", *The Guardian* (Manchester), 24 April 1999.

10 Ibid.

11 All quoted in ibid.

12 Ibid.

13 All quoted in ibid.

14 Ibid.

15 Ibid.

16 Joffe, "At War with NATO".

course journalists."[17] However, by the 18 April (six days of frustrating bombing campaign later), Shea was saying "I think the time has come to take a closer look at the Serb state media. It is not really a media at all, it is part of President Milošević's war machine."[18] In other words, transmitters were now an 'integral part of a military apparatus', even though it can be argued that the Geneva Convention means things other than 'propaganda' when referring to 'military operations', and the Convention's emphasis on military 'command and control' reflects this. On the 21 April, NATO General Giuseppe Mariani confirmed that NATO was in the business of "disrupting the regime and degrading the FRY propaganda apparatus."[19]

Within two weeks 'transmitters as such' had become 'propaganda machines', hence part of a 'military apparatus', whilst what Shea previously recognised as civilians (journalists, and therefore not targets) had become part of that apparatus, hence, military personnel. This resulted in Sir Ian Garnett's view according to which a 'propaganda machine' – by definition part of an 'overall military structure' – is composed of *both* transmitters *and* 'studios from which the information is transmitted'. So, when is a TV station not a TV station? When is a civilian not a civilian, but a part of 'military apparatus'? More importantly, when is freedom of expression not freedom of expression but 'propaganda'? The limit, the threshold between the meaning of a word and its opposite, has to be negotiated, calculated.

Ljiljana Bererina, a survivor of the attacks released the following declaration: "What does RTS represent for me? An interesting job. You can't imagine what it means to be in a poor country under an embargo to deal with international relations, to be in contact with foreign colleagues. But at home we never watched the news on RTS, we switched on the TV only when there was football."[20] Ljiljana also stated that most of those killed vehemently opposed Milošević's government.

On 19 December 2001, the European Court of Human Rights (ECHR) dismissed a case against the NATO bombing of RTS on the grounds of jurisdiction. The Former Republic of Yugoslavia (FYR) was outside of the Court's 'jurisdiction'. To be sure, the Court had previously claimed jurisdiction on territories other than those belonging to signing parties in cases of 'military occupation' by those signing parties.[21] A question related to the issue of jurisdiction emerges: how can a Court dealing with Universal Human Rights be qualified by a geographical – and therefore by definition exclusive – element (Europe)? And such a contradiction is evident in its own denomination: '*European* Court of *Human* Rights'. Should it not be renamed – 'Court of Rights for European Humans'? Again, the limit – even the limit of the 'Universal', of the 'Human' – has to be negotiated, defined. The idea

---

17 Ibid., emphasis added.

18 Ibid.

19 Ibid.

20 Ibid.

21 The question of ECHR jurisdiction is a complex one and will be studied at length in Chapter 5.

of a European Court of Human Rights is in itself reminiscent of a very peculiar mode of thinking whereby a Universal is – paradoxically – defined in terms of its own exclusion. The title that Slavoj Žižek chose to assign to the second part of his compendium is in essence indicative of this: *The Universal Exception.*[22]

Richard Holbrooke's account of the Dayton peace process offers a similar account regarding the delimitation of meaning and the 'technicalisation' of conflict – of how conflict needs to be framed within limits before it can be calculated and resolved.[23] First, there is the story of the maps. After intense days of negotiation at Dayton, Milošević had made an important number of territorial concessions on behalf of the Bosnian Serbs (referred to as 'Pale Serbs', and often differentiated from the more moderate 'Banja Luka Serbs' in the account). Without realising it, during these concessions Milošević had altered the proposed partition of Bosnia to a ratio of 55 per cent for the Bosnian-Croat Federation side and 45 per cent for the (Pale) Serbian side, whilst the pre-condition agreed by all parties for negotiating at Dayton was a distribution of land equivalent to 51 per cent for the Federation side and 49 per cent for the Bosnian Serbs.

When Milošević realised this he was rather upset. Talking to Holbrooke, he said "You tricked me…how can I ever trust you again?…I can do many things, but I cannot give you more than 51%…I can't force Pale to accept a deal for less than 49%. Please believe me. This is the end of the matter."[24] This is particularly interesting, as throughout the account it emerges that Milošević exerted a considerable amount of pressure on the Pale Serbs, effectively dictating terms to them. Holbrooke makes numerous references to Milošević's 'charm offensives' aimed at the Pale Serbs, while Milošević is repeatedly alleged to have referred to them in less than flattering terms, calling them 'pigheaded' and 'stupid' quite a few times. But on the percentage issue, he did not seem to have much room for manoeuvre. In a tragi-comical way, Milošević apparently burst into a desperate monologue, stating "Give me anything, rocks, swamps, hills – anything, as long as it gets us to 51–49."[25]

As Holbrooke put it, the 51–49 issue had taken on 'an almost theological force'.[26] This reference to theological (metaphysical) force is rather interesting in the context of the epistemic framework this book seeks to elucidate, and in relation to Complexity-inspired opposition. But how do we get to a situation in which numbers – the necessarily abstract representation of reality – become the precondition for a (real) settlement? How can such an issue assume a *sine qua*

22 See Slavoj Žižek, *The Universal Exception* (London: Continuum International Publishing Group, 2005). Žižek's argument will be analysed at length in the relevant chapters (3 and 5 in particular).

23 Richard Holbrooke, *To End a War* (New York: The Modern Library Editions, 1998).

24 Ibid., 295–96.

25 Ibid., 302.

26 Ibid., 296.

non status in diplomatic negotiations, to the extent that the nature, or quality, of the question in object (land) is no longer relevant (rocks and swamps)? Holbrooke begins to provide an answer:

> The most disturbing aspect of this obsession with 51–49 was that it revealed how little each other trusted the political aspect of the Dayton agreement to which they had both agreed. As Izetbegovic once said, a 'mountain of corpses' between the two sides prevented trust. The argument over the land was, in effect, a continuation of the war in Dayton, while the political discussions were a tentative effort to build a political framework for a joint future. We were all too aware of the internal contradiction, but there was nothing that could be done about it.[27]

Numbers take over once the immanent reality (the mountain of corpses) renders an agreement – any agreement – 'undecidable'. The metaphysical nature of negotiations is revealed once the failure to deal with the problems at the level of immanence becomes apparent. Indeed, this is evident in the Pale Serbs' insistence on the 51–49 ratio.[28] Given the perceived ethnic composition of the province (44 per cent Muslim, 31 per cent Serb, 17 per cent Croat, 6 per cent Yugoslav), it would have been impossible for the Croat-Muslim Federation to accept anything that could not be presented as less than the 'majority' of Bosnia's territory. On the other hand, a partition that reflected the perceived ethnic balances of Bosnia would have been unacceptable to the Serbs: you cannot fight a war and claim to have won it if you are left with 31 per cent (Serb), or even 37 per cent (Serb plus 'Yugoslav') of the territory. In other words, the Pale Serbs may have presented the Dayton agreement as the result of a military 'victory' if the partition ratio reflected the fact that barely a majority of the territory will be assigned to the enemy, which can be presented as an inevitable factor given the presence of third party mediators: but nothing more. Those few percentile points in territory, thus, become the borderline of what can be acceptable to both parties: on the one hand, the possibility of presenting the result as something that guarantees the majority principle enshrined

27 Ibid., 297.

28 David Campbell exposes the constructed character of the 1991 Yugoslav census (44 per cent Muslim, 31 per cent Serb, 17 per cent Croat, 6 per cent Yugoslav – see page 79 of the book cited below), which provided most of the 'data' for negotiations in the region. Furthermore, Campbell analyses (Chapter 5 of the book cited below) the ontopological assumptions that emerged in relation to the nexus that is assumed to exist between identity and territory. The idea that such nexus exists and that it ought to be used as a ground for peace negotiations was a principle that was driven by the international community as much as it was by Belgrade. The ontopological assumptions that statistically summarise the nexus of territory and identity are epistemic in nature, for they underpin the mechanisms in which relevant knowledge is produced and deployed. See David Campbell, *National Deconstruction: Violence, Identity and Justice in Bosnia* (Minneapolis: University of Minnesota Press, 1998).

in the perceived composition of the population, and the principle that a war was not 'lost' since no more (or barely more, that is, a negligible 1 per cent) than half of the province's territory was lost. In other words, the number 51 indicates a majority – but just, barely, a majority – and its symbolic value derives from the fact that such a notion of 'limited' majority would have enabled the relevant Pale leaders to claim that they had not 'lost' the war, whilst enabling the Bosnian-Croat Federation to claim that a majority of the province's territory was secured. This is precisely why the peace needed to be calculated, as both parties sought to secure what they could not achieve through military means in the negotiation process: that is, something they could present as a 'decisive victory'. It is worth noting that earlier proposals put forward by non 'Yugoslavs', that is, plans that sought to present a more *super partis* proposal, suggested a 43 (Serb): 57 (Federation) ratio (Vance-Owen Plan),[29] whilst plans proposed by constituents which did not have to deal with the constraints of a nationalist-dominated public opinion at home (the Bosnian proposal, which was promptly withdrawn) went for a 67 (Federation): 33 (Serb) deal (which comes a lot closer to the perceived ethnic reality on the ground as depicted by the 1991 census).[30] In the end, the mathematics of the agreement had to be worked out by the two players upon whom specific (epistemic) nationalist-discursive constraints applied the most: Tudjman and Milošević.[31]

As Holbrooke put it, this was a perfect example of politics constituting the continuation of war by other means, which was characterised by an attempt to impose constraints that were present at the immanent level (the Pale Serbs' imperative to be perceived as the side that had 'won' the war) to a context that sought to do precisely the opposite, that is, negotiate away such 'red line' requirements.

Richard Holbrooke's *To End a War* is an interesting read not only because of its vivid description of the Dayton negotiations, but also because it illustrates how these negotiations were preceded, or framed, by Holbrooke's attempts at calculating the right conditions for the talks. Consider, for example, the quote below, which refers to a conversation held between the American envoy and Croat officials:

> As we left the meeting, I pulled Defense Minister Susak aside. "Gojko, I want to be absolutely clear," I said. "Nothing we said today should be construed to mean that we want you to stop the rest of the offensive, other than Banja Luka. Speed is important. We can't say so publicly, but please take Sanski Most, Prijedor, and Bosnaki Novi. And do it quickly, before the Serbs regroup![32]

29 See David Owen, *Balkan Odyssey* (New York: Harcourt Brace, 1995), 121.

30 See Carl Bildt, *Peace Journey* (London: Weidenfeld and Nicolson, 1998), 140.

31 Gearóid Ó Tuathail and Carl Dahlman, "The Clash of Governmentalities: Displacement and Return in Bosnia Herzegovina", in *Global Governmentality: Governing International Spaces* (London: Routledge, 2004), 145.

32 Holbrooke, *To End a War*, 166.

The conflict in Bosnia engendered situations in which, according to a senior United States negotiator, it was necessary to secure further conflict in order to secure the peace. The peace had to be calculated, and the variables had to be in place.

The TV station that is no longer a TV station, the map (the signifier) that no longer represents a tool to settle an object of dispute (land – the signified), but it becomes in itself the object of dispute, a court of justice whose (Universal) focus is limited by (particular) territorial jurisdictions, and the need to secure further conflict in order to secure the peace: all of these contradictions represent various facets of a particular mode of thought that characterises the way in which knowledge is produced and deployed in modern IR. It is the objective of this work to examine what the main tenets of this configuration of knowledge are, to understand their most inner workings, and to explore – with the help of a Complexity-informed epistemic approach – whether such workings are being challenged. It is the purpose of this work to trace the evolution of this modern configuration of knowledge, to understand how it has permeated through the realms of society and policy-making on this particular occasion (the Kosovo crisis), and to examine how it is being challenged by alternative configurations of knowledge. At the practical level, these issues always remain intimately related to questions faced in the day-to-day practice of crisis management: what makes the thought that peace can only be achieved with further conflict possible? What makes a map an object of 'theological obsessions'? What makes a young journalist who only switches to RTS to watch football part of a 'propaganda machine' and thus part of a 'military apparatus/target'? Are these all incidences of metaphysics as power (or metaphysics of power)? These are only examples related to a limited dimension of the conflict. The final chapters of the book will, for example, look at the formation of the ethno-nationalist discourse in the region in some detail.

The Architecture of an Argument

Chapter 1 will proceed to examine the evolution of scientific epistemology in general and the rise of Complexity in particular in the context of the Western/Continental intellectual tradition and through the epistemic lenses that will be fully presented in Chapter 2. As such, the chapter will provide some hints on the epistemic significance of Complexity that will be fully explored in Chapter 2. It will be argued that Complexity – understood as an epistemic configuration – represents a break from the modern episteme insofar as it posits non-linear (thus non-contingent) temporality at the heart of theorising, thus directly challenging what Foucault called the 'Age of History' (modernity).

There is more. Historians such as Eric Hobsbawm identify Natural Philosophy and German Romanticism as the precursors of Complexity – whilst noticing the role that such approaches to knowledge played in the 'Epistemic Civil War', which was fought all over Europe during the 'Age of Revolutions'. It thus becomes possible to argue that Complexity has the potential to re-introduce the great 'modern' debate that was at the heart of such Epistemic Civil War. The debate, to put it crudely, regards the question of what should be the role of Reason after the Enlightenment. Once it becomes possible to demonstrate that Complexity can be understood in this way, the implications for the theory and practice of IR become immediately obvious – approaches that see the role of Reason as being that of enabling us to cope with uncertainty, rather than that of providing us with certainty, will generate knowledge practices which radically differ from current interpretations of human affairs, including human conflict.

There is an additional sense of urgency in any attempt to critically assess the impact of Complexity in the way we generate and deploy knowledge, particularly as the concept of Complexity itself is being constantly abused by dubious claims to knowledge (both in academia and elsewhere) that seek to re-justify themselves under its aegis. By Googling 'Complexity' these days one will find hundreds of hits explaining how a business' sales can be dramatically improved thanks to the latest insights of the new science, or sites claiming that better dating techniques can be acquired thanks to Complexity Science. Or how we can now better understand 'globalisation', or regional security regimes, since these things are also 'complex'. The idea that Complexity in itself represents an important challenge to our modern configuration of knowledge, and that as such it re-opens the question of how we should handle conscious, rational thought in the post-Enlightenment era, does not seem to come up. Just as a prelude of what will be discussed in this chapter, it is interesting to note that Foucault predicts that philosophers such as Bergson and Deleuze will precipitate the collapse of the modern episteme, whilst the most important theorists of Complexity Science in fields as diverse as particle physics, biology and cognitive neuroscience observe the affinity there is between their claims and philosophers such as…Bergson and Deleuze. Needless to say, Foucault sees in these thinkers a challenge to the modern episteme precisely because of their alternative conceptualisations of time. In other words, parallelisms between Complexity and post-structuralist (and post-Bergsonian) philosophy will be made. Chapter 1 will thus argue that Complexity could be seen as overcoming the modern episteme and its genesis is shown to be compatible with Foucault's description of the evolution of the sciences – indeed, it will argue that Foucault's archaeological method provides a very rigorous tool for understanding the evolution of Complexity.

Chapter 2 will seek to present the methodology through which the rise of Complexity, and the evolution of IR (theory and practice), are to be examined. Foucault's archaeological method will be presented, and the main underlying features of the modern episteme will be outlined. However, it may be useful to present some of the main arguments here in order to emphasise the role and importance that Complexity plays in the context of novel and epistemic approaches to conflict.

As a whole, this work will argue that the tragic events in Kosovo are characterised by a metaphysical understanding of conflicts and human relations. This metaphysical approach is responsible for the particular way in which the

Kosovo conflict was understood, and consequent solutions calculated. The work will seek to demonstrate that the metaphysical nature of our times is to be detected not only in the realms of diplomacy, but in every conceptualisation that characterises contemporary Western thought. Two questions arise: 1) How is it possible to back such a claim: what tools do we have at our disposal to elucidate this fundamental trait in IR and in the day-to-day practice of diplomacy and policy-making? 2) Besides, what has 'Complexity' got to do with any of this? To what extent can we speak of a new Complexity-based *episteme* as a break from the current configuration of knowledge?

The underlying configuration of knowledge, the ensemble of rules that characterise the way in which we, as humans, approach and generate knowledge, is what Michel Foucault referred to as an *episteme.* According to Foucault, the modern episteme emerges once the underlying assumptions of the classical episteme no longer provide legitimate grounds to claims on the nature of knowledge. Whilst in the classical episteme the nature and order of things (including humans) was determined according to how these stood in relation to each other, indeed according to how they represented each other: Modernity brings forward an epistemic configuration that no longer requires this representational attitude when producing and deploying knowledge. In the modern episteme, things will be examined as self-coherent and self-sufficient wholes, their organic structure becomes more relevant than their representation of other objects, and their limits are imposed by an analytic of finitude. The study of 'Man' becomes possible only when 'Man' can be delimited, and regarded as something which is *produced* as well as something that *produces*. Thus, the 'Birth of Man' is related to the birth of the 'humanistic sciences' and vice-versa, and the nature of these phenomena is epitomised in Marx's classical maxim: Men produce their own history but not in the conditions of their choosing.

On the other hand, the birth of such subjects of study focus our attention on these objects' inner, organic structures: these are always inaccessible to humans but they ground all claims to knowledge. It is this analytic of finitude that determines when a TV station ceases to be a TV station, for example. The analytic is always present in discursive formations, and its limits are constantly negotiated. According to Foucault, such an analytic of finitude necessitates a concept of linear history to take place. In fact, the analytic is supposed to negotiate the limits of things, but since they can no longer do so in terms of their representational power, an alternative explanatory source must be found. This source is the concept of linear history, which reveals the intrinsic and inner limits of all things. Since the ultimate purpose of linear history is to assist an analytic of finitude in placing contingency, its linear and unidirectional nature must be maintained. Thus, a concept of linear history is of fundamental importance for the process of negotiating the limits of things.

This work will, thus, argue that *the two axes of modernity identified by Foucault's epistemic analysis are responsible for understanding the nature of the Kosovo conflict, and for the way in which IR theory and practice are constituted to provide such understandings*. The two axes include an *analytic of finitude*, which is responsible for defining the meaning of concepts in the modern organisation of knowledge, and *historical linearity*, which is responsible for placing contingency upon such finitude. In other words, this work is an attempt to understand how the Kosovo conflict was handled in our age, which Foucault calls the 'Age of History', precisely because of the nature of the modern episteme: an episteme that is defined by a concept of historical linearity (history), which comes to dominate all discursive formations. These two axes will provide the lenses, or the tools, through which this work will elucidate how a particular conceptualisation of events led to consequent actions in the context of the Kosovo crisis, and how IR theory and practice have evolved to underpin precisely such kind of conceptualisation. As Chapter 1 will have elucidated, notions such as historical linearity and analytical finitude are simply and literally unthinkable in the new approach to knowledge provided by Complexity, hence the argument that Complexity represents a decisive break from standard approaches to knowledge, including those that are dominant within IR.

Chapter 3 will apply the theoretical insights gathered in the previous two chapters to the development of academic IR theory. These developments are particularly important as they concretely show how Foucault's epistemic approach can, in a very powerful way, account for the intellectual trajectory of specific disciplines and concepts, and how such trajectory is a mirror of underlining epistemic shifts that will be identified in the analysis of the evolution of scientific theorising (Chapter 2). In other words, Chapter 3 will tangibly show how the epistemic approach, and the related understanding of the evolution of the sciences presented in Chapters 1 and 2, can account for the way in which knowledge is produced and deployed in IR. Needless to say, it was such an approach to knowledge that grounded our understanding of the Kosovo conflict. The chapter will seek to examine the evolution of modern ethical discourse in the same way.

In sum, the theoretical argument of this work can be presented as follows. Our current understanding of conflict is characterised by epistemic constraints that condition the generation and deployment of knowledge. Such constraints are themselves characterised by the rules of the modern episteme, which, according to Foucault, inaugurate the 'Age of History'. This is because such episteme relies on a notion of analytical finitude, which requires the adoption of historical linearity. Overall, the modern episteme relies on historical linearity to function and to generate consequent discourses, or knowledge practices. As it happens, the formation of all human sciences can be analysed on the bases of the evolution of the modern episteme. IR theory (and practice) clearly evolved along the lines of the modern episteme too, and this is evident in the a-historical nature of some of its most salient analytical frameworks (Neorealism). On the other hand, Complexity challenges the rules of the modern episteme, and it does so precisely through an alternative understanding of time, and therefore history. Thus, we now have a conceptual framework that may first allow us to challenge the epistemic constraints imposed on the generation of knowledge regarding conflict and IR, and to second proceed to generate alternative frameworks of knowledge leading to alternative understandings and actions. Finally, Kosovo provides a good case study for testing these claims as it represents a number of novelties that have emerged in the context of the international system. Kosovo, as such, exemplifies a transition period in which all the contradictions of the modern episteme – which in this case are applied to our understanding of IR – come to light. It thus offers a good opportunity to carefully dissect the inner workings of the modern episteme – and to challenge them through what will be presented as an alternative to such episteme (Complexity).

An Intermezzo is strategically placed between the theoretical and practical focus of the current work. It is hoped that the few pages it occupies will represent a useful roadmap for the reader whenever the links between the different components of the study are not immediately clear. Indeed, the Intermezzo seeks to summarise the theoretical insights and to outline how these base considerations on the events that unfolded in the context of the Kosovo crisis.

Following the theoretical perspective elucidated above and developed in Chapters 1–3 it will be possible to examine two particular concepts surrounding the Kosovo crisis, that is, the way in which the two axes of modernity operated in this particular case (and in the way contemporary IR theory and practice understood the case): 1) the application of an analytic of finitude in the context of international law (and ethics, see Chapter 5); and 2) the role of historical linearity in constructing the object of enquiry ('Kosovo', see Chapter 6). It will be argued throughout Chapters 5 and 6 that a concept of historical linearity translated into the belief that the conflict was characterised by perennial and persistent 'ancient ethnic hatreds', whilst analytical finitude mutated into a notion of 'Universal Exclusion' in legal and ethical discourses. In the case of our analysis of the juridico-ethical aspect of the crisis, Chapter 5 will implement a study grounded on the understanding of the analytic of finitude, which echoes a perspective (Universal Exclusion) that can be found in Žižek's thought:

> In the chapter "Hegel's 'Logic of Essence' as a Theory of Ideology", Žižek makes the case for the importance of Hegel's notion of 'positing the presuppositions' for any serious work in ideology analysis. He also looks at the way Hegel reconceptualizes Kant's notion of the 'sublime' not as some transcendental 'beyond' out there but as a kind of fantasy image brought about by a split in here. This strange logic, which Žižek will go on to connect with a certain feminine 'not-all', as opposed to a masculine 'universality produced through exception', will have the widest implications for the rest of Žižek's work. It will allow him to criticize, for example, *the usual notion of human rights as a universality only possible on the basis of a series of exclusions (women, children, the mad, the primitive), a universality from which ultimately everybody is excluded*, as opposed to a conception of human rights as non-universal but applying precisely to these exceptions.[33]

33 Rex Butler, *Slavoj Žižek: Live Theory* (New York: Continuum, 2005), 8, emphasis added.

In a nutshell, this perspective will be tested against the experience of the crisis as revealed in a number of documentary monuments, which all reveal the exclusionary nature of a Universality that had to be constructed according to the limits imposed by an analytic of finitude, which is in itself inherent in the rules of the modern episteme.

Chapter 4, on the other hand, will begin by presenting an overview of current scholarship on the Kosovo conflict. As such, it seeks to provide the building blocks for subsequent arguments and to identify gaps in our current understanding of the Kosovo crisis. It will be argued that whereas a substantial amount of work has been published in a great number of disciplines related to the issue at hand (from political science and IR to international law, via military analysis and media studies, just to name a few), very little has been done to synthesise such approaches through an epistemic perspective so as to gather the intrinsic novelty inherent in what has come to be defined as the Kosovo crisis. Thus, works tend to be compartmentalised in their respective disciplines and the underlying constraints that characterise phenomena go unnoticed. For example, the contradictions that characterised military strategy (in terms of the obvious dissonance that existed between the stated objectives and the means that were chosen to implement them) were also present in subsequent legal reasoning – both contradictions can be traced to the same epistemic constraints.

Chapter 6 will also provide a detailed account of some aspects of what happened in Kosovo using the analytical tools developed in the first part of this work, and it will offer some generic reflections on how the epistemic approach presented here can enhance our understanding of the events and on how a Complexity-informed analysis can help us to identify ways in which the relevant epistemic constraints are being challenged. Curiously, Benedict Anderson has addressed the role of linear temporality in the construction of nationalisms. One of the objectives of our case study will be to demonstrate that Anderson's arguments can not only be applied to the subjects experiencing the processes of identity formation, but that it also conditions how others, outsiders, frame and identify a particular group. In Anderson's classical study of nationalisms[34] an entire section (appropriately entitled "Apprehensions of Time") is dedicated to the analysis of linear time as a fundamental component in the construction of national and ethnic identities.[35] Consider for example the following claim:

> Our own conception of simultaneity has been a long time in the making, and its emergence is certainly connected, in ways that have yet to be well studied, with the development of the secular sciences. But is it a conception of such fundamental importance that, without taking it fully into account, we will find it difficult to probe the obscure genesis of nationalism? What has come to take the place of the medieval conception of simultaneity-along-time is, to borrow again

34 Benedict Anderson, *Imagined Communities* (London: Verso, 1991).

35 Ibid., 22–36.

> from Benjamin, an idea of 'homogenous, empty time', in which simultaneity is, as it were, transverse, cross-time, marked not by prefiguring and fulfilment, but by temporal coincidence, and measured by clock and calendar.[36]

According to Anderson, without an emerging concept of 'homogenous, empty time' it would be difficult, if not impossible, to imagine oneself as being part of a coherent community. Can we also say that without this notion it would be equally difficult to imagine 'others' as being part of 'other' coherent communities? Is this the notion that characterised the conceptualisation of the 'Kosovars' and the 'Serbs', for example, from Rome to Washington via, Paris, Madrid and London? Interestingly, Anderson notes that the emergence of linear time is probably related to the creation of modern secular sciences but that this link is yet to be well studied. This represents an odd omission, especially when one thinks that the emergence of such concept of linear time, in precisely those terms, was identified by Foucault in a book (*The Order of Things*) subtitled *An Archaeology of the Human Sciences* – sciences which Foucault characterises as being strictly modern and secular. It remains unclear to what extent Anderson was aware of Foucault and to what extent the latter influenced the former. Although Anderson refers to a 'Foucauldian sense of abrupt discontinuities of consciousness'[37] when comparing the notion of time in nationalistic and non-nationalistic works of literature, no explicit references to what would appear to be the most relevant work (i.e. *The Order of Things*, where the notion of epistemic breaks and the rise of historical linearity is formulated) appears to be made in *Imagined Communities*. The last part of this work will seek to bridge that gap.

The theoretical insights of *Imagined Communities* leads this study to conclude by revealing why and how a modern approach to the Kosovo crisis has tended to frame and understand the conflict in terms of ancient ethnic rivalries, and to explain the particularly violent nature of the Yugoslav wars on the bases of such historically linear views. It will be noted that this temporally linear perspective characterises the practice of IR (the 'ancient ethnic hatreds' argument) as well as IR theory (Neorealism's concept of continuity, or the 'striking similarity in the quality of international life over the last millennia'): an epistemic approach will reveal that this is not coincidental, and that the two visions of temporal linearity are mutually constituted. A Complexity-guided approach, on the other hand, allows us to understand that it was precisely the absence of such intrinsic ethnic hatreds and nationalist feelings which led to the extreme levels of violence in the region.

---

36 Ibid., 24.
37 Ibid., 28.

Chapter 1
Complexity and the Modern Episteme: Epistemological Outline of a New Science

> What is the role of time?...Time prevents everything from being given at once...Is it not the vehicle of creativity and choice? Is not the existence of time the proof of indeterminism in nature?
>
> Henri Bergson, *The Possible and the Real*[1]

Introduction: French Philosophy and the Modern Episteme

This chapter will present how Complexity challenges the modern epistemic configuration, a configuration which will be fully outlined in the next chapter, and which it will be shown to underpin approaches to knowledge in contemporary IR theory and practice. The current chapter will thus provide the lenses that will enable the current work to analyse how the Kosovo crisis may have been framed, understood and acted upon differently had Complexity-based approaches been adopted in contemporary IR. This chapter is guided by the Nietzschean belief according to which only things that do not have a history can be defined. Thus, we are not seeking to define Complexity; rather, we will use Foucault's understanding of epistemes to capture Complexity's ethos and significance. Towards the end of the chapter the reader will be able to compare the results of presenting Complexity in such a way to other attempts at defining Complexity on the bases of essential properties (the 'checklist approach', as we call it).

A good way to begin our journey is to tell the story of a strange discovery: *the philosopher who Foucault argued would herald the end of the modern configuration of knowledge, Henry Bergson, happens to be the same philosopher who inspired crucial works in the philosophy of Complexity science*. It is this discovery that will allow an understanding of Complexity as a postmodern episteme to take place.[2]

As Michel Foucault describes the birth of the modern episteme, however detailed the account is, the reader cannot fail to notice that something is missing.

---

1 Henri Bergson, *Oeuvres* (Paris: Presses Universitaires de France, 1959), 1331, my translation.

2 It is worth noting that we absolutely want to move away from vacuous definitions of 'postmodernism', and, for that matter, of 'Complexity'. It is for this reason that Chapter 2 will fully outline what is meant by Foucault's – rather rigorous – understanding of modernity.

Foucault explains that as the era of representation withers, paving the way for the modern episteme, the realm of philosophy finds itself divided into three distinct areas of enquiry – but Foucault maintains that this division is only valid until a figure appears in philosophy: "The criticism – positivism – metaphysics triangle of the object was constitutive of European thought from the beginning of the nineteenth century to Bergson."[3] Bergson? Why Bergson? Are we to understand that Henri Bergson was the first thinker to push Western philosophy beyond the modern organisation of knowledge? Foucault does not say, at least not within *The Order of Things*. Presumably, it is important to have enough knowledge of Bergson to gather the significant differences between this philosopher and the recently presented modern episteme.

Bergson, a fascinating figure, also happens to appear, intriguingly, in a seemingly unrelated book: The End of Certainty.[4] In this exciting work Ilya Prigogine, a Nobel prize winner in biology and one of the emblematic figures of a loosely defined 'Complexity Science', explains why and how the deterministic scientific era, characterised by Newtonian principles of certainty embedded in the reversibility of Time, is coming to an end. Prigogine, incidentally, declares that his work in the natural sciences has been deeply influenced by philosophical inquiry. He even goes on to declare: "The dream of my youth was to contribute to the unification of science and philosophy by resolving the enigma of time."[5] This is a unification of two realms of knowledge that, as the next chapter will show, Foucault argues have been divided as a consequence of the end of representation and the birth of modernity. Furthermore, Foucault argues, as outlined in Chapter 2, that the single most important phenomenon that characterises the collapse of representation and the consequent birth of the modern episteme is precisely centred on emerging and contrasting notions of linear temporality and history, an emergence that caused the fragmentation of knowledge into different forms of enquiry.

But what should really be of interest in this bizarre literary detour is that the problematic of time within Prigogine's arguments brings us back to...Bergson. Consider: "The results of nonequilibrium thermodynamics are close to the views expressed by Bergson...Indeterminism, as conceived by Whitehead, Bergson, and Popper, now appears in physics."[6] So, a general problematic starts to emerge, a problematic that should be of particular interest for IR theorists and for any student of the Kosovo crisis. Is IR not the discipline, after all, in which Kenneth Waltz's dominant neorealist paradigm is constantly accused of a 'scientistic' a-historicism? Does the culprit not defend his positions in the name of 'scientific' methodology? Moreover, recent works in IR theory coincidentally seek to adjust these 'scientistic' fallacies by introducing the notion of historical research to the

3 Foucault, *The Order of Things,* 245.

4 Ilya Prigogine and Isabelle Stengers, *The End of Certainty: Time, Chaos, and the New Laws of Nature* (New York: Free Press, 1997).

5 Ibid., 72.

6 Ibid., 72 and 108.

discipline.[7] It would seem that if Bergson is considered to mark the limit of one precise configuration of knowledge through a specific concept of temporality on the one hand, and to found the bases upon which new knowledge is being produced on the other hand, it would be useful for us to understand where fields of enquiry related to IR and to the Kosovo crisis stand, epistemologically and ontologically, in relation to these developments.

Is there a possibility that recent and not so recent debates concerning the nature of 'scientific IR' are built upon fundamentally misleading notions of 'science' and 'history'? How is all of this related to our understandings and judgements, of crucial events such as the intervention in Kosovo? Do various interpretations of the Balkans in general not suffer – in their attempts to emulate 'scientific rigour' – from a systematic 'historical reductionism'? More importantly, is a 'pseudo-scientistic' approach, reminiscent of modernity's attempt to construct transcendental philosophies of objects, determining the way we conceive arguments such as 'human rights', 'humanitarian intervention' and 'history'?[8]

This chapter is a modest attempt to begin answering these tricky questions. First, it will put them in order. To do so, a general framework of understanding, which will be fully outlined in the next chapter, will be used. This is the principal reason why the present chapter will use Foucault's analysis of epistemic fluctuations, and general concepts provided by contemporary French philosophy, as a way of understanding the epistemic differences that exist between modern transcendental philosophies of objects and Complexity. This framework should equally allow us to fully grasp the significance of Bergson's philosophy. Consequentially, the present chapter shall first explore the links that exist between Bergson himself, this break from modernity, and scientists such as Prigogine. Second, it will analyse the genesis of Complexity through the epistemic lenses provided by the next chapter. This should allow Chapter 3 to understand the consequences of all of these arguments for the social sciences in general and for the discipline of IR in particular. It will be demonstrated that the scientific bases which have founded much of 'scientific IR' theory (and practice) are being seriously undermined by developments within the epistemology of science. It will be equally necessary to show that many of these notions (such as temporality), boil down to the notion of freedom of action, or, to put it in fashionable terminology, to the structure and agency debate. This is the question that, after all, has fascinated philosophy since its inception: to what extent is human action contextually (i.e. historically, socially, economically, psychologically, etc.) determined?

---

7 See Barry Buzan and Richard Little, *International Systems in World History: Remaking the study of* International Relations (Oxford: Oxford University Press, 2000).

8 Chapter 2 will fully outline the notion of 'transcendental philosophies of the object': it is, essentially, the main mechanism through which metaphysical approaches to knowledge in the modern empirical sciences are deployed.

Keeping this in mind, Gary Gutting describes French philosophy in the twentieth century as the 'Philosophy of Freedom'.[9] This author offers an account that describes how "from Bergson through the existentialists and poststructuralists, individual human freedom was itself a radical starting point that required no philosophical foundation."[10] This can explain why, for example, French philosophy of science occupied such an elevated status: the desire to demonstrate that deterministic science was compatible with human individual freedom was indeed a major motivation for philosophers such as Boutroux, Poincaré, Le Roy and others.[11] As we shall see, Bergson's ideas emerged from initial debates within this current of thought. The need to relativise the determinism with which the scientific method is often associated perhaps explains the fact that authors such as Bachelard and Canguilhem have preceded Thomas Kuhn's description of scientific revolutions by more than 30 years.[12] Foucault's *The Order of Things* was also, to a certain extent, a history of epistemic revolutions. Within these contexts, we will see how he explored the way in which 'scientific' disciplines such as biology were constituted.[13]

The Thought of Henri Bergson

As noted above, Gutting explains that the philosophers of the Third Republic had an intense interest in science. Indeed, it would seem that while we "can think of philosophy's pre-modern period as the time, before the scientific revolution, when it was identical with science, when philosophy was simply the enterprise of understanding the world in all its aspects."[14] The task of philosophy after the triumph of the 'scientific revolution' is relegated to justify a role for itself. As Gutting puts it, the argument is that after the incredible success of scientific discovery philosophy had to demonstrate that a number of phenomena were not explainable through the 'scientific method' alone.

9 Such is the title of the conclusive last chapter of Gary Gutting, *French Philosophy in the Twentieth Century* (Cambridge: Cambridge University Press, 2001).

10 Ibid., 380.

11 Ibid., 26 and 40.

12 Ibid., 87. Similarly, when Foucault was accused of omitting Kuhn's arguments from his *Order of Things*; he replied that since his book made several references to Canguilhem, further references of Kuhn were not necessary. See Gutting, *French Philosophy in the Twentieth Century*, 39.

13 Foucault has been undoubtedly influenced by the work of historians of science, especially Canguilhem and Bachelard. Indeed, Gutting believes that the ideas of these two thinkers are crucial for an accurate understanding of Foucault's arguments. Moreover, it was Canguilhem who proposed the very terminology 'Archaeology of Knowledge' to Foucault. See Gutting, *Michel Foucault's Archaeology of Scientific Reason*, 1–54.

14 Gutting, *French Philosophy in the Twentieth Century*, 49.

Philosophy's task was to show that in order to pursue the abstraction that modern science must necessarily adopt, some non-quantifiable aspects of our experience are ignored. Philosophy, thus, must exhibit that it "can and should root itself in an experience with an immediacy or concreteness that escapes the abstractions of modern science."[15] And, as the following paragraphs will illustrate, these abstractions are produced because of the metaphysical nature of modern science, and its drive to formulate a posteriori transcendental philosophies of objects.[16] Note how this corresponds to Foucault's arguments regarding the fragmentation of knowledge and the new role of philosophy as a discipline that seeks to recover the lost uniqueness of wisdom (see Chapter 2).[17]

Henri Bergson is in this respect one of the most important figures within the spiritualist tradition, a tradition that advocated the presence of a distinctive philosophical experience. Bergson followed with a lot of interest the developments that were taking place within the philosophy of science. More precisely, Poincaré's initial doubts concerning the infallible objectivity of science and his disciple's (Le Roy) reinforcement of these doubts must have played an essential role in the constitution of Bergson's thought. At the core of Bergson's philosophy of science lies the conviction that the scientific method adopts a cinematographical view of temporality, which implies, as Gutting puts it, "that science views reality not as a continuous flux (the duration that in fact is) but as a series of instantaneous 'snapshots' extracted from this flux."[18]

Science's cinematographical view of duration is due to the fact that it is primarily concerned with action. As thought that is primarily concerned with practice, science must abstract from that concrete reality that we experience, in which temporality is not simply another form of space, but a "wholly qualitative multiplicity, an absolute heterogeneity of elements which pass into the other."[19] For Bergson, in the real continuum of duration there are no distinct elements that precede or follow real points in 'time'. In this context, it becomes meaningless to speak of an a priori or an a posteriori: Bergson envisages a notion of temporality as a "continuous flux of novelty in which nothing is ever fixed, complete or separate. In this flux, anything that we can say exists 'now' also incorporates into a qualitative whole everything we can say is 'past', a whole that is itself being incorporated into the new synthesis of the 'future'."[20] The distinction between the synthetic and the analytic disappears in the flux of time, for it is precisely this continuous temporal vortex that is responsible for the formation of things (a posteriori) and their essential reality (a priori) – as Chapter 2 will show, this

15 Ibid., 50.

16 See John Dupré, *The Disorder of Things: Metaphysical Foundations of the Disunity of Science* (London: Harvard University Press, 1995).

17 Foucault, *The Order of Things*, 217–49.

18 Gutting, *French Philosophy in the Twentieth Century*, 51.

19 Ibid., 57.

20 Ibid.

division between a posteriori and a priori phenomena is an essential characteristic of modern approaches to knowledge. This is the main postulate of what has been referred to as Bergson's 'superior Empiricism' (more on this below). And again, it is precisely this refusal to deal with transcendentalisms that characterises Bergson's drive for an immanent reality that can be experienced but that cannot be cut into bits and abstracted. Clearly, the emergence of such ontology revolutionises the bases of the modern episteme, which, as Chapter 2 will demonstrate, is based on analytically and historically delimitated metaphysical approaches.

Bergson equally argues that it is misleading to view modern science, through differential calculus, as a method that alters the basically static notion of time. Modern science differs from classical science insofar as the former democratises the notion of temporality: while classical science privileged some 'moments' over others, modern science seeks to explain phenomena from any temporal standpoint. In this sense, because all temporal standpoints are considered, time 'appears' in modern science, much in the same way as 'man' appears once it becomes an object of knowledge. Nonetheless, the assumption that the flux of time is divisible into isolated elements is not altered. Bergson also refuses the idea that modern science has given time a fundamental role. The argument contested is that modern science has made temporality an independent variable of deterministic mathematical equations, and that this represents a major qualitative shift from Aristotle's static physics. Bergson, in contrast, argues that the problem lies precisely in turning temporality into a parameter. The flux of time is not just a quantifiable parameter that can be isolated and used as a variable, but a constitutive process characterised by sheer heterogeneity and multiplicity.[21] In other words, time is not something thanks to which things happen (a variable), but it is rather something in which things happen, something, thus, that establishes the very parameters and laws according to which events unfold. In this sense, temporality is not something that places contingency, but precisely the opposite: that which ensures perpetual transformation, a process of becoming without being – again, the ways in which modernity requires temporality to place contingency on objects of analysis will be fully explored in Chapter 2. The concept of being, by definition, necessitates a set of parameters to define its existence, the notion of becoming, on the other hand, necessitates a concept of continuous and non-linear time to ensure that the becoming process never produces a definite being.

Having established the fact that science fails to tackle the issue of real temporality, Bergson argues that philosophy might have been expected to occupy this empty ground. However, this was not to be. Much as Foucault has argued, philosophy has attempted to resolve problems inherent in the modern episteme, instead of attempting to surpass them. Modern philosophy, Bergson argues, has not challenged the view of time as "nothing more than a fourth spatial dimension,

---

21 The argument is rather different when it comes to Bergson's positions on relativity. See Keith Ansell Pearson, *Philosophy and the Adventure of the Virtual: Bergson and the Time of Life* (London: Routledge, 2002), Chapter 2.

which could readily be viewed as having no creative efficacy, as merely the vehicle for the automatic unrolling of a nomologically determined sequence."[22] This modern scientific vision of time, as Prigogine maintains, is all but dead.

Bergson argues that a philosophy that sought to adopt a more immanent approach to temporality would reveal how the very notion of time is inherent to any conceptualisation of human freedom. To expose the point, Bergson attempted to present just how problematic a divisible notion of time is when applied to the analysis of psychological states. In his doctoral thesis, Bergson posited the problem as follows: accepting the notion that our decisions, feelings and emotions occur at identifiable isolated 'spaces in time', the determinists will maintain that human will is never free because determining causes exist. On the other side of the spectrum, non-determinists either deny the existence of these casual determinants (libertarianists) or argue that the presence of these does not infringe human freedom (compatibilists). Bergson's thesis is that to view the self as a constitution of separate psychological states, which might be linked by causal connections, leads us to an unsolvable paradox of human freedom. On the contrary, "a description of the self that accords with the immediate givens of consciousness shows it to be an organic whole that creatively produces its future, and this production is precisely what we mean by freedom."[23]

Now we can start to understand how Bergson goes beyond the modern episteme. His conceptualisation of temporality refuses the a priori/a posteriori distinction upon which the modern organisation of knowledge is based. His rejection of transcendentalism, coupled with his insistence on the realm of immanence, has produced, amongst many, challenges to the modern notions of abstraction, temporality, empiricism, science and freedom.[24] It is precisely by demolishing the modern episteme's understanding of all possible paths and conditions for the attainment of knowledge that Bergson issues a challenge to Kant's revolution in philosophy and in science, for "unlike the transcendental procedure of Kant, [Bergson] does not refer to the conditions of all possible experience; rather, it is moving toward 'the articulations of the real' in which conditions are neither general and abstract nor are they broader than the conditioned...Bergson insists upon the need to provide a genesis of the human intellect."[25]

In order to advance in the critique of the Kantian revolution Bergson introduces the ideas of virtual multiplicities, of temporality and of intuition as means of thinking beyond the human condition as opposed to means of thinking within such condition. These rather complex issues need to be tackled carefully. Therefore, this section will only briefly introduce these notions and present them

22 Gutting, *French Philosophy in the Twentieth Century*, 57.

23 Ibid., 58.

24 For Bergson's 'superior empiricism', see Pearson, *Philosophy and the Adventure of the Virtual: Bergson and the Time of Life*, 12.

25 Ibid., 11–13, emphasis added.

as a critique of the Kantian epistemic revolution,[26] while we will focus on more precise definitions as the study proceeds to describe Deleuze's philosophy of Life in relation to Complexity science.

The Kant – Bergson nexus is of course important for any interpretation of Complexity through epistemic lenses as Foucault considers Kant as a fundamental thinker for the modern episteme, while considering Bergson as the first postmodern philosopher. We can begin to see the similarities and differences that exist between Kant and Bergson by focusing on the antinomies that are inherent in Kant's critique of pure reason. These antinomies arise, according to Kant, when "reason oversteps the bounds of sense and understanding and freely speculates on issues it is not equipped to adequately deal with",[27] thus generating a number of contradictions. Such a contradiction, for example, is embedded in the following statement: "Man has complete freedom" and "There is no freedom since everything operates in accordance with natural necessity". As we have seen, Bergson does tackle this issue by maintaining that human freedom can only be conceived of in terms of duration. In IR, this discussion has usually been referred to as the structure and agency debate.

However, to put it bluntly, Kant denies that we can ever think in terms of duration, for that would imply thinking beyond the human condition, and that is not possible because…we are finite beings. All the Kantian elaboration of the conditions and possibilities of knowledge are grounded on an analytic of human finitude, this being the reason why Kant can be legitimately defined by Foucault as the turning point of modernity. Moreover, Foucault has also identified this finitude as the very source of historical linearity, that is, the contingency that makes finitude possible. But this should be looked into in more detail, for, as the study will seek to argue later on, especially using recent literature on the argument, not only is the latest wave of 'scientific' (Waltz) and 'social' (Wendt) IR theory purely Kantian, but so is our perception of the causes of conflicts and our related actions – especially the justifications for such actions. Foucault teaches that it is precisely the Kantian finitude, his insistence on the limits of the human bodily apparatus to perceive and ground all possible paths to knowledge, which produces historical teleology. Only thinking beyond the human condition can allow us to

26 Although it would be relevant to fully elucidate the nature of Bergson's analysis of time as opposed to Kant's, we do not have the space for this here. For a succint presentation of Bergson's views, see two important pages in what is probably his most relevant work in this context: Henri Bergson, *Matter and Memory* (New York: Cosimo Classics, 2007), 280–82. Considerations on the nature of time play a crucial role in Kant's *Critique of Pure Reason*: indeed, the whole of Section II of Part 1, which deals with transcendental aesthetics, is dedicated to the notion of time: Immanuel Kant, *Critique of Pure Reason* (Indianapolis: Hackett Publishing, 1999), 88. It should be noted that Bergson dedicates an entire chapter to the criticism of Kant's understanding of space and time and the relationship these have with the notion of freedom and intellect. See Henri Bergson, *Creative Evolution* (Mineola, New York: Courier Dover Publications, 1998), 356–63.

27 Ibid., 115.

fully appreciate history as becoming, as the non-linear process which fully reflects the nature of the vortex of time.

It is important to specify that there is, nearly by definition, something intrinsically intuitive in the way Bergson tackles these antinomies. Bergson's very first work on psychological states, and later works on matter and memory, attempt to legitimise an intuitive (as opposed to purely rational) form of knowledge. Not that an intuitive approach lacks of rigour: on the contrary, Bergson's superior empiricism is seen as a more rigorous, because of its immanent nature, methodology than many purely metaphysical proceedings. As we have seen, 'rational' proceedings need to subdivide the flux of time into quantifiable strata: only intuition can perceive temporality as the heterogeneous and continuous flux that it in fact is (for example, Bergson argues that out of all our senses, sight is the most prone to subdivide duration, while hearing comes closer to the appreciation of the totality that time represents).

Such intuitive proceedings are related, for example, to the way memory works. Marcel Proust, who was Bergson's student until 1894 in the Sorbonne, has immortalised this vision of memory as a purely intuitive exercise in his main work *Remembrance of Things Past (In Search of Lost Time)* in which the author explores not rational and voluntary memory, which is controlled by our intelligence and rationality, but involuntary memory, which arises from unexpected stimuli, from events that appear to be insignificant but that reveal the darkest corners of our psyche, and through the association of internal feelings and intuitive actions, the enormous inner and hidden construction that is our memory. There is something purely unconscious and intuitive that characterises our existence and our ways to know: this is Bergson's response to the rationalistic categorising of all possible conditions for the attainment of knowledge.

Bergson and Complexity Science: Ilya Prigogine

There are at least two ways in which the scientific developments elaborated by Prigogine can be broadly understood within a Bergsonian framework. First, Prigogine quickly acknowledges the cinematographical nature of pre-complexity science and second, indicating how this precise view is caused by the notion of time as an illusion, Prigogine relates the problematic of the reversibility of time with the conceptualisation of human freedom. For Prigogine it is precisely the positing of temporality as the creative drive inherent in the living and inert elements of nature that pushes a number of thinkers, including himself, to equate Complexity science with 'freedom'.

On the other hand, numerous philosophers within the framework of post-structural thought have also been enormously inspired by the Bergsonian time/freedom nexus. Amongst these, one of the more striking examples is Deleuze. Whilst the links between Bergsonism and Deleuze have been covered extensively elsewhere,[28] as indeed have been the relations between Deleuze/Guattari and Complexity science;[29] the purpose of the current work is to situate all these relations within a Foucauldian framework. And it is precisely Foucault's concise definition of 'modernity' as an organisation of knowledge that shall provide some parameters for the understanding of these relations: it seems obvious, for instance, that much debate concerning the nature of Complexity science is flawed precisely because it lacks a general philosophical landscape within which notions such as 'modernity' can be situated.

Prigogine articulates the idea that contemporary science uses a static notion of time principally by making reference to Einstein and Hawking. Einstein famously declared that "time is an illusion". More recently, "in his Brief History of Time, Hawking introduces 'imaginary time' to eliminate any distinction between space and time."[30] Thus, Classical and Modern physics have maintained a spatialised vision of time that is basically static, and, even today, scientists assume as a "matter of faith that as far as the fundamental description of nature is concerned, there is no arrow of time."[31]

For Bergson, as we have seen, the cinematographical view of time is adopted because of science's primary concern with action. To a certain extent, Prigogine agrees. For it is the desire of immediate practical results that the technique of reductionism is adopted: looking at things on the smallest scale, it is thought, confers a deeper and therefore practical knowledge concerning the object under study. However, it is not principally reductionism that facilitates the immobilisation of time. Fundamentally, what reductionist and 'practical' science requires in order to justify the idea of static temporality is...a metaphysical dimension. In the following arguments, the relevance of Foucault's description of the modern frameworks of knowledge and Dupré's description of the metaphysical nature of science, which will be outlined in the next chapter, should become apparent.

Prigogine argues that "Nature involves both time-reversible and time-irreversible processes."[32] Reversible processes exclude temporality as a constitutive

---

28 Deleuze himself wrote a book on Bergson, see Gilles Deleuze, *Bergsonism* (New York: Zone Books, 1988). For other works on Deleuze and Bergson see, for example: Constantin Boundas, "Deleuze – Bergson: An Ontology of the Virtual," in *Deleuze: A Critical Reader*, ed. Paul Patton (Oxford: Blackwell Publishers, 1996); Paul Douglass, "Deleuze's Bergson: Bergson Redux," in *The Crisis in Modernism: Bergson and the Vitalist Controversy*, eds, Frederick Burwick and Paul Douglass (Cambridge: Cambridge University Press, 1996), 47–61; Paul Douglass, "Deleuze and the Endurance of Bergson," *Thought* Vol. 67, no. 264 (1992). For an interesting piece in Italian consider: 67–71.

29 See Manuel De Landa, *Intensive Science and Virtual Philosophy* (London: Continuum, 2002). Guattari's last book deals with the relations between his and Deleuze's work and Complexity theory: Felix Guattari, *Chaosmosis: An Ethico-Aesthetic Paradigm* (Bloomington: University of Indiana Press, 1995).

30 Prigogine and Stengers, *The End of Certainty,* 58.

31 Ibid.

32 Ibid., 18.

apparatus of the process. Examples of these processes can be found in Newton's formulation of classical physics and in Schrödinger's basic equation of quantum mechanics. In both cases, equations are invariant with respect to time inversion. Contrarily, time irreversible processes break time symmetry. In these processes temporality does affect how the general rules of motion will impact the system in a precise temporal context. More importantly, time irreversibility produces entropy. An example of time irreversible processes is the second law of thermodynamics. However, Prigogine argues that time reversibility is produced first because we accept the reduction of the analysis to an elementary level (isolationism), and second because we abstract: "Reversible processes correspond to idealizations: We have to ignore friction to make the pendulum work reversibly."[33] In Foucault's words, these metaphysical transcendentalisms adopt reductionism because they "must deploy the deductive forms only in fragments and in strictly localised regions" (see Chapter 2).

Once Prigogine dismisses the idea that entropy might be caused by insufficient data or faulty examination, the ideas that follow from his arguments suggest that, if we bear Foucault in mind, time reversibility is a particular cause of a transcendental philosophy of objects, that is, a metaphysical system that, as Kuhn puts it, ignores elements which do not happen to coexist with the basic premises of a paradigm. This causes the need to discard incompatible elements (precisely such as the second law) on the grounds of humanity's imperfect observation capacities (due to its finitude?) or on the inadequacy of its instruments. However, "The results presented thus far show that the attempts to trivialize thermodynamics… are necessarily doomed to failure. The arrow of time plays an essential role in the formation of structures in both the physical sciences and biology."[34]

Time irreversibility becomes undeniable once, on the one hand, we adopt a more immanent approach to nature and on the other hand, once we look at populations and not at single elements that compose them. In a sense, this approach is very similar to what Deleuze has described as "Bergson's superior empiricism". Pearson describes one of its features as follows: "Instead of chopping up experience into atomistic sensations, which can then only be brought into union with one another in terms of a purely abstract principle that swoops down upon them from high and folds them in its own conjunctive categories (Bergson's empiricism) recognizes a continuity and concatenation between things."[35] The apparently contradictory pulls towards immanence and connectivity are resolved through the continuum of time and this notion of empiricism. This would be a crucial starting point for any Complexity-inspired approach to IR theory and practice.

To present this point, we must illustrate Prigogine's proposals for a unified theory of quantum mechanics. Quantum theory is in a very paradoxical state. Despite providing some remarkable predictions since its formulation about 60

33 Ibid.

34 Ibid., 71, emphasis added.

35 Pearson, *Philosophy and the Adventure of the Virtual,* 12.

years ago, the scope and meaning of the theory are still widely discussed. As Prigogine explains, this is unprecedented in the history of science. The ambiguity of quantum theory can be exposed through its principal calculus, that is, the Schrödinger equation. This equation is both time reversible and deterministic, but Prigogine explains that it presents us with a paradox:

> The basic assumption of quantum theory is that every dynamical problem can be solved at the level of probability amplitudes exactly as every dynamical problem in classical mechanics was traditionally associated with trajectory dynamics. But strangely, in order to attribute well-defined properties to matter, we have to go beyond probabilities amplitudes; we need probabilities themselves [what Deleuze would call immanent actualities].[36]

Thus, by presenting an example using the Schrödinger equation, Prigogine shows that

> ...initially we started with a single wave function Ψ, but we still end up with a mixture of two wave functions, u1 and u2. This is often called the 'reduction' or 'collapse' of the wave function. The Schrödinger equation paradoxically seeks to transform a wave function into another wave function, but it ends up moving from a 'pure state' (the wave function) to an ensemble, or mixture.[37]

As Prigogine sees it, the problem is that "we need to move from potentialities described by the wave function Ψ to actualities that we can measure." This is a problem that De Landa describes quite well as he presents the processes that characterise the shift from the non-metric virtual to the metric real within the Deleuzian ontology.[38] As both Deleuze and Prigogine argue, these actualisations occur through the breaking of time symmetry. We should remark that the problem of moving from a potentiality, expressed in probabilistic rather than essentialist terms, to an immanent reality, corresponds to what Gutting considers French philosophy's call, to which Bergson vividly adhered, for a form of thought that "can and should root itself in an experience with an immediacy and concreteness that escapes the abstractions of modern science."[39]

Prigogine's solution for the dual status of quantum theory involves, thus, a more immanent approach to nature as well as an apparently contrary trend towards anti-reductionism. This is, in the fullest meaning of the term, a flat epistemology: The whole is treated as a unit, but without higher, transcendental, levels of analysis

36 Prigogine and Stengers, *The End of Certainty*, 47.

37 Ibid., 48.

38 De Landa, *Intensive Science and Virtual Philosophy,* Chapter 3.

39 The analysis of how we move from a potentiality to an immanent reality should be of interest to anyone who argues that the events in Kosovo are a simple actualisation of a crisis that was simply waiting to happen.

such as motionless essences or metaphysical assumptions. Prigogine proposes to substitute the function that results from Schrödinger's equation with Poincaré's resonances, the crucial point being that these resonances involve populations and not individual wave functions. In Prigogine's words:

> Through Poincaré's resonances, we achieve the transition from probability amplitudes to probability proper without drawing on nondynamical assumptions [that is, metaphysical]...Only by going beyond a reductionist description we can give a realistic interpretation of quantum theory. There is no collapse of the wave function, as the dynamical laws are now at the level of ρ [populations], the density matrix, and not [individual] wave functions Ψ. Moreover, the observer no longer plays any special role. The measurement device has to present a broken time symmetry. For these systems, there is a privileged direction of time, exactly as there is a privileged direction of time in our perception of nature, it is this common arrow of time that is a necessary condition of our communication with the physical world; it is the basis of our communication with our fellow human beings.[40]

The crux of all this is that the 'probabilising revolution' (which characterises the proposed Poincaré's resonances) is ending up demonstrating that probabilistic results do not follow from an imperfect human knowledge but represent a real state of affairs in nature. This situation, Prigogine keenly maintains, produces an end of certainty, which should be welcomed as enhancing a new conceptualisation of human freedom that has not been possible since the famous Epicuru's Dilemma.[41] And, more importantly still, time plays a crucial role in this new conceptualisation of the basic laws of nature and human freedom. Prigogine is happy to demonstrate that his conclusions concord with Bergson's conceptualisation of temporality:[42]

> I am certainly not the first one to have felt that the spatialization of time is incompatible with both the evolving universe, which we observe around us, and our own human experience. This was the starting point for the French philosopher Henri Bergson, for whom 'time is invention or nothing at all'...I mentioned one of Bergson's later articles, "The Possible and the Real"...where he expressed his feeling that human existence consists of 'the continual creation of unpredictable novelty', concluding that time proves that there is indetermination in nature.[43]

40 Prigogine and Stengers, *The End of Certainty*, 54, emphasis added.

41 Ibid., 10.

42 For a more detailed account see Damian Popolo, "French Philosophy, Complexity, and Scientific Epistemology: Moving beyond the Modern Episteme", *Emergence* Vol. 5, no. 1 (2003), 77–98.

43 Prigogine and Stengers, *The End of Certainty*, 54.

What is important to understand is the relevance of all of this with Deleuzian and Bergsonian ontology. For Deleuze, the wave function would not represent merely 'probabilities', but it would be a striking example of the virtual, and the virtual, which expresses itself through time-breaking symmetries, is real: "The virtual is real without being actual, ideal without being abstract."[44] In short, Pearson describes such ontology as follows: "With Deleuze and Bergson we have the distinction between virtual (continuous) multiplicities and actual (or discrete) multiplicities, a conception of the evolution of life as involving an actualisation of the virtual in contrast to the less inventive or creative realization of the possible."[45] Prigogine's need to move from probability amplitudes to probability proper (real, existing) entails a conceptual shift from the realisation of the (essentialist – metaphysical) possible to the actualisation of the (immanent – multiple) virtual. Moreover, Prigogine stresses that the achievement consists in moving from probability amplitudes (that is, possibilities) to probability proper without relying on 'non-dynamical assumptions', that is, on metaphysical concepts separated from the immanent actuality. In this case, the famous collapse of the wave function represents a striking example of the natural shift from the non-metric continuous (but Real) virtual to the metric concrete actual. Interestingly, Bergson declared that the new science of space-time required a concept of "immediate and constantly varying duration" if it was to avoid remaining abstract and deprived of any meaning.[46] In short, with this ontology we understand that the virtual multiplicities are real without necessarily having been actualised, and this presents a sharp contrast with the rules of the modern episteme, which is characterised by transcendental philosophies of objects or subjects.

Prigogine notes that his main objective is to demonstrate that the spatialisation of time is incompatible not only with the physical world, but also with 'our own human experience'. Following Foucault, we can understand how the crucial component of modernity, that is, the analytic of finitude, characterises scientific epistemology as a transcendental philosophy of the object that necessitates a linear concept of time. Through Prigogine we have an example of a new science that, via Bergson, goes beyond the modern episteme in terms of our understanding of the physical world. However, given the interests of both Bergson and Prigogine, it may also be useful to understand how a Complexity methodology can underpin our understanding of 'our own human experience'.

It is interesting to observe how contemporary cognitive research deals with problems related to the concept of human freedom. Indeed, most research on consciousness and the brain is characterised by the famous Kantian deadlock described above – with the slight difference that the phenomenal is to be located in the very material space of the brain, while the noumenal consciousness is precisely that which cannot be explained through research on the brain alone. It

44 Pearson, *Philosophy and the Adventure of the Virtual*, 1.

45 Ibid.

46 Ibid., 11.

goes without saying that 'freedom' (or 'transcendental imagination') is assumed to be located in this noumenal aspect: on the contrary, consciousness (and all other properties) would have to be understood in terms of mechanical bio-chemical reactions. An interesting work of analytical philosophy demonstrates how most attempts to understand consciousness in the neurosciences derive precisely from this false division between the phenomenal (the brain) and the noumenal: Bennet and Hacker show that such attempts are flawed precisely because of efforts in attributing the brain with all exclusive competences with regard to the phenomenal notion of 'consciousness'.[47] The problem may lie, however, in the fact that brain dynamics are studied in terms of traditional 'snapshot' methodology, while its emergent properties may indeed be only understood if such dynamics are analysed in terms of duration.[48] Contemporary cognitive research is also increasingly finding an inspiration in the thought of Bergson.[49]

A (Short) Genesis of Complexity

Before broadly assessing the implications of Complexity's epistemic revolution in terms of its relationship with a postmodern (in Foucauldian) or post-structural understanding of life – and for their related understandings of the Kosovo conflict – we should bear in mind Michael Dillon's warning. To 'compare' complexity inevitably leads to the temptation of defining it. Dillon, however, also reminds us of the Nietzschean belief according to which only things which do not have a history can be defined.[50] Complexity, as a set of loosely defined principles, does have a history, a history which enables us to capture its ethos rather than its precise (and necessarily abstract, or necessarily essentialist) definition. Since a critical assessment of Complexity is becoming more and more urgent, it is equally urgent to give careful consideration to the genesis of Complexity's underpinning ideas.

The urgency is due to the fact that in recent years there has been an explosion of work concerned with the implications of Complexity Science. There is no subject that has remained unscathed. Within the areas covering IR, it seems that

47 Max Bennett and Peter Hacker, *Philosophical Foundations of Neuroscience* (London: Blackwells, 2003).

48 Roger Lewin, *Complexity: Life at the Edge of Chaos* (Chicago: University of Chicago Press, 2000), Chapter 8: The Veil of Consciousness.

49 For an excellent example of a modern-Kantian deadlock in cognitive neuroscience, and of a solution that is clearly inspired by Bergson, see Stephen Robbins, "Semantics, experience and time," *Cognitive Systems Research* Vol. 3, no. 3 (2002), 302. A summary is presented in Damian Popolo, "Complexity as an Epistemic Revolution: Considerations on the New Science in the Context of Western Intellectual History", in *Philosophy and Complexity – Worldviews, Science and Us*, ed. Carlos Gershenson. London: World Scientific, 2007.

50 Michael Dillon, "Poststructuralism, Complexity and Poetics," *Theory, Culture and Society* Vol. 17, no. 5 (2000), 1–26.

everything can be understood in novel ways thanks to the insights of Complexity. We have discovered that Complexity can provide insights to better understand the dynamics of globalisation,[51] of war[52] and even of regional security regimes.[53] Theorists have attempted to construct models of international politics on Complexity-inspired concepts of turbulence[54] and system interaction.[55] In one way or another, Complexity has fascinated and influenced the work of scholars whose names are well known to the IR research community, such as Robert Cox,[56] Janet Abu-Lughod,[57] Immanuel Wallerstein[58] and John Lewis Gaddis.[59] This is not to mention the enormous impact of Complexity on other branches of social sciences, especially sociology.[60]

---

51 John Urry, *Global Complexity* (Polity Press, 2002).

52 David Alberts and Thomas Czerwinski eds, *Complexity, Global Politics and National Security* (Washington DC: National Defense University Press, 2003). See also Alan Beyerchen, "Clausewitz, Nonlinearity and the Unpredictability of War", *International Security*, Vol. 17, no. 3 (Winter, 1992), 59–90.

53 Walter Clemens, ed., *The Baltic Transformed: Complexity Theory and European Security* (New York: Rowman and Littlefield Publishers, 2001).

54 James Rosenau, *Turbulence in World Politics, a Theory of Change and Continuity* (New Jersey: Princeton University Press, 1992).

55 Robert Jervis, *System Effects: Complexity in Political and Social Life* (New Jersey: Princeton University Press, 1999).

56 Consider: "Even the notion of the haphazard can be contested, as scientists now perceive order within chaos [footnote referencing Gleick]". Robert Cox, *Approaches to World Order* (Cambridge: Cambridge University Press, 1996), 148.

57 Consider: "The traditional 'same cause yields same effect' logic that underlies positivist social science seems sadly ill-equipped to deal with systemic change. Instead, the theories of chaos (recently described by Gleick) may be more pertinent". Janet Abu Lughod, *Before European Hegemony: The World System A.D. 1250–1350* (Oxford: Oxford University Press, 1989), 369.

58 Consider: "The importance of complex systems analysis for the analysis of social science is far-reaching". Immanuel Wallerstein, *Open the Social Sciences: Report of the Gulbenkian Commission on the Restructuring of the Social Sciences* (Stanford: Stanford University Press, 1996), 63.

59 Consider: "The moment was one of what chaos theorists call 'sensitive dependence on initial conditions:' had things occurred differently on a personal scale at this particular time, vast differences on a collective scale would have followed from them. Contingency created circumstances in which Wilson and Lenin defined mutually hostile ideological visions, imposed them upon the countries they led, and then departed from their positions of leadership, leaving it to less visionary successors to determine what their legacies were to be". John Lewis Gaddis, *We Now Know: Rethinking Cold War History* (Oxford: Oxford University Press, 1997), Chapter 1, Section II.

60 Note interesting reflections on the nature of Complexity in relation to the notion of freedom in the Foreword in Raymond Eve, Sara Horsefall and Mary Lee eds, *Complexity and Sociology: Myths, Models and Theories* (London: Sage Publications, 1997).

Yet, with so much debate over relatively novel terms, there is a serious risk that the term 'Complexity Science', and with it the concept, will eventually be diluted to a set of rather shallow notions. At best, the term would then be considered to be useful only insofar as it can provide appealing metaphors for old concepts that one may want to present in original ways. Worse, the term could be adopted to justify rather dubious concepts as having benefited from the latest insights of the new science.

It is in these contexts that the most simple questions, such as 'what is Complexity Science?', tend to become the most difficult to answer. These are the questions that increase the temptation for a standard, and therefore inadequate and confusing, definition. This is evident in the latest round of the 'Science Wars', in which Sokal attempts to deliver us from the heresy of a humanities-based interpretation of Complexity by stating that Complexity is, contrary to what it may seem, essentially Newtonian.[61] This is, of course, in contradiction with the arguments of other well-established scientists who, despite disagreeing on what Complexity 'is', agree on what it is not: Newtonian.[62] Sokal's neat definition of Complexity seems to be at odds, for example, with Prigogine's.

Moreover, an avalanche of volumes, both in 'popular science' and in academia seek to neatly present Complexity as a set of strictly defined concepts. The creation of a 'Complexity checklist' used to label research as 'Complexity research' is all too evident, for example, in Albert's and Czerwinski's work.[63] These quests for precise criteria, which seem to be in line with the (modern?) nature of our times, are not only artificial but contribute to a general failure to critically assess the philosophical, historical and indeed epistemic impact of Complexity – worse, this failure prevents us from analysing how understandings of conflicts may have differed had they been based on an epistemic assessment of Complexity. The objective of producing a short genesis of Complexity is not therefore related to the task of 'defining', or indeed 'presenting' the object, but to capture its inherent ethos.[64]

A timely reminder of Complexity's origins can be found in the works of Eric Hobsbawm. Hobsbawm rightly asserts that the principles of Complexity did not 'appear' but re-appeared under the misleading tag of 'chaos theory'. The re-appearance of such ideas was possible thanks to the increasing calculating powers of computers. According to Hobsbawm, the re-emergence of 'Complexity' has profound implications for the concept of causality. Such an approach does have

61 Alan Sokal and Jean Bricmont, *Fashionable Nonsense: Postmodern Intellectual's Abuse of Science* (New York: Picador 1999), Chapter 7.

62 See Prigogine and Stengers, *The End of Certainty.*

63 Alberts and Czerwinski, *Complexity, Global Politics and National Security*, Chapter 1.

64 This is very much in line with the findings in Dillon, "Poststructuralism, Complexity and Poetics".

the potential to undermine several 'political, economic and social' assumptions,[65] including – as the current study argues – assumptions on the nature of the Kosovo crisis.

Apart from thoroughly describing the effects of Complexity in the world of the natural sciences, Hobsbawm proceeds to describe how, drawing on Max Planck, scientific and social, economic and political history are necessarily intertwined: indeed, Hobsbawm shows how social events are underpinned by the way in which scientific methodology portrayed itself as a new path towards certainty from the beginning of the 'short twentieth century'. Hobsbawm masterfully demonstrates how modern science, seen as a path to certainty, and the 'Age of Catastrophes' (or the 'short twentieth century') are inherently related.[66] Crucially, Hobsbawm identifies the genesis of Complexity in the truly European 'epistemic civil war', which was characterised by two contrasting interpretations of the role of reason after Enlightenment, and therefore of modernity. In particular, Hobsbawm identifies in German Romanticism and Natural Philosophy – and in the work of Goethe – important inspirations for the precursors of chaos theory (Feigenbaum and Libchaber). This is important as it reveals how Complexity emerges out of a very (anti-Newtonian) embryonic 'modernity', which was at odds with contrasting (Newtonian) epistemes.[67] Hobsbawm retrieves this crucial information on Goethe's fundamental influence on the two precursors of Complexity in Gleick's seminal book.[68] Such an account of contrasting 'modernities' is also present in Negri's and Hardt's Empire.[69]

The genesis of Complexity is therefore to be located in a moment of dislocation between two opposing visions of 'scientific' knowledge, ultimately based upon two different visions regarding the role of reason after the Enlightenment: whereas

65 Eric Hobsbawm, *L'Age des Extremes* (Brussels: Editions Complexes, 1999), 697.

66 Ibid., Chapter 18.

67 Consider: "Developments within 'chaos theory' in the 1970s and 1980s are not without commonalities with the emergence, in the beginning of the 19th century, of a 'romantic scientific school', of which Germany was the primary focus (Naturalphilosophie); that reacted to the dominant 'classical' science, essentially represented by practices in France and in Great Britain. It can be interestingly observed that two eminent pioneers of the new science (Feigenbaum and Libchaber) were in fact inspired by Goethe's – radically anti-newtonian – theory of colours, and also by Goethe's treatise '*On the Transformation of Plants*', which can be considered as a precursor of anti-Darwinian and anti-evolutionist theories." Hobsbawm, *L'Age des Extremes,* 756, my translation. The corresponding quote can be found in page 542 of the version in English, *The Age of Extremes* (London: Vintage, 1996).

68 James Gleick, *Chaos: Making a New Science* (New York: Viking Penguin, 1987).

69 Consider: "The origins of European modernity are often characterized as springing from a secularising process that denied divine and transcendent authority over worldly affairs. That process was certainly important, but in our view it was really only a symptom of the primary event of modernity: the affirmation of the powers of *this* world, the discovery of the plane of immanence". Michael Hardt and Antonio Negri, *Empire* (Cambridge MA: Harvard University Press, 2000), 71.

one school of thought regards reason as that which can provide ultimate certainty after the collapse of theology, the other would argue that the role of reason is to enable us to deal with uncertainty, which is a natural and irreducible feature of the world around us.[70] What we are referring to in here is the re-introduction of German romanticism in modern science through the emergence of Complexity. It is tempting to interpret recent developments within the epistemology of science as the re-introduction of romanticism's ethos, should we say, 'through the back door'. As such, the future of Complexity should be seen in terms of the 'longue durée' as one of the possible paths to knowledge opened by the European intellectual heritage.

The broad intellectual movement referred to as Natural philosophy is credited with being the main influence on the precursors of Complexity, yet, it is important to note that it played an important role in shaping the modern European system of thought. Hobsbawm locates in the 'classicism – romanticism' nexus another battleground for the 'dual Revolution' in the 'Age of Revolutions', namely the economic (industrial revolution) and political (French revolution), developments that re-configured every aspect of thought in the Old World. As Hobsbawm explains:

> The main currents of general thought in our period have their correspondence in the specialised field of science [note Foucault's account on the creation of fragmented fields of knowledge], and this is what enables us to establish a parallelism between sciences and arts or between both and socio-political attitudes. Thus, 'classicism' and 'romanticism' existed in the sciences, and... each fitted in with a particular approach to human society. The equation of classicism (or, in intellectual terms, the rationalist, mechanist Newtonian universe of the Enlightenment) with the milieu of bourgeois liberalism, and of romanticism (or, in intellectual terms the so-called 'Natural Philosophy') with its opponents, is obviously an over-simplification, and breaks down altogether after 1830. Yet it represents a certain aspect of truth. Until the rise of theories like modern socialism had firmly anchored revolutionary thought in the rationalist past, such sciences as physics, chemistry and astronomy marched with Anglo-French bourgeois liberalism. For instance, the plebeian revolutionaries of the Year II were inspired by Rousseau rather than Voltaire, and suspected Lavoisier (whom they executed) and Laplace not merely because of their connections with the old regime, but for reasons similar to those which led the poet William Blake to excoriate Newton. Conversely, 'natural history' was congenial, for it represented the road to the spontaneity of true and unspoiled nature. The Jacobin dictatorship, which dissolved the French Academy, founded no less than twelve research chairs at the Jardin des Plantes. Similarly, it was in Germany, where classical liberalism was weak, that a rival scientific ideology to the classical was most popular. This was Natural Philosophy...it was speculative and intuitive.

70 I offer a more detailed reflection in Popolo, "Complexity in a Complex Europe".

> It sought for expressions of the world spirit, or life, of the mysterious organic union of all things with each other, and good many other things which resisted precise quantitative measurement or Cartesian clarity.[71]

Few doubt that in the end it was the 'rationalist, mechanist Newtonian universe of the Enlightenment', and its 'particular approach to human society' that prevailed. Some attribute to this triumph of rationalism the worse crimes of the twentieth century[72] – particularly with regard to the metaphysical essence of this approach.[73] Finally, Hardt and Negri see a constant cleavage between metaphysics and philosophies of immanence throughout European history, a cleavage that is also embedded in the 'classical – romantic science' nexus.[74] It is also important to note the influence of German philosophy on the development of Natural Philosophy, Romanticism and Complexity science.[75]

Complexity, Post-Structuralism, and the Modern Episteme

The nucleus of the argument presented in this chapter is that Foucault describes modernity precisely through the birth of temporality, and that it is this changing notion of time that Foucault argues has been revolutionised by Bergson who, in turn, is fundamental for the thoughts of Prigogine – a standard bearer of Complexity Science – and post-structuralist philosophers such as Deleuze. Bearing this in mind, the question that follows from a reading of Prigogine's arguments, which explain how Bergson's ideas are now being introduced into physics, has to ask whether or not physics is surpassing the modern episteme. The interest for this question is somehow reinforced when one thinks that the path undertaken by modern science broadly corresponds to Foucault's description of modernity: on the one hand, 'representational' empiricism seems to have been outmanoeuvred

71 Eric Hobsbawm, *The Age of Revolutions* (London: Abacus, 2003), 335, emphasis added.

72 Consider: "Bauman argues that the Holocaust was not a *novum* in history but the outcome of technological rationalism of modern society and the attendant normative socialisation of modern subjects". Anthony Gorman, "Whither the Broken Middle? Rose and Fackenheim on Mourning, Modernity and the Holocaust", in *Social Theory after the Holocaust*, eds, Robert Fine and Charles Turner (Liverpool: Liverpool University Press, 2000), 49.

73 Consider: "Drawing on the ontology of Martin Heidegger, philosophy even imputed the murderous tendencies evinced in the Holocaust to the metaphysics of the subject and to the hubris of Western humanism". Robert Fine, "Hannah Arendt: Politics and Understanding after the Holocaust," in *Social Theory after the Holocaust*, eds, Robert Fine and Charles Turner (Liverpool: Liverpool University Press, 2000), 35.

74 Hardt and Negri, *Empire*.

75 We do not have the space to elucidate such links here. For a more detailed account, see Popolo, "Complexity as an Epistemic Revolution".

by 'metaphysical' science (a development which, as we shall see, Waltz is eager to imitate), whilst on the other hand, history appears in modern science but it has a strictly linear and homogenising character: much as the time envisaged by Ricardo. We shall also be tempted to affirm, following Foucault, that both developments are linked (see Chapter 2).

Thus, the argument that the current work wants to make is that any attempt to understand the nature of Complexity, and Complexity's potential impact on other branches of knowledge, which does not give a central role to its notion of time, necessarily produces mixed results. Moreover, such an attempt should also have a contextual backing for its arguments, otherwise, words such as 'time' and 'modernity' run the serious risk of being nothing but convenient terms deprived of any meaning.

Much of the debate surrounding the question of whether Complexity can be seen as a manifestation of 'postmodern' science is focussed around vacuous notions of 'postmodernity' and 'complexity'. The Foucauldian framework presented here has the advantages of giving a coherent context for the understanding of modernity's ethos, without necessarily 'defining' it, whilst allowing us at the same time to consider as 'postmodern' (strictly in this Foucauldian sense) any construct of knowledge that does not adhere to modernity's conceptualisation of time, for modernity is defined as the 'age of (a precise form of) History', and this precise understanding of History was responsible for the way in which Kosovo was understood (see Chapter 6), and for the way in which IR is currently constituted. As many authors have noticed, defining what Complexity Science is exactly meant to be constitutes a daunting task. Many perceive Complexity as being simply the manifestation of what Lakatos would call a 'progressive paradigm'. The emergence of notions such as 'deterministic chaos' suggest that Complexity is nothing more than a more sophisticated tool for the unfolding of real patterns that just happen to appear as being completely random.[76] Others suggest that Complexity, in a number of fields, has changed many paradigmatic assumptions to the point of legitimately claiming to be a proper Scientific Revolution in the Kuhnian sense.[77] As it should be clear, this chapter suggests that Complexity Science, understood as the set of knowledge practices which, as in Prigogine's case, postulate the central importance of time irreversibility, could be understood as an epistemic revolution. Thus, Foucault allows us to put some order in the debate by characterising Complexity not simply as that which looks for indeterminist, as opposed to deterministic, scientific laws, not simply as a field of knowledge that calls for interdisciplinary inquiry and recognises the non-linear character of the

---

76 Byrne, for instance, considers Complexity exclusively for its potential in quantitative social science, and believes that the new science will 'eradicate postmodernism'. See David Byrne, *Complexity Theory and the Social Sciences: An Introduction* (London: Routledge, 1998). Byrne seems to ignore Prigogine's references to Bergson and Goethe's role in inspiring the discovery of strange attractors.

77 For complexity as a paradigmatic revolution see Gleick, *Chaos*, 37–9.

interconnectedness of all things, but as a set of practices which depart in their quest for knowledge on the 'postmodern' assumption that the arrow of time exists, and that time is irreversibly a constitutive element in the formative processes of things and not simply a convenient parameter.

It is precisely this characterisation of time that is described in De Landa's chapter 'The Actualisation of the Virtual in Time'.[78] In this exciting work, De Landa acknowledges the link between Complexity Science and Deleuze within a general problematic of temporality. Thus, after quoting a passage of Prigogine in which a reference to Bergson is made, De Landa notes that Complexity's link with some fundamental aspects of Deleuzian ontology "is not a coincidence, since Deleuze was greatly influenced by those philosophers (such as Henri Bergson) who were the harshest critics of the reversible and uncreative temporality of classical science."[79]

As an example of the utility of these Foucauldian arguments, we could consider Dillon's important contribution. In an audacious attempt to understand the relation between Complexity and Post-structuralism, Dillon's main line of argument is that both share important intellectual grounds, but that ultimately what divides them is still fundamental.[80] Dillon argues that if we attempt to capture Complexity's and Post-structuralism's respective ethos we would realise that what these two currents of thought share is a commitment to the 'anteriority of radical relationality'. This means that "nothing is without being in relation, and that everything is – in the way that it is – in terms and in virtue of relationality."[81] Nonetheless, this commitment differs depending on whether this anteriority of radical relationality is seen as being simply that, as it is the case for Complexity, or whether the anteriority of radical relationality is relationality with the radical non-relational. Here, the radical non-relational is the "utterly intractable, that which resists being drawn into and subsumed by relation albeit it transits all relationality as a disruptive movement that continuously prevents the full realisation or final closure of relationality, and thus the misfire that continuously precipitates new life and new meaning.[82]

For Heidegger, the radical non-relational is death. For Levinas, it is the Other. For Derrida, it is Alterity, while for Lacan, it is the Real.[83] Ultimately, it is because of the presence of these radical non-relationals that post-structuralism assumes a Poetic character, while Complexity is still entangled in its technical quest for

78 See De Landa, *Intensive Science and Virtual Philosophy*, 82–117.

79 Ibid., 84. However, Deleuze's relation to Bergson is a complex one, and cannot be fully detailed here. Pearson, for instance, correctly reminds us that "It is inadequate to describe Deleuze as a Bergsonian, not simply because of the many and varied sources he draws upon, but rather because of the highly innovative character of his Bergsonism." See Pearson, *Philosophy and the Adventure of the Virtual*, 167–204.

80 Dillon, "Poststructuralism, Complexity and Poetics."

81 Ibid., 4.

82 Ibid., 5.

83 As argued by Dillon in ibid.

an "implicate orderliness – the orderliness as such even if the notion of order is developed in novel ways – of the anteriority of radical relationality."[84]

However, we can argue that following Dillon's description of the radical non-relational, Complexity does seem to have a perfect candidate to assume this role: Temporality. The arrow of time is constitutive and present in all formations, but the virtual that the arrow of time represents is never fully actualised: the process never stops. As De Landa describes the ontology of Deleuze and Prigogine, these are philosophies of becoming without being.[85] And it is precisely the fact that no process ever fully 'becomes' something, following Prigogine, that the arrow of time can ensure 'the continuous precipitation of new life and new meaning'. Furthermore, it is precisely the presence of temporality as a radical non-relational that makes Complexity 'poetic'. Guattari has explored the notions of chaos theory and their relation to his own work in psychoanalysis, and has argued that, following Complexity, "In this conception of analysis, time is not something to be endured: it is activated, orientated, the object of qualitative change…in these conditions, the task of the poetic function, in an enlarged sense, is to recompose artificially rarefied, resingularised Universes of subjectivation."[86] Foucault's categorisation of epistemes allows the observer to understand the centrality of the notion of time as that which characterises the qualitative difference inherent within Complexity science.

Other attempts to relate Complexity with 'postmodernism' have mainly dealt with issues concerning connectivity[87] and/or the possibility of effective prediction,[88] but have generally failed to address the central notion of temporality, which, as we have seen, should be central to any discussion surrounding the nature of 'modern' or 'postmodern' knowledge.[89] One notable example of a study which does address the potential of Complexity in terms of a Derridean approach to philosophy can be found in Protevi.[90] However, apart from efforts outlined above, most other debates do suffer form a clear lack of conceptual rigour when addressing the notions of Complexity and 'modernity'. To exacerbate the confusion and the shallowness of such debates, the Review of International Studies has published a recent interview

---

84 Ibid., 4.

85 As opposed to essentialist practices of being without becoming, De Landa, *Intensive Science and Virtual Philosophy*, 84. Note that this is reflected in the title of one of Prigogine's most important books, Ilya Prigogine, *From Being to Becoming: Time and Complexity in the Physical Sciences* (San Francisco: W.H. Freeman, 1980).

86 Guattari, *Chaosmosis: An Ethico-Aesthetic Paradigm*, 18–19.

87 Paul Cilliers, *Complexity and Postmodernism* (London: Routledge, 1998).

88 Goktug Morçol, "What Is Complexity Science? Postmodernist or Postpositivist?," *Emergence* Vol. 3, no. 1 (2002), 104–19.

89 Byrne, for example, commentates with surprise that Cilliers' exploration of Complexity and postmodernism did not entail an absolute relativism…see JASS book review, http://jasss.soc.surrey.ac.uk/2/2/review1.html (accessed 26 April 2008).

90 John Protevi, *Political Physics: Deleuze, Derrida and the Body Politic* (London: Continuum – Athlone, 2001).

with Robert Jervis that can be mentioned as an example.[91] In the interview, Jervis talks about Complexity and 'postmodernism' without ever defining what he means by either 'modernism' or 'postmodernism'.

Nobody quite agrees on whether Complexity could really be seen as a 'Poetic' science, or whether Complexity is just another classical quest for scientific laws, albeit indeterminist, but laws nonetheless. It would be hard to describe the situation better than Turner:

> Large divisions are beginning to arise – between those who study 'deterministic chaos' and those who allow an element of the random into the picture; between those who believe it can be useful only when strictly confined to mathematical descriptions and those who hold that it marks the one way bridge from math into physical reality; between those who see it as something that can take place within the traditional framework of space as we understand it and those who feel it demands new definitions of space itself; between those who regard the field as reconcilable with classical notions of time as a space like dimension and those who see it as confirming the uniqueness and irreversibility of time, between those who see it as a new piece of content within science and those who regard it as implying modifications in the scientific method; between those who see it as a supplement to the mechanism of evolution and those who regard evolution itself as a special case of nonlinear emergence; and between those who see it as a confirmation of human freedom and responsibility and those who see it as another scientific reduction of the human to the mechanistic.[92]

Thus, we would argue, the need for some sort of 'criteria'. However, these standards are not meant to strictly 'define' what Complexity 'is': these criteria should allow us to better capture a certain ethos, or, 'historical significance'. A philosophical understanding of the concept of modernity, as elaborated by Foucault, as well as an appreciation of the genesis of Complexity, as presented by Hobsbawm, should enable us to fully and critically assess the implications of Complexity. Complexity may not simply be a revolutionary epistemology: it may indeed represent an ethos that fundamentally challenges our perception of modern life and human interaction, including assumptions in IR theory and practice, and perceptions on the Kosovo crisis.

---

91 Thierry Balzacq, "Interview with Robert Jervis", *Review of International Studies* Vol. 30, no. 4 (October 2004), 559–82.

92 Frederick Turner, "Foreword," in *Chaos, Complexity, and Sociology: Myths, Models, and Theories*, eds, Raymond Eve, Sara Horsfall and Mary E. Lee (Thousand Oaks, California: Sage Publications, 1997), 22, emphasis added.

Conclusion

The next chapter will demonstrate that modernity, as Foucault describes it, allows for a number of epistemic configurations and paths to knowledge. That chapter will show that the Vienna Circle marks the moment in which scientific methodology fluctuates towards the transcendental pole of the modern episteme: logical positivism, as the Vienna theorists formulated it, is nothing but a transcendental philosophy of objects. Such chapter will, thus, seek to demonstrate that transcendental philosophy rests upon what we may refer to as the two 'axes of modernity', these being an analytic of finitude and historical linearism.

This chapter, on the other hand, has argued that a number of recent developments within scientific epistemology – inspired by Bergson – have rejected both axes of modernity in favour of an immanent approach to the object of analysis. This is significant for at least two reasons: first, because, as Chapter 3 will show, the discipline of IR was constructed as a 'modern (American?) social science',[93] as a transcendental philosophy of the object modelled on the conclusions reached by the logical positivist in Vienna. Second, as the final two chapters will seek to illustrate, other concepts related to the Kosovo conflict were based on the two axes of modernity that characterise the dominant discourse in present international affairs. The path to knowledge elucidated in Vienna can be seen therefore as the dominant discourse in both formal academia and in the everyday interpretation of events, whilst developments outlined in the pages above (the emergence of Complexity Theory) constitute a robust challenge to the very epistemic rules that make Vienna – and the subsequence knowledge practices – possible. Furthermore, the challenge is centred round the specific role of time, the linear interpretation of which Foucault explains is necessary for the modern episteme to exist. Chapter 3 will seek to bring these discussions from meta-theory to the level of specific disciplines, that is, the disciplines of IR and Humanitarian Law/Ethics. Such chapter will, thus, outline what the theoretical insights presented until now mean in the context of IR theory and Ethics by providing a genesis of the disciplines: it will be shown that the formation of such disciplines broadly corresponds to the patterns outlined by Foucault in relation to other empirical sciences. The current work will conclude by bringing these insights down to a further level, that is, the level of practice, by outlining how the frameworks presented until now conditioned the way in which the Kosovo conflict was framed and acted upon by IR theory and practice. Such outlining will simultaneously present how alternative, Complexity-based understandings would have warranted different interpretations and actions.

93 For a recent analysis of Stanley Hoffman's famous definition, consider Steve Smith, "The discipline of international relations: still an American social science?", *The British Journal of Politics and International Relations* Vol. 2, no. 3 (2000), 274–402.

Chapter 2
An Archaeology of Modernity

> Preludes of Science: Do you really believe that the sciences would ever have originated and grown if the way had not been prepared by magicians, alchemists, astrologers, and witches whose promises and pretensions first had to create a thirst, a hunger, a taste for hidden and forbidden powers? Indeed...the whole of religion might yet appear as a prelude and exercise to some distant age.
>
> Friedrich Nietzsche, *The Gay Science*[1]

Introduction

This chapter will outline Foucault's epistemic approach in general and Foucault's analysis of the modern episteme in particular. The modern episteme will provide the theoretical lenses through which all remaining material will be approached. The chapter will conclude with an application of Foucault's description of the modern episteme to the evolution of scientific epistemology. A thorough outline of the modern episteme is necessary for a number of reasons. First, because the next chapter will outline how much IR knowledge and practice was influenced by such evolution. Such chapter will show that the contemporary production and deployment of knowledge in fields such as IR and Human Rights Law is reminiscent of the modern episteme: these developments follow epistemic rules and evolve on the bases of the constraints imposed by the modern episteme. Second, because such an analysis will allow us to better grasp the novelty inherent in Complexity science, which has been presented as a departure from the modern episteme in the previous chapter. Such chapter has argued that a solid understanding of the modern episteme could ground better conceptualisations of notions such as Complexity, modernity and postmodernity. Third, the two axes of the modern episteme that will be thoroughly outlined below (historical linearity and an analytic of finitude) will be shown to have characterised the way in which the Kosovo crisis was understood and acted upon (Chapters 4, 5 and 6). Finally, a presentation of developments in Kosovo will reflect on how alternative, postmodern (strictly in the Foucauldian sense, that is, approaches that break from the modern episteme as described by Foucault) and Complexity-inspired approaches may have warranted different interpretations and different responses. In other words, a solid understanding of the modern episteme lies at the heart of

1 Friedrich Nietzsche, *The Gay Science: With a Prelude of Rhymes and an Appendix of Songs* (New York: Vintage Books Edition, 1974), 240.

all claims the current book is making, and constitutes, essentially, a methodology for the analysis of Complexity, IR theory and practice, and these two elements in relation to the Kosovo crisis.

The immediate reactions of most of those who come across Michel Foucault for the first time are characterised by an unusual mix of fascination and despair. The detailed analysis of crucial texts and the magnitude of erudition required to produce those paragraphs incite the former, but the idea that our efforts to understand the world around us are inexorably anchored to fluctuating *epistemes* is, at first glance, hardly comforting. Nonetheless, if we accept the basic premises of this argument, if we accept that all knowledge is contextualised, and that contexts evolve, the methodological programme elaborated by Michel Foucault in *The Order of Things* and in his *Archaeology of Knowledge* can prove to be extremely useful.[2] An accurate reading of these two texts would suggest that their author did not write them with the intent of dismissing all claims to knowledge, as he did not set out to adopt a quintessential relativist position. Indeed, the opposite is true: the archaeological method is characterised by analytical rigour. As Gutting well explains, there are three things that should be kept in mind when confronting Foucault: first, archaeology does not simply emanate from Foucault, but is the result of a much longer tradition in the French study of thought, a tradition that includes Bachelard and Canguilhem.[3] Second, archaeological studies are grounded on the study of historical practice and not on philosophical theory. Third, "...archaeology is not...an engine of universal scepticism or relativism, undermining all pretensions to truth and objectivity. The project...does not, in itself, question the objectivity or validity of a body of knowledge to which it is applied."[4]

Thus, at second glance, the fact that the study of changing *epistemes* has been provided with such a rigorous analytical tool should provoke enthusiasm. The task that lies ahead is to understand the fields related to IR and to the Kosovo crisis through this perspective. This should not take exclusively the form of adapting Foucault's concepts that were elaborated for the precise study of social reality as

---

2 Michel Foucault, *Les Mots et les Choses* (Saint Amand, Cher: Gallimard, 2001) and *L'Archeologie du Savoir* (Mayenne: Gallimard, 2001). Note that the texts have been studied in French and that all citations are extracted from the French originals (my translations). Occasionally editions in English are used – when this is the case the English text is cited and referred to. Overall, the chapter makes extensive use of primary sources (that is, of Foucault's texts themselves) and secondary authors (such as Gary Gutting, cited below) are mainly used as an aid to paraphrase (or indeed translate) key passages from Foucault's original. Although the final parts of the section offer a brief overview of debates surrounding alternative interpretations of Foucault's work, the current effort attempts to remain as faithful as possible to the primary sources and to offer an interpretation based mainly on such sources.

3 See also Dominique Lecourt, *Marxism and Epistemology: Bachelard, Canguilhem, Foucault* (London: New Left Books, 1975).

4 Gutting, *Michel Foucault's Archaeology of Scientific Reason, Modern European Philosophy* (New York: Cambridge University Press, 1989), 11.

was, for example, the concept of power related to the analysis of the prison, to the study of global politics and economics.[5] It should not exclusively attempt to detect a causal relationship between a precise configuration of knowledge and a parallel configuration of power.[6] It should also, and primarily, constitute a comprehensive attempt to chart the evolution of the relevant disciplines and the representations that these have created of international practice in archaeological terms, which is what the present book seeks to do. Only then, Foucault's insights could be fully applied to the understanding of the present state of international theory and practice.[7]

The first part of this study wishes to outline and apply Foucault's understanding of the general frameworks of knowledge that have characterised modernity. This will be of crucial importance for the general argument of the present work. In fact, it will be argued that an understanding of modernity such as Foucault's can facilitate the comprehension of many theoretical and practical advances within human knowledge and activities. In order to accomplish this analysis it will be necessary for this chapter to first introduce Foucault's general examination of the birth of the modern configuration of knowledge. Foucault presents these arguments as he sets out to analyse the second epistemic break, in which the classical episteme fades, paving the way for modernity, in Chapter 7 of *The Order of Things*.

Following this introduction to Foucault's thought we will expose how Foucault applied these theoretical insights to the analysis of those empirical sciences which are based on the modern episteme. In *The Order of Things*, Foucault illustrates his arguments through the archaeology of modern political economy, biology and

---

5 James Keeley, "Towards a Foucauldian Analysis of International Regimes," *International Organization* Vol. 44, no. 1 (1999), 83–105.

6 Brian Blair, "Knowledge, Power, and the Modern State: Towards a Genealogy of Universal Productionist Order, 1500–1815" (Phd thesis, University of Newcastle, 1997).

7 Michel Foucault has had an enormous impact on the academic disciplines which relate the most to the current study (IR and Critical Geopolitics). Yet, our study is not the right place to provide a survey of how Foucault has been appropriated by these disciplines for mainly two reasons: first, we will use Foucault as a provider of (meta-theoretical) epistemic lenses through which theory can be developed and applied. For this reason, the current research does not seek to understand what a Foucauldian analysis can bring to the understanding of Kosovo, rather, we are more interested in triangulating Foucauldian meta-theory with a detailed discussion on the nature of modernity and modern understandings which, in turn, will base a Complexity-inspired analysis of the Kosovo crisis as an alternative methodology. There have been attempts to discuss the implications of Foucault for IR in the light of the specifically Foucauldian analysis of modernity: the most relevant work in such context is provided by John Gerard Ruggie, "Territoriality and Beyond: Problematizing Modernity in International Relations", *International Organization* Vol. 47, no. 1 (1993), 139–74. Second, the appropriation of Foucault by scholarship in IR is not unproblematic, but a critical and detailed analysis of such challenges has been conducted elsewhere: see Jan Selby, "Engaging Foucault: Discourse, Liberal Governance and the Limits of Foucauldian IR", *International Relations* Vol. 21, no. 3 (2007), 324–45.

philology. The analogies will be restricted to what Foucault considers to be the most crucial elements defining modern knowledge: the substitution of Order with History, and the necessity of constructing an anthropological and historical analytic of finitude around the newly born 'man'. Finally, the chapter shall argue, in two parts, that modern scientific epistemology has evolved through patterns similar to those exposed by Foucault. In other words, the chapter will conclude by arguing that the metaphysical nature and the historical linearity of modern science, and of modern IR, have emerged within a much broader epistemic context – that is, the context of modernity. This is important because we are presenting Complexity as a new episteme that challenges the foundation of the old – as such, it challenges the foundations of all knowledge practices including those present in the fields related to the study of IR and of the Kosovo crisis.

The Modern Episteme

After having examined the classical episteme, or the representational age, Foucault sets out to determine how from the nineteenth century a second epistemic break characterised the modern organisation of knowledge. This epistemic break is due to the appearance of the concept of *organism* in the general architecture of knowledge. Relatively suddenly, just as when the realm of representation replaced the episteme that was based on similitude, a new epistemic configuration allows to see the same things in different ways, to elaborate different concepts through which reality will be examined. This major configurational shift is due to the presence of 'organic organisation' within the episteme. While in the age of representation things were ordered by the concepts of identity and difference, that is, by the place they occupied in the general *taximonia* and *mathesis*,[8] in the modern age things will no longer be defined by the position they take in these orderly tables, but by the place they take within identified and isolated organisms. Things will from now on take the shape of organised wholes, and elements will be defined by the functions they fulfil within these. The concept of function now becomes fundamental: this is what guarantees the survival of the organism and what therefore determines the identity of elements. The very concept of a general unified body of knowledge, organised through taximonia, is replaced by the idea of isolated but internally coherent organisms.[9]

Nonetheless, representation has not ceased to exist. Rather, it has stopped being the defining organising principle of knowledge. As Gutting explains (quoting Foucault): "representation has lost the power to provide a foundation… for the links that can join its various elements together. No composition, no

8 For Foucault's description of *taximonia* and *mathesis* consider Chapter 3 in *The Order of Things*, for a comprehensive summary, see Gutting, *Michel Foucault's Archaeology of Scientific Reason,* Chapter 4.

9 Foucault, *Les Mots et les Choses*, 230.

decomposition, no analysis into identities and differences can now justify the connections of representations one to another". This power is now to be sought "outside representation, beyond its immediate visibility, in a sort of behind the scenes world even deeper and more intense than representation itself."[10] With the death of representation that which gives significance to things is now inaccessible to our immediate senses: it is hidden in the very deepest core of the organism. This is due to a particular relation between representation and sensory experience, which shall be explored after.

This has several consequences, and one of the most important among these is the substitution of Order with History. In the realm of representation, the purpose of taximonia was to show that there was Order, while Order, in turn, allowed a general taximonia to organise knowledge. Within organisms, the functional determinants of things imply that similarities between functionally alike elements are to be detected by their proximity in the temporal succession of things, and not by their proximity in spatial classificatory tables. As Foucault bluntly states, "History *gives place* to analogical organic structures, just as Order opened the way to *successive* identities and differences."[11] From the nineteenth century History will deploy, in temporal series, analogies that link different organisms. This History will therefore impose its laws on the analysis of economic production, of living organisms and of linguistic groups (the three empirical sciences analysed by Foucault). Not surprisingly, Foucault calls modernity the 'Age of History'.[12] As we will see, this immobilisation of time that enables History to emerge is crucial for contemporary understandings of never-chancing ancient ethnic hatreds, and for the very birth of nationalism as an ideology (see our analysis of Benedict Anderson's arguments in Chapter 6).

In the process of rendering representation obsolete and replacing it with something deeper Foucault sees Kant as being of primordial importance. Kant does assume that empirical knowledge is mainly representational, but "...he does not accept the Classical assumption that all thought (and hence all knowledge) is by its very nature representational...his critique questions representation on the basis of its rightful limits and thereby sanctions for the first time...the withdrawal of knowledge and thought outside the space of representation."[13] For Kant, representational thought is just one of the possible paths to knowledge, knowledge which must from now be founded on something more fundamental than representation itself. The empirical sciences analysed by Foucault follow the Kantian tradition in the sense that their knowledge is conscious of their objective limits: these limits are embedded in philosophies of Life, Labour and Word: modern empirical science no longer simply considers things that 'represent': money is

10 Gutting, *Michel Foucault's Archaeology of Scientific Reason*, 182.

11 Foucault, *The Order of Things: An Archaeology of the Human Sciences*, 219.

12 Ibid., 217.

13 Gutting, *Michel Foucault's Archaeology of Scientific Reason*, 182.

no longer the representation of value and work through exchange, morphological features and words are no longer representations of living entities and meanings.

When things withdraw from the taximonia and enter their own spaces in order to be organised according to their own hidden, non-perceivable laws, they become elements established according to the *internal* laws of organisms, which for the observer, become *external*. The replacement of representations by organisms has the effect of creating the internal/external dichotomy in the realm of knowledge. From now on, "there will be things, with their own internally coherent organisation, their secret nervous systems, the History that produces them; and their representations".[14] But representation no longer defines things: representation is where inner forces are only partially expressed, where these expressions are inexorably subject to interpretation and subjectivity. Organisms isolate knowledge and are in turn defined by isolation; structures are organised around irreducible notions situated in the deep core of the organism (Life, Labour, Word…and as we will argue in the following chapter, Anarchy).

Among the many consequences of these events described by Foucault two should receive particular attention. First, knowledge becomes fragmented. While in the Classical age mathematics, philosophy and empirical studies all belonged to a general science of order (taximonia and mathesis), from the nineteenth century empirical sciences, for example, no longer needed to bother with questions of their own representation (philosophy):

> …The epistemological field exploded in different directions and could no longer be understood as a linear series of inquiry employing the same basic method in different domains. Rather there were three distinct dimensions to the space of knowledge. One was that of mathematical sciences…another was what Foucault calls empirical sciences…the third dimension was the philosophical dimension.[15]

The decline in representation provokes the split, through the appearance of History, between analytic (a priori) and synthetic (a posteriori) knowledge. On the contrary, "an analysis of representations in terms of identities and differences was at the same time a connection [synthesis] of them in the ordered tables that express their essential reality [analytical nature]".[16] Therefore, in the analysis of the mathematics – empirical sciences – philosophy split, we understand that the "analytic knowledge of mathematical and logical sciences becomes sharply separated from the synthetic knowledge of empirical sciences".[17] One deals with the essential reality of things, the other deals with their synthetic nature.

14 Foucault, *Les Mots et les Choses*, 252.
15 Gutting, *Michel Foucault's Archaeology of Scientific Reason*, 183.
16 Ibid., 184.
17 Ibid.

Mathematics		**Empirical Sciences**
Analytic (a priori)		Synthetic (a posteriori)
	Philosophy:	
	Deals with the appearance of 'man'	

Figure 2.1 The mathematics/empirical sciences split

While we have analysed the mathematics/empirical sciences split, it is also important to note the developments that occurred within the realm of philosophy. Foucault argues that what becomes one of philosophy's main tasks in the modern episteme – the analysis of the human mind's power to represent objects – has a considerable influence on the other two epistemological realms. For what concerns the empirical sciences, for example, we have noted that knowledge is ordered around irreducible notions. This requires precisely the formulation of transcendental philosophy. Without transcendentalism, Life, Labour and Word would not be irreducible notions around which bodies of knowledge could be established: "The new positivity of biology, of language and of economics is in correspondence with the construction of a transcendental philosophy".[18] The problem now relates to the following question: how are we to link the emerging transcendentalism with the empirical world and with representation?

Foucault notes that modern philosophy has elaborated three solutions. The first questions the conditions of a relationship between representations from that which makes them possible: in doing so we open a transcendental field where the subject determines in its relationship with any object all the possible conditions for experience. In other words, this is the analysis of the transcendental subject, the very subject that opens up the possibility of elaborating a foundation for the analysis of relationships between representations. The other form, which is diametrically opposed, questions the condition of a relationship between representations from the objects that are being represented. That is how we look for the possibilities of experience in the conditions of the represented object's existence. As Gutting puts it:

> Representation is essentially a relation between a subject and the object it thinks and *experiences*. One approach to a philosophical account of representation begins from the side of the experiencing subject and seeks in it the conditions for the possibility of objects of representation. Here the idea is that the mind is a transcendental reality that constitutes the objects of representative knowledge. This, of course, is the approach taken by Kant in his transcendental philosophy of the subject. But…it is also possible to approach the question from the side of the object. Here the idea is to find in the object the conditions of the possibility of the subject's representational experience, thereby developing a

18 Foucault, *Les Mots et les Choses*, 257.

> transcendental philosophy of the object. Such philosophies particularly focus on life, labour and language, which…are introduced in the empirical sciences as non-representational sources of representational systems.[19]

What is important is that both approaches assume that it is necessary to link representations in such a way that our experience occurs in function of either a subject or an object that lies *outside* that experience but that grounds the possibility of understanding such experience.[20]

Foucault explains that in the second case, where transcendentalism is to be found on the side of the object, work, language and life become that which makes possible the objective knowledge of living things, of production laws and of language forms. Modern empirical sciences are thus organised around transcendental notions of objects, because it is in these objects' terms that the relationships with the subjects are viewed. In their essence, these transcendental notions of modern empirical science (Life, Will, Word, and, as we will later argue, Anarchy) are outside the possibility of human knowledge: but they are, at the same time, the necessary conditions to attain knowledge: they correspond to Kant's discovery of a transcendental sphere (just like in the first case), but they differ in two ways. First, as we noted, they are situated on the side of the object. Second, and consequently, they imply that knowledge is an a posteriori phenomenon: they do not focus on the a priori requirement to elaborate an *analytic* of transcendental knowledge. The first difference is what creates the possibility of elaborating 'pre-critical' metaphysics. The second difference explains the birth of positivism.[21]

The fact that transcendental notions concern a synthesis of a posteriori phenomena means that a whole sphere of events is given to experience, experience of which the rationality and the causality lies on objective foundations that cannot be 'discovered'.[22] As Foucault explains, through positivism, "we cannot understand substances but phenomena, not the essence of things but the laws that govern them, not the things as such but their regularities."[23] From here, we obtain a major schism between those philosophies that deal with things that cannot be objectified (metaphysics), and those philosophies that have the task of exclusively observing that which is analysable through positive knowledge. As Gutting explains, after having considered the two options to deal with transcendental notions (to analyse the relationship transcendental/empirical representation from either the side of the object or the subject):

19 Gutting, *Michel Foucault's Archaeology of Scientific Reason*, 185, emphasis added.

20 Ibid.

21 Foucault, *Les Mots et les Choses*, 257–58.

22 Ibid., 258.

23 Ibid. As Chapter 3 will argue, this is exactly the sort of argument that Kenneth Waltz deploys to defend the limitations of his Neorealist approach.

> Foucault points out another option: simply to restrict ourselves to our *experience*, with no effort to provide it with any transcendental grounding. This amounts to accepting what Kant would call the 'phenomenal' world as the only domain of which we can have any knowledge. This, Foucault says, is positivism, the third form of modern philosophical reflection.[24]

As Foucault understands it, this positivism is based on empiricism (for we can understand only that which we experience), a reflection that does not require transcendental metaphysics to operate. Empirical positivism fails to relate the representational to the transcendental, and denies that any such access to the transcendental world (if there is any) is possible. Positivism is simply defined as a rejection of all transcendental notions. In this sense, Foucault considers himself a 'Positivist'.[25]

Thus, the triangle of modern philosophy is composed by critique – positivism – metaphysics. One should not regard these categories as having strict boundaries: indeed, Foucault states several times that these are not categories as such, but rather poles of modern philosophy within which forms of knowledge can be located. These three poles of modern philosophy influence the general configuration of knowledge which, as we have seen, is determined by the emergence of mathematics, empirical sciences and philosophy itself. These three – just like the three poles of modern philosophy – are not strict categories but rather epistemic extremes. For instance, what Foucault calls the human sciences are to be found within these three axes of knowledge: they attempt to elaborate mathematical formalisations, they borrow models from the empirical sciences and they are concerned with the conceptualisation of 'man', something they share with philosophical thought. Their conceptualisation of 'man' can be located within the three poles we examined: for example, a 'positivistic' conceptualisation of man will differ from a 'metaphysical' conceptualisation…this will be explored in greater detail in the following paragraphs. What is important to understand is that modern empirical science, and, as following chapters will demonstrate, contemporary theories of ethics, IR, and understandings of the Kosovo conflict are constituted according to the modern ordering of knowledge and that, in this triangular organisation, they are located in the metaphysical pole.[26]

The appearance of 'man' in the modern episteme is therefore due to the decline in representation: this break means that man, the subject of representational knowledge, becomes an object of 'organical' knowledge.

This is particularly true in the modern empirical sciences, where the transcendental philosophy of the object allows man to 'appear', that is, to be

---

24 Gutting, *Michel Foucault's Archaeology of Scientific Reason*, 185.

25 Indeed, Foucault states that "if rejection of a transcendental approach means that one is a positivist, then I'm quite happy to be a one", see Gutting, *Michel Foucault's Archaeology of Scientific Reason*, 242.

26 Gutting, *Michel Foucault's Archaeology of Scientific Reason*, 186.

Subject
Criticism

Object
Metaphysics
Modern Empirical Science

Positivism
Concerned exclusively with
the phenomenal world

Figure 2.2 The triangle of modern philosophy

studied in terms of the transcendental objects it experiences. Now that man exists, modern philosophy has to deal with how it relates to that which it experiences. We have seen that modern empirical sciences study man from the objects that it experiences: nonetheless man cannot be simply viewed as that which is constituted by the objects it perceives – it also has to be seen, to a certain extent, as that which constitutes the world around him. Foucault notes that "the study of man, precisely as a constituting subject, is the central concern of modern philosophical reflection and, in another way, of the modern human sciences."[27]

We are still dealing with the relationship between transcendental notions. However, this is no longer the attempt to relate a transcendental subject with transcendental objects, but rather the attempt to reconcile, once we accept viewing the subject through the objects it experiences the notions of man as an object that constitutes other objects and man as an object that is constituted:

> Man as an object – that is, of the empirical sciences – appears as a finite being, limited by the environment, forces of production, and linguistic heritage that have formed him. As Foucault sees it, the question for modern philosophy is how such a being can also constitute the world of objects in which it is included. He says that the general answer, first proposed by Kant, is that this is done precisely in virtue of the very finitude that characterises man as an object. Kant argued that the very factors limiting our knowledge – its restriction to the forms of space and time and the framework of categories – are also the conditions for the possibilities of knowledge.[28]

In the realm of empirical sciences this means that, for example, the limits imposed by the forces of production (or Anarchy) on man are the very same ones that will allow an understanding of how production shapes and constraints the actions of subjects. This phenomenon is what Foucault calls the process of 'analytical finitude' – finitude as that which founds is the fundamental, while finitude as that which is founded is the positive.[29] As we will see when we proceed to present

27 Ibid., 199.

28 Ibid., 200.

29 Foucault, *Les Mots et les Choses*, 326.

Foucault's analysis of empirical science, History contributes enormously in constructing analytical finitude – in fact, History is that which provides contingency to analytical finitude. Indeed, the analytic of finitude is both Anthropological and Historical. Foucault explains that the attempt to construct an analytical finitude must establish a relationship between the fundamental and the positive, and that three options have been considered. However, for the purposes of this research, we will only illustrate the solutions constituted by the creation of the 'empirico-transcendental' doublet, as these are the solutions which, according to Foucault, the modern empirical sciences (including, as the rest of this book will demonstrate, IR and related understandings of Kosovo) have adopted.

Following Kant, Foucault argues that the first solution to relate the fundamental with the positive takes the form of an empirico-transcendental doublet. In this doublet, the approach (advocated by Kant) consists in reducing the transcendental to the empirical. This, in turn, can be done in two ways: "The alternative of basing philosophical truth on empirical truth Foucault calls 'positivist', and that of basing empirical truth on philosophical truth he calls 'eschatological'."[30] In order to relate man as the finite being that can only be understood as the product of the objects it experiences and man as the positive being that constructs the objects it perceives, the empirical option will firstly establish man's finitude in terms of his biological and sensorial limitations to represent. Thus, the limitations posed by our biological apparatus are also the conditions that allow us to experience. This approach "took our (empirical) biological knowledge of the human body as the basis of a positivistic rendition of a transcendental aesthetic…this was taken to show that human knowledge had an (empirical) nature that determined its character and, at the same time, made it an object of our empirical knowledge."[31] As we will argue, modern philosophy of science is based on both a notion of anthropological finitude (embodied in the dogmas of empiricism) and on a notion of historical finitude (embodied in the reversibility of time).

Another approach is to present History as that which is founded as well as that which founds, or in Marx's words, men make their own history but not in the conditions of their choosing. In this case, the limitations and possibilities of our knowledge are expressed through historical contingency. This eschatological alternative (the grounding of empirical truth on philosophical truth) is obvious in the Marxist dialectic, and shows that "knowledge had historical, social, or economic conditions…in short that there was a *history* of human knowledge which could both be given to empirical knowledge and prescribe its forms."[32] These insights concern most current theoretical debates in IR theory. Statements such as "States act according to self help determined by conditions of Anarchy" (Kenneth Waltz) and "Anarchy is what states make of it" (Alexander Wendt) are nothing but variations of the fundamental problem related to the connection

30 Gutting, *Michel Foucault's Archaeology of Scientific Reason*, 201.

31 Ibid.

32 Ibid.

of representations that has emerged as a consequence of Kant's discovery of the grounds for the attainment of knowledge. Both statements above are two sides of the same coin, both belong to the same epistemic formation, both are characterised by finitude and linear historicism. In similar vein, we could argue that statements such as "the Kosovo conflict was characterised by historical determinants and ancient ethnic hatreds" and "Kosovo's history is what the relevant actors make of it: history is thus a phenomenon that is constantly re-constituted in the present in order to justify specific political positions" take place in an identical epistemic context.

Foucault suggests that modern empirical sciences take the eschatological form:[33] indeed, by forming transcendental philosophies of the object, they become organised around irreducible notions (which are embedded in historical thought) that determine the limitations and possibilities to understand man through what he experiences. *The fundamental message of Michel Foucault is that all transcendental philosophy must be based on notions of historical and anthropological finitude, for the only way to examine a subject through 'metaphysical', 'transcendental', and 'artificial' principles, is to impose parameters of study (both spatial and temporal) on the represented subject of enquiry*: this insight is to be kept in mind as we will present arguments concerning the metaphysical nature of modern science. As we will proceed with illustrations presenting how this epistemic configuration contributes to the formative discourses that characterise modern knowledge, the relationship between analytical finitude, anthropological finitude and historical finitude should become more apparent.

Discourse Formation in the Modern Empirical Sciences

Foucault exposes how the decline of representation gives way to organic knowledge in three empirical sciences: economics, biology and philology. For the purposes of our argument, we will restrict the analysis to the disciplines of economics and biology, for they both offer important insights that will ground an analysis of the 'scientification' of IR, that is, of the formation of IR as a truly 'modern' empirical science – this, in turn, will reveal how the Kosovo crisis was understood on the bases of relevant epistemic constraints. A particular focus will be put on Foucault's description of the formation of economic thought, as it clearly demonstrates that the emergence of linear historicism is a consequence of a metaphysical sort of theorising which is developed through a transcendental notion of labour.

This very notion of labour will provide an important analogy as we will proceed to describe the similar process of formation of 'scientific' IR: the positing of anarchy will be presented as another transcendental notion through which events are to be understood. On the other hand, Foucault's analysis of the formation of biology reveals that, not only does metaphysical theorising produce

33 Foucault, *Les Mots et les Choses*, 330.

linear historicism, but it also generates an analysis which is primarily concerned with the notion of function. Thus, we shall also argue that the emergent concepts of 'function' and 'unit' evolve within similar epistemic formations both in biology and in 'scientific' IR.

Foucault proceeds in his analysis of economic thought by focusing on two key writers who can be seen as the founders of economics as a separate empirical science: Smith and Ricardo. With Adam Smith, a new concept enters the arena of economic thought: the notion of work. To be sure, previous economic thought had already dealt with this notion: nonetheless, the physiocrats considered work to be one of the many factors that can reduce exchange to need and commerce to the primitive exercise of barter, that is, they considered work as that which could represent value. For Smith, on the other hand, work becomes the irreducible notion around which all values will be measured:

> Suddenly, wealth will no longer establish its interior order of equivalence by comparing exchangeable objects, nor by estimating the power of every object to represent another object of need (of which the most irreducible example is food); but it will be organised around the units of work which really produces it. Wealth remains a representational element that functions: but that which it finally represents, is no longer an object of desire, but work.[34]

Thus, Smith modifies the notion of work and turns it into the irreducible factor which measures wealth. Nonetheless, his notion of work is still entangled with classicism: the function of work is still to *represent* (and not determine thanks to its inner organic nature) values which are ultimately reduced to exchange and need:

> Smith did not define (as had earlier thinkers who employed the concept) labour in terms of the needs and desires that are represented by commodities in the system of exchange. He used it as an irreducible measure of value. To this extent, Foucault sees him moving beyond purely a representational view of wealth. On the other hand, Foucault holds that Smith never decisively broke with the Classical approach. Even though he viewed labour as the measure of a commodity's value, he still held that the commodity had value only because of its connection with the representational system of exchange.[35]

Despite this, labour becomes the transcendental notion which isolates and organises all remaining elements within the newly defined area of economics. As we will argue in the next chapter, a similar process (the debates between Aron and Waltz) ensured that the realm of IR came to be regarded purely through the notion of anarchy, and this determined the underlying rules of knowledge production within the field. This matters not so much because of a perhaps naïve belief that IR theory

34 Ibid., 235.

35 Gutting, *Michel Foucault's Archaeology of Scientific Reason*, 187.

somehow influences practice. Rather, it matters because theory and practice (or knowledge and power) are embedded within the same modern epistemic context. The tracing of such ideas can thus reveal the underlying assumptions of practice, and serve as guides for genealogical enquiry – which is what will be done through an analysis of the Kosovo crisis.

Smith's new transcendental notion of labour is precisely that which limits and consequentially grounds the possibility of understanding man as an economic subject, and it does so by introducing the crucial notions of linear History and temporality. Smith's answers to arguments criticising labour's new role exemplify the way in which labour became – through Smith – the absolute irreducible notion grounding and limiting the new 'organism' of economics. For instance, how can labour be the measure of everything since work itself has a price, which is even variable? Indeed, where there is an abundant workforce labour will be cheaper, and vice-versa.

Foucault notes how Smith handles this issue. For Smith this was indeed true, but market circumstances influenced what could be purchased with an hour of work, and not the unit of labour itself. Similarly, the fact that different units have different capabilities to deal with the impositions of anarchy does not mean that Anarchy, as that which determines the 'international system', ceases to influence the actions of all actors involved. Demand and supply mean that a day of work can buy more or less, but for the experiencing subjects, for working men, a day of work remains the same. And this is precisely because they are limited by time, pain and fatigue: the temporality of labour, the importance of this finite life, mean that a day's work is always a day's work, no matter how much this day can buy. Thus, Foucault highlights Smith's fundamental quote, "The equal quantities of work are always the same for those who work."[36]

But how can hours of work remain equal regardless of what they can buy considering that changes in working practices, such as the introduction of new technologies, alter the productive capacity, the pain and fatigue, and, thus, the nature of labour itself? Again, Smith argues that labour as such does not change: what changes is the relationship between work and production. Labour, understood as time, pain and fatigue is a fixed numerator: only the denominator is variable. When technological advances are introduced, the productive power of labour is multiplied, that is, the number of objects that are being produced increases dramatically in what remains one labour unit (a day, for example). Therefore, the value of these objects will diminish and such objects will now be able to acquire objects which embody a proportionally lower amount of labour (note here how the measure of value through work is still dependent on the representational system of exchange). However, in this process, work has not diminished in relation to the products, but it is the products that have lost value in their relationship with labour.

---

36 Foucault, *Les Mots et les Choses*, 235.

Thus labour is not 'invented', but it has changed its function within economic thought and within what has now become an economic organism. It has become a transcendental measure of economic value through which the economic factors experienced by economic agents are analysed. This establishment of labour as the new unit of measurement required a decisive break from the representational order of value constituted by exchange, which was in turn rooted in the notion of need:

> ...within exchange, with the order of equivalence, the measure that establishes equality and difference is not of the same nature as the notion of need. This measure is no longer linked to the desire of men...it is an absolute measure, as it does not depend on men's hearts or needs, but it is a measure that is imposed upon them from the outside: it's their time and their pain...if according to men, what they are exchanging is objects of need, for the economist, that which circulates in the market in the shape of objects, is work; and not objects of need that are represented by other objects, but time and pain which are transformed, hidden, and forgotten.[37]

Similarly, anarchy broke the established dogma which believed that the causes of war were to be found in either the 'representational' notion of human nature or in the intrinsic nature of particular states: it is the system, organised through anarchy, that externally 'imposes' its rules on the agents. Anarchy was not 'invented' by Waltz, but Waltz did change its fundamental organising task within 'scientific' IR.

Finally, we can remark how the irreducible notion of the object, which defines and limits the possibility of economic knowledge, *necessitates* a History to justify the orders of value it creates:

> The equivalence between objects of desire is no longer established through the intermediary of other objects and desires, but they are defined by a transition to what is, for them, radically heterogeneous; if there is an order within wealth, if this can buy that, if gold is worth two times more than silver...it is because all men are submitted to time, to pain, to fatigue, and, taken this to its logical extreme, to death itself. Men exchange because they have desires and needs; but they can exchange and organise values because they are submitted to time and to great external fatalities.[38]

From Smith on, it is the temporal succession that labour represents which will found and limit the possibility of understanding economic agents in terms of the work they have to experience. Thus, Foucault insists that from Smith on, we can witness the creation of a kind of anthropology within economic thought, and that this conceptualisation of man as an economic agent is possible thanks to the

37 Ibid., 236.
38 Ibid., 237.

history that limits the existence of man itself. Moreover, it will be History that will determine the laws of value through the transcendental notion of labour. To conclude with Smith, Foucault reminds us that "From Smith on, the time of the economy will no longer be cyclical, rather, it will become the internal time of an organisation which grows according to its own needs and develops according to its own autochthonous laws – the laws of capital and of production regimes."[39]

The decisive step towards modernity is articulated as Ricardo presents labour not only as a measure of value but also as the *sole source* of value. From this moment "value ceases to be a sign, it becomes a product."[40] Ricardo represents the solution to the confusions of Smith's thought, which are caused by an ambiguous position between two epistemes. Smith had to satisfy one condition in order to measure value through labour: he had to assume that the amount of work necessary to produce an object was equal to the amount of labour that this object could buy in the representational system of exchange. This creates a major confusion, as there is no difference between labour as a productive force and labour as a commodity. Every product represents a certain amount of work, and labour had to represent a certain amount of products: value, in this case, is still a sign. However, Ricardo argues that any value of any object originates *exclusively* from the work that was required to produce it. Value is no longer determined by whatever an object can represent in the system of exchange, as the physiocrats – who were still trapped in the Classical episteme – wanted us to believe. Value is equally no longer determined, as Smith argued, by the representational power of labour as a service that can be exchanged and quantified like a commodity. Ricardo goes the extra mile in proving the veracity of his claim on labour as the exclusive source of value, for

> ...the 'value' of things increases proportionally to the amount of work that is necessary to produce them, while it does not vary according to the rise or decline of the wages that are paid in the system where labour is exchanged as any other merchandise...from Ricardo on, the possibility of exchange is based upon work, and a theory of production now necessarily precedes a theory of exchange.[41]

Similarly, once anarchy is 'discovered', a theory of IR must precede a theory of foreign policy (see the Waltz–Aron debate in the next chapter).

Three important consequences follow from this qualitative change in the notion of value. The first consequence is the emergence of a casual series which radically differs from anything known in the age of representation. During the classical age, casual phenomena were always cyclical because these concerned exclusively the representation of objects, which represented one another in circular manner. Thus, prices increased when representative elements grew faster than the represented objects: "this is because value is always related to the system of exchange, in

39 Ibid., 238.
40 Ibid., 266.
41 Ibid., 266–67.

which any change in value is always correlated with inverse change in other values. Since the system always involves a finite number of correlated values, changes can only be cyclical."[42]

The notion of History, and the notion of 'man' (as either a transcendental subject or object), does not exist in the representational episteme. From Ricardo on, labour – once it establishes itself at the very core of economic knowledge and allows no place for representation – organises value according to a causality of its own. This system of causality, on the other hand, is totally dependent on historical thought. Since labour is what determines value, and labour itself is dependent on forms of production, and forms of production change the ultimate value of an object is the result of a linear process of historical causality. Forms of production are composed by the division of labour, the quantity and quality of tools, the amount of capital invested...all of these factors are determined by work that has already been conducted. This, as Foucault explains, is a crucial development, as:

> ...we witness the birth of this grand *linear and homogenous* series which is the process of production...this kind of serial accumulation breaks for the first time the reciprocal determinations which alone appeared in the classical analysis of wealth. This introduces at the same time the possibility of *a continuous historical time*, even if, as we shall see, Ricardo only thinks this history in terms of a persistently slower axis of time, and eventually, he sees *a total suspension of history*.[43]

This quote is of fundamental importance for the overall argument of our work. The birth of a transcendental philosophy of the object introduces linear historical analysis in economic thought. The very possibility of such an economic understanding must be based on analytical finitude, and that is precisely why the emerging historical thought must necessarily be linear. History imposes finitude on man in an eschatological manner (man works, but it produces with means that precede it), and it also explains, linearly, why labour confers a certain value to an object in a given time: had the relationship been non linear (or Complex...), History could not have limited and therefore not explained the relationship between labour and value in a given moment, precisely because non linear relationships offer a multiplicity of options, whilst what History really needs is the capacity to be contingent, to limit and explain the economic subject man through the transcendental notion of labour that is experienced by such, and to reconcile man as that which produces with man as that which is produced.

This development also causes the 'birth of man': during the classical age man was analysed simply in terms of how it stood in relation to the general taximonia and mathesis: thus, man's needs and labour were only regarded in relation to equivalents in man's needs and desires. In turn,

42 Gutting, *Michel Foucault's Archaeology of Scientific Reason*, 187.

43 Foucault, *Les Mots et les Choses*, 268, emphasis added.

> ...modern economics deals with the factors that have caused men to form such representations – for example, with the barrenness of nature that forces us to work, with the bodily deficiencies and the external threats that limit our ability to produce...modern economics is ultimately based not on an analysis of representations but on an 'anthropology' of human finitude.[44]

Another important consequence relates to the *linear evolution* of the economy. To illustrate this point, Foucault exposes how Ricardo dealt with the notion of land rent. While Smith and others saw these profits as a sign of the earth's fruitfulness, Ricardo shows that a proper theory of value should consider the bareness of land. It is the labour employed in the cultivation of the most difficult terrain that establishes the general value of food. As populations increase and less fertile lands have to be cultivated, and proportionally more labour employed, humanity slowly reaches a point at which values will be stabilised by the relationship between scarcity and the possibility of human existence, a relationship which is totally founded on a linear view of History. At that point,

> ...the tide of History will at last become slack. Man's finitude will have been defined – once and for all, that is, for an indefinite time. Paradoxically, it is the historicity introduced into economics by Ricardo that makes it possible to conceive of this immobilisation of History...it is the cumulative time of population and production, the uninterrupted history of scarcity, that makes it possible from the nineteenth century onwards to conceive of the impoverishment of History, its progressive inertia, its petrification, and, ultimately, its *stony immobility*. We see that History and anthropology *are playing in relation to one another*. History exists (that is, labour, production, accumulation and growth of real costs) only in so far as man as a natural being is finite: a finitude that is prolonged far beyond the original limits of the species and its immediate bodily needs, but that never ceases to accompany, at least in secret, the whole development of civilisations... History does not allow man to escape from his initial limitations – except in appearance, and if we take the word limitation in its superficial sense; but if we consider the fundamental finitude of man, we perceive that his anthropological situation never ceases its progressive dramatisation of his History, never ceases to render it more perilous, and to bring it closer, as it were, to its own impossibility. *The moment History reaches such boundaries, it can do nothing but stop, quiver for an instant upon its axis, and immobilise itself forever.*[45]

Thus, we can equally conclude with Foucault's statement:

44 Gutting, *Michel Foucault's Archaeology of Scientific Reason*, 188.

45 Foucault, *The Order of Things: An Archaeology of the Human Sciences*, 259, emphasis added.

> What is essential is that at the beginning of the nineteenth century a new arrangement of knowledge was constituted, which accommodated simultaneously the historicity of economics (in relation to the forms of production), the finitude of human existence (in relation to scarcity and labour), and the fulfilment of an end to History...History, anthropology, and the suspension of development are all linked together in accordance with a figure that defines one of the major networks of nineteenth century thought...*Finitude, with its truth, is posited in time; and time is therefore finite*. The great dream of an end to History is the utopia of causal systems of thought, just as the dream of the world's beginnings was the utopia of the classifying systems of thought.[46]

The sentence "*Finitude, with its truth, is posited in time, therefore time is finite*" is a maxim characterising modern understanding, and a maxim characterising all knowledge – including knowledge on the Kosovo crisis – based on the modern episteme. Continuous historical time and historical linearity are also epistemic formations that allow the idea, according to which persistent ethnic hatreds characterise conflict, to be actually thought.

This is an understanding which arises from a modern attempt to establish the possible grounds of human knowledge, and represents the opposite pole of other attempts to think beyond the human condition (as the following chapter will elucidate, Bergson's effort to think beyond the human condition entails a non-linear concept of temporality, and the replacement of the concept of 'possible' with the concept of 'virtual').

Just like the analysis of wealth, the analysis of nature was based on a system of representation, that is, species were classified in taxonomic tables according to their identities and differences. The revolution in economic thought caused by Ricardo's displacement of labour as that which provides value but lies outside any possible representation, is paralleled by Cuvier's modification of the notion of 'organic structure' as a notion that lacks any form of representation. From Cuvier on, the internal link which makes all structures dependent on each other is no longer to be found at the representational level: the internal link becomes the very foundation upon which all correlations will be analysed. For Cuvier, organic structure had a role prior and independent of taxonomic classification, or, as Geoffroy Saint Hilaire put it: "Organic structure is becoming an abstract being...capable of assuming numerous forms."[47] That is how we find the new role given to the concept of function. In the classical age, an organ was defined by its structure and by its function; it was like a system which could be analysed from either the role it played or from that of its morphological value:

> ...the two modes of decipherment coincided exactly, but they were nevertheless independent of one another – the first expressing the utilisable, the second the

46 Ibid., 262–63, emphasis added.
47 Ibid., 264.

> identifiable. It is this arrangement that Cuvier overthrows: doing away with the postulates of both their coincidence and their independence, he gives function prominence over the organ – and to a large extent – and subjects the arrangement of the organ to the sovereignty of function.[48]

This event in the architecture of knowledge – the primacy of function as the defining feature of elements – is rendered possible by the replacement of representation with a transcendental notion (Life) which orders functions. Life, as that which defines and limits the study of nature, is that which functions must ultimately ensure.

Indeed, it is only when we consider the organ's relation to the function that we identify similarities there where there is nothing identical at the superficial, or representational, level:

> ...a resemblance that is constituted by the transition of the function into evident invisibility...it matters little, after all, that gills and lungs may have a few variables of form, magnitude, or number in common: they resemble one another because they are two varieties of that nonexistent, abstract, unreal, unassignable organ, absent from all describable species, yet present in the animal kingdoms in its entirety, which serves for respiration in general.[49]

In biology, what to classical eyes were merely differences juxtaposed with identities must now be ordered and conceived on the basis of a functional homogeneity which constitutes their hidden foundation, "when the same and the other both belong to a single space, there is natural history; something like biology becomes possible when this unity of level begins to break up, and when differences stand out against the background of an identity that is deeper and, as it were, more serious than the unity."[50] Moreover, this primacy of functionality implies that new relations emerge: those of coexistence, of internal hierarchy, and of dependence with regard to the level of organic structure.

Cuvier, thus, introduces some important developments. Foucault argues that

> ...this pre-eminence of one function over the others implies that the organism, in its visible arrangements, obeys to a structure....it is understandable, then, how the species can at the same time resemble one another and be distinct from one another. What draws them together is not a certain quantity of coincident elements; it is a sort of focus of identity which cannot be analysed into visible areas because it defines the reciprocal importance of the various functions; on the basis of this imperceptible centre of identities, the organs are arranged in the body...Animal species differ at their peripheries, and resemble each other at their

48 Ibid.
49 Ibid., 265.
50 Ibid.

> centres; *they are connected by the inaccessible, and separated by the apparent. Their generality lies in that which is essential to their life; their singularity in that which is most accessory to it...*[51]

Scientific IR describe States as functionally alike units, which differ only insofar as they have different capabilities for the accomplishment of the same task: survival. The inaccessible organic structure orders elements through a transcendentalism that occults the generality but exposes the singularity. In other words, what links them is invisible functionality, what separates them is how they perform their common function, and this is how academic IR explains intervention in Kosovo.

This new primacy of functionality also has several implications for how we start thinking about life. Life, of course, is no longer a feature, or a quality, that can describe an element in the natural world, but becomes the foundation and the limitation of what a 'science of nature' can seek to discover: that is how the notion of 'order' disappears as the basis for a general science of nature. Instead of having a unified table of classification, we will have a discontinuous reality characterised by how the maintenance of life can be achieved through varying forms of functionality. Thus,

> ...there is opposition between identities and differences: they are no longer of the same fabric, they are no longer established in relation to each other on a homogenous surface: the differences proliferate on the surface, but deeper down they fade, merge, and mingle, as they approach the great, mysterious, invisible focal unity, from which the multiple seems to derive, as though by ceaseless dispersion. Life is no longer that which can be distinguished in a more or less certain fashion from the mechanical; it is that in which all the possible distinctions between living beings have their basis.[52]

This, as Foucault explains, *legitimises* the criteria of isolation in modern anatomy, for it is this anatomy that "gives rise to an *interior space*...it is a matter of an anatomic disarticulation; the major functional system has to be isolated; it is now the real divisions of anatomy that will make it possible to form the great families of living things."[53] This is, also, how the international system finds itself to be 'anatomically' isolated: the international is characterised by its main 'functional system': self help in conditions of anarchy.

Foucault demonstrates how Cuvier and Ricardo are both subject to the same notion of temporality, and how this emerging History is needed once representation becomes obsolete and transcendental philosophies of the object are formed. Foucault explains that because living things are now defined by functional factors, it becomes impossible to order them in continuous taxonomic tables: "There is no

51 Ibid., 266, emphasis added.

52 Ibid., 269.

53 Ibid.

possibility of ordering the variety of functional systems in a continuous series… as a result, the continuum of Classical orders is replaced by a discontinuous proliferation of species of life."[54] Consequently, the pressure of environmental forces determines the discontinuity between different functional systems:

> For natural history, distinctions of species were explained by pre-established differences expressed in the taxonomic tables. The differentiation of species was not produced by any external causal factors operating on real plants or animals. But for Cuvier and those who came after him [consider Darwin], the separation of living things into different classes is due to the different ways that living things are linked to the surroundings on which they depend for survival…for modern biology, the nature of a species is causally dependent on the environment in which its members exist.[55]

This allows us to understand how temporality is introduced into biology: "Precisely because living things are scattered into discontinuous groups that have been formed by the pressure of environmental forces, they are essentially tied to the time in which these forces and their effects exist…with Cuvier…life is essentially tied to time; it is a thoroughly historical reality."[56]

But what is the nature of this temporality? What follows is crucial to understand how History as a tool for analytical finitude fundamentally determines any modern empirical science based on transcendental philosophies of objects. The quote that follows could be regarded as the 'manifesto' of epistemic modernity:

> Historicity, then, has now been introduced into nature…It took the suspension, and, as it were, the placing between parentheses, of that kind of history to give the beings of nature and the products of labour a historicity that would enable modern thought to encompass them, and subsequently to deploy the discursive science of their succession…from the nineteenth century [chronological sequences] express…the profoundly historical mode of being of things and men.[57]

The suspension of history is needed because, as knowledge becomes fragmented and isolated, a requirement of analytic finitude is necessary. Since this requirement is embedded in history, history becomes finite, and together with the anthropological finitude of man, places contingency on the experiencing subject. These developments are related to the project of developing a transcendental philosophy of the object. How did these epistemic constraints limit the specific ways in which the Kosovo crisis was interpreted? Was an analytic of finitude – a conceptual isolation of the crisis – responsible for ultimately creating a historically

54 Gutting, *Michel Foucault's Archaeology of Scientific Reason*, 191.

55 Ibid.

56 Ibid., 192.

57 Foucault, *The Order of Things*, 276, emphasis added.

linear understanding of the conflict in order to use such understating to justify the limits of such analytic? Is this not the sort of continuous time Benedict Anderson argues is responsible for allowing a concept of nationalism to emerge?[58] These will be the main questions that subsequent chapters will seek to address.

Science and Fragmentation: The End of Empiricism

In concentrating on the Vienna Circle this study shares Steven Smith's position regarding the successive stages of 'positivism' and their influence on the discipline of IR – and, as we will argue, their influence on our framing of the Kosovo crisis. Smith argues that we can discern three waves of positivism:

> The first variant is that developed by Auguste Comte in the early nineteenth century,…the second variant is that of logical positivism, which emerged in the 1920s in what was known as the Vienna Circle…the third variant is the one that has been most influential in the social sciences in the last fifty years. It emerged out of logical positivism, but moved away from its extremely stark criteria for what counts as knowledge…[59]

As Smith explains, the third influential variant is the result of the mixed conclusions of the Vienna Circle: it emerged from it, but it formulated quite different interpretations of science. These different formulations are the consequence of the end of empiricism as the dominant epistemic position within the philosophy of science.

More importantly, it is crucial to consider the Vienna Circle because the following sections will argue that it is possible to discern in the Circle's most fundamental conclusions the schisms that have characterised all social sciences: for what concerns IR, it will be demonstrated that the arguments which oppose Waltz to Aron, for example, should be viewed in terms of the realist/anti-realist schism that resulted from the Vienna Circle. This argument will be expanded in the fourth chapter, when Waltz's constant references to the Circle's ideas will be shown to represent the thrust of his efforts to actualise the epistemological status of 'scientific' IR. On the other hand, it will be demonstrated that Aron was accused of not considering the Circle's conclusions on the role of empiricism in the formulation of hypothesis: thus resulted the accusation of being a *backward* positivist. Subsequent chapters will show that debates relating to the principles and practicalities of the Kosovo conflict – indeed, debates on the ways in which the conflict should be framed – are equally reminiscent of such crucial epistemic debates.

---

58 See Chapter 6.

59 Steve Smith, "Positivism and Beyond," in *International Theory: Positivism and Beyond*, eds, Ken Booth, Steve Smith and Marysia Zalewski (Cambridge: Cambridge University Press, 1996), 15.

It is fundamental to understand the Circle's arguments, and their successive influence on the epistemology of IR, in terms of Foucault's description of the modern episteme. For what does the end of empiricism in scientific methodology represent if not the break from a certain kind of representation? As outlined above, Foucault demonstrates how modernity is characterised by a break-up of representation in three distinct modes of enquiry: the formulation of a transcendental philosophy of the object (metaphysics), of the subject (criticism), and the birth of positivism. Metaphysics results from an a posteriori analysis of the subject in terms of the objects it experiences, while Criticism results in the a priori contextualisation of the experiencing subject. Positivism is defined by Foucault as the refusal to engage with any transcendental philosophy. The fundamental question, which is to be kept in mind in the following presentation of the Vienna Circle, is: to what extent is Foucault's positivism distinct from the classical episteme's bases of representation?

Gutting considers this very problem as follows:

> ...positivism might seem a reversal to classical modes of thought. Is it not, after all, the identification of reality with the world of representations? Should we not, therefore, regard it as a mere revival of the empiricist philosophies of the Classical age? Although Foucault does not raise this question, he might respond by maintaining that it is not possible to separate positivism from the critical turn that it rejects. The point would be that, once this turn has been made, there are, in contrast with the Classical age, alternatives to regarding thought as merely a system of representations. Positivism may maintain that in fact this is all our thought is, that there is nothing beyond the phenomenal realm. But it does so in a context that, in contrast to the Classical age, at least allows the possibility of other construals of thought.[60]

Once the turn has been made, there is no going back: and the turn – that is, the collapse of the 'dogmas of empiricism' – has occurred, as Willard Van Orman Quine maintains, in Vienna.[61]

Indeed, the philosophers of the Circle introduced the problematic that frames the empiricist dilemma as a base for their formulation of logical positivism. The first message of the Circle was that if we think of science as being concerned exclusively with general phenomena, and if we also assume that a general proposition can be considered as a scientific hypothesis only after empirical validation, we have to accept the fact that it is not possible to directly experience generalities. This is the main paradox upon which an alternative scientific methodology, a more 'coherent' one, had to be built. This paradox, in fact, leads us to believe that it is impossible

60 Gutting, *Michel Foucault's Archaeology of Scientific Reason*, 185.

61 Willard Van Orman Quine, "Two Dogmas of Empiricism," in *From a Logical Point of View*, ed. Willard Van Orman Quine (Cambridge MA: Harvard University Press, 1951).

to justify scientific hypotheses on empirical experience...precisely because of the biological finitude of human beings. This, ultimately, relates to the exact link that can be established between the generic, or Universal, hypotheses and phenomenal, or particular issues: this, thus, represents yet another epistemic constraint that characterised many of the debates surrounding intervention in Kosovo.

The debates that took place were all attempts to conceptualise alternative (logical as opposed to empirical) foundations for scientific enquiry.[62] For instance, the philosopher Fries proposed to the Circle the argument that there were three possible solutions to this empirical problem. The first one was to accept hypotheses on the grounds of the intellectual authority of those scientists who had produced them. This position is qualified as 'dogmatic'. The second proposition was to regress *ad infinitum* in order to empirically certify the bases upon which all theoretical constructs were built. This option ('regressionism') was obviously not viable. The third solution was the one that Fries advocated: it was possible to logically deduct propositions which were based on facts that had been previously empirically tested. Fries' proposal was categorised as a 'foundationalist' solution.

Carnap also proposed an alternative variant of foundationalism. He argued with Wittgenstein, that the meaning of all complex propositions depends on the meaning of the elementary concepts that compose them. Moreover, Carnap agreed that the meanings of propositions are dependent on the context of truth within which they are situated. Nonetheless, Carnap argued that some propositions were irreducible, independent from other propositions, inherently true and objective. These are what we will call irreducible propositions. According to Carnap, these propositions did not need to be justified, and could serve as the basis for all consequent scientific theories. Nonetheless, the idea of irreducible propositions had to be abandoned after the powerful critique of Neurath. The same criticism led Neurath and Carnap to adopt a common position that expressed the impossibility of formulating foundational propositions derived from sensory experience.

Foundationalism, moreover, was vividly rejected by the other fellows of the Circle, most notably by Popper. Popper restated that we cannot affirm the validity of any facts, even if these are empirically detectable, if we want to use them in order to formulate general propositions. We cannot, as individuals, experience multiple phenomena at the same time. The generality to which science aspires and the individual's limited empirical experience that is supposed to justify its propositions constitute an irreducible paradox – a paradox that characterises all (epistemic) modern knowledge. In a sense, we are faced with Foucault's description of the struggle to relate the transcendental with the representation of empirical experience, and with the limitations imposed by our own biological finitude. In this sense, the empirical stance of reducing philosophical (theoretical scientific propositions) truths to empirical truth is, in Popper's eyes, untenable.

62 For the debates within the Circle see Anouk Barberousse, Max Kistler and Pascal Ludwig, *La Philosophie Des Sciences Au Xxe Siècle* (Manchecourt: Flammarion, 2000), Chapter 1.

Indeed, Popper later famously announced that scientific enquiry could only proceed through 'conjectures and refutations'.[63] Normal sciences were then facing the very uncertainty principle that many social sciences still face. This situation was characterised by the nearly total unreliability, unavailability or unwillingness to use empirical data for the formulation of scientific hypothesis. This also caused the famous schism that gave birth to the opposition between realism and anti-realism in science.

Significantly, some members of the Circle concluded that foundationalism had to be abandoned because it was intrinsically paradoxical. In fact, foundationalism (both in its logical and empiricist mould) seeks to establish irreducible propositions which are supposed to satisfy two important requirements. As Davidson explains: "The foundations of knowledge must be simultaneously objective and subjective, that is, certain but nevertheless subject to eventual refutation."[64] The problem is that these two requirements (objectivity and subjectivity) are simply not compatible, and cannot be satisfied by an irreducible proposition. As Barberousse notes, "from this moment the road taken by Neurath and Carnap leads to the opposite direction to the one taken by Schlick."[65]

The turn had been made. In fact, this paradox encouraged some philosophers such as Carnap and Neurath to argue that it was more adequate to renounce the idea of an absolute foundation of knowledge in order to maintain the objectivity of science (relativism), while other members of the Circle, headed by Schlick, considered absolute foundations indispensable, thus rejecting the idea that foundations must necessarily be objective. As we noted, this paradox terminated, via scientific fragmentation, reductionism in science, a philosophy that sought to reduce the whole of science to experienced singular phenomena. This was one of the two dogmas of empiricism detected by Quine.[66] From our perspective, this schism is fundamental as it encourages scientific theorising to move away from the epistemic pole of empirical positivism as defined in Foucault's description of the modern triangular configuration of knowledge. The move towards metaphysical theorising is, on the other hand, something that has characterised and continues to characterise the generation and deployment of knowledge in IR in general, and in relation to the Kosovo crisis in particular.

The schism has had an enormous importance on scientific theorising over the past decades. For scientific 'realists', who attempted to satisfy the objectivity requirement by questioning basic assumptions, do not really envisage the task of theorising as 'anti-realists', who postulate the crucial importance of absolutes do. This is particularly true when it comes to differentiating general 'real' patterns from accidental ones:

---

63 Karl Popper, *Conjectures and Refutations: The Growth of Scientific Knowledge*. London, Routledge, 2002.

64 Ibid., 30.

65 Ibid., 29.

66 Quine, "Two Dogmas of Empiricism".

> ...Realist theorists believe that...it is necessary to elaborate *metaphysical* theoretical constructions in which...non-observable entities must be postulated in order to explain generalities. On the other hand, empiricists affirm that it is not possible to postulate an absolute capable of explaining generalities if the construction of this absolute has to take place outside the scientific process itself...[67]

Vienna marks the beginning of an era in which metaphysical construals are viewed as *legitimate* bases for the scientific enterprise – in the same way that metaphysical justifications may come to be viewed as legitimate bases for bellicose endeavours. Of course, this metaphysical stance is rejected by the empiricists, those who Foucault describes as 'positivists'. Nonetheless, this positivism is no longer regarded as the *only* path to scientific understanding, and it is precisely this path that Quine describes through the notion of 'dogma'. Following Gutting's arguments, this schism should be taken as marking the definite break-up with representational modes of thought within the philosophy of science. And there is no better way to demonstrate this than by fully grasping the consequences of the following quote, describing the conclusions of the Vienna Circle:

> The logical analysis demonstrates that pure thought cannot be a source of empirical knowledge: the possibility of an a priori synthetic knowledge, which is fundamental in Kant's philosophy, is strongly rejected. Only two kinds of propositions have a legitimate claim within science: those which are a priori, but tautological (that is, with no real meaning) and those that are synthetic, but always a posteriori, of empirical science.[68]

In Foucault's epistemic triangle, Vienna marks a new configuration of scientific thought in which transcendental philosophies of the subject are rejected in order to render legitimate only metaphysical or 'positivist' claims to scientific understanding. Indeed, tautological (metaphysical) claims are meaningless because these transcendental notions, as Foucault reminds us, are outside the possibility of knowledge: but they ground, by this very virtue, all possible claims to knowledge. The a posteriori claims, on the other hand, only consider as legitimate observations that follow from empirical observation. To reinforce the argument that the modern epistemic fracture translates, in the philosophy of science, into the debates that took place in Vienna, it is possible to read the following assertion through the arguments exposed above. Gutting, in maintaining that positivism is distinct from representation, indicates that

---

67 Barberousse, *La Philosophie Des Sciences Au Xxe Siècle*, 90, emphasis added (my translation).

68 Ibid., 298.

> …of course, the positivist can try to exclude these other construals (as, for example, meaningless). But how can he do this except by methods (for example, the appeal to a principle of verification) that themselves go beyond the resources of thought limited to the phenomenal realm? Thus positivism seems to face the alternative of either making the merely dogmatic assertion that thought is to be identified with representation or else falling in incoherence by attempting to establish this assertion.[69]

Is this not, after all, what characterises the empiricist stance since the Vienna Circle? And since, as Smith argues,[70] the bulk of academic IR is based on a specific understanding of 'positivism', what are we to make of related developments and related understandings of the Kosovo conflict?

The Metaphysical Foundations of Modern Science

One of the main contributions of twentieth century philosophy of science was to demonstrate how the scientific method is not characterised, as it was generally thought, by the mere objective observation and experimentation of reality. If we apply Foucault's definition of the modern organisation of knowledge, arguments such as Popper's and Kuhn's make us realise that what we often brand as 'science' is not located within the analytic or positivist epistemic poles. Rather, the 'scientific method' is centred on presuppositions, or conjectures, that have more to do with metaphysical transcendental theorising than with positivistic experimentation or mathematical/logical essences. In this sense, the realist 'scientific method' should be regarded as a transcendental philosophy of the object, for the subjects of scientific enquiry are ultimately examined by how they stand in relation to the basic presuppositions of the paradigm, and not vice-versa.

There is a difference to be noted, however, and this is that whilst Vienna marks the beginning of a new epistemic context, a context in which metaphysical presuppositions are regarded as legitimate grounds for the scientific enterprise, arguments such as Kuhn's indicate that, in a sense, there has always been a strong metaphysical dimension within scientific thought. Kuhn argues that science has always been paradigmatic: scientists always relied on assumptions to make sense of their research. However, it can be argued, as Kuhn does, that the social sciences, including IR, were at a pre-paradigmatic stage. The adoption of paradigmatic science also implies the adoption of all its inconveniences.[71] Kuhn's *Structure of*

69 Gutting, *Michel Foucault's Archaeology of Scientific Reason*, 186.

70 Smith, "Positivism and Beyond".

71 The application of Kuhnian arguments to IR has caused important controversies. For a more detailed argument see Stefano Guzzini, *Realism in International Relations and International Political Economy: The Continuing Story of a Death Foretold* (Florence: European University Institute Press, 1992), 27–30.

Scientific Revolutions explores the notion of 'paradigm' and what is at stake in the claim to knowledge made by paradigmatic science:

> ...they constitute what I'm here calling normal science. Closely examined, whether historically or in the laboratory, that enterprise seems an attempt to force nature into the preformed and relatively inflexible box that the paradigm supplies. No part of the aim of normal science is to call forth new sorts of phenomena; indeed those that will not fit the box are often not seen at all. Nor do scientists normally aim to invent new theories, and they are often intolerant of those invented by others. Instead, normal-scientific research is directed to the articulation of those phenomena and theories that the paradigm already supplies.

The benefits and disadvantages of paradigms in the natural sciences, explains Kuhn, lie respectively on the possibility of deep inquiry and on the limitations imposed by a paradigm:

> ...perhaps these are defects. The areas investigated by normal science are, of course, minuscule; the enterprise now under discussion has drastically restricted vision. But those restrictions, born from confidence in a paradigm, turn out to be essential to the development of science. By focusing attention upon a small range of relatively esoteric problems, the paradigm forces scientists to investigate some part of nature in a detail and depth that would otherwise be unimaginable.[72]

The study of reality seems to *follow* from metaphysical assumptions. How does this correlate to Foucault's arguments on modernity's desire to supersede taximonia and mathesis by studying the deep core of the organism? Is this deep core not ultimately inaccessible, do we not always need, in the end, to replace these hidden truths with metaphysical assumptions? Does this depth and detail that would otherwise be unimaginable, not correspond to a general trend aiming at discarding the superficial nature of representation in order to fully grasp what causes such representations? Are paradigms being introduced as the equivalents of those 'nonrepresentational sources of representational systems' in the empirical sciences? In other words, does this necessity to study the order of things from the representational source, not necessarily entail the creation of a metaphysical system of thought? What is this inflexible box into which nature is forced to comply, if not an example of a tool that allows the study of things from that which they experience? Is a paradigm not, after all, a perfect example of a transcendental philosophy of a metaphysically constructed object? Does this inflexible paradigmatic box not perfectly illustrate the notion of analytic finitude inherent to all projects wishing

72 Both quotes in Thomas Kuhn, *The Structure of Scientific Revolutions* (Chicago: University of Chicago Press, 1970), 24.

to constitute a transcendental philosophy of the object? Finally, the fundamental question, which will be tackled in the next chapter: does this transcendental philosophy of the object necessitate linear historicism in scientific methodology as it does in economics, biology and philology – and in IR? To what extent did this characterise the way in which the Kosovo crisis was framed? And to what extent are these constraints being challenged?

Dupré, in a book with a very pertinent title, seeks to illustrate the "dependence of *modern* science on metaphysics" arguing that "science itself cannot progress without powerful assumptions about the world it is trying to investigate…without… a prior metaphysics."[73] In a way, his project is similar to the main arguments of our work. Dupré insists on the fact that a scientistic approach to social events, and 'scientific' approaches that are characterised by metaphysical foundations, produce precise ways in which we think of, for example, the political and economic realms. Thus, Dupré proceeds to demonstrate how the three main consequences of metaphysical science (essentialism, reductionism and determinism) have characterised the 'scientific' analysis of social events.[74] It is important for us to take note of Dupré's arguments:

> To lead to the most significant consequences, the thesis that scientific belief depends always on background assumptions not all which can be equally subject to empirical warrant must apply not merely to more or less theoretical beliefs, but also to what are taken to be the empirical data on which scientific beliefs might be founded.[75]

Conclusion

The project to develop a distinct archaeological methodology was conducted as Michel Foucault attempted to frame his previous and future works in a coherent research programme. In this sense, the project of *The Archaeology of Knowledge* is entirely consistent with the findings of *The Order of Things* as it effectively constructed a methodology that would deal with the emergence of 'man' in the modern episteme by eliminating the importance of the human subject in the structural analysis of thought.

The purpose is not to study epistemes because they necessarily determinate that, for example, empiricism and reductionism are philosophies which, by epistemic definition, were destined to disappear once A or B happened. The purpose is, rather, to understand what allows for challenging philosophies of science to emerge, how these are formed, how these influence intellectual and practical

73 Dupré, *The Disorder of Things: Metaphysical Foundations of the Disunity of Science*, 1–2, emphasis added.

74 Ibid., 244–64.

75 Ibid., 246.

outputs and how these relate to the production of knowledge on the Kosovo crisis from a 'scientific' IR perspective, for example. Waltz's 'scientific IR' will not be thoroughly analysed because of the influence that it may have had on diplomatic practice, rather, the theory will be presented as a 'monument' to the modern episteme, whose underlying axes – the analytic of finitude and historical linearity – influence the way events themselves are interpreted (in this case, the Kosovo crisis). This, in turn, will allow a second part to show how the most important traits of this configuration can be discerned in the practice of IR (the shift from a purely descriptive analysis of an episteme to an explicative analysis – that is one which tackles the power/knowledge nexus – is often translated by Foucault in terms of a shift from archaeology to *genealogy*).

By now, it should be clear what we mean when we refer to Complexity science as a 'postmodern science', as we have investigated the revolutionary potential of Complexity within an epistemic framework. Complexity is postmodern strictly in this epistemic sense, as it does away with the 'Age of History' and, as Prigogine argues, places *non-linear* temporality at the heart of theorising. In the following chapter we shall make a supplementary effort to present pre-Complexity science as a transcendental philosophy of constituted objects, and to show how IR theory and practice have been developed as transcendental philosophies of objects, which rely on linear time as a provide of contingency and which are thus fundamentally undermined by the ethos of Complexity.

At this point, it would be important to state that there have been many interesting debates surrounding Foucault's innovative intellectual project.[76] Whilst it is not the intention to ignore such debates, which have been considered in the formulation of the analysis, the current study requires that a specific understanding of Foucault's definition of modernity is provided in order to concentrate the analysis on what defines modernity and Complexity: that is, a diametrically opposed understanding of temporality. The importance and requirement to concentrate on this issue leaves very little space for a detailed consideration of secondary literature.

76 See, for example, the aptly named work of Béatrice Han, *Foucault's Critical Project: Between the Transcendental and the Historical* (Stanford: Stanford University Press, 2002) and Hubert Dreyfus and Paul Rabinow, *Michel Foucault: Beyond Structuralism and Hermeneutics* (Chicago: University of Chicago Press, 1983).

Chapter 3
Complexity, International Relations and Ethics from an Epistemic Perspective

> Cause and effect: such a duality probably never exists, – in truth we are confronted by a continuum out of which we isolate a couple of pieces, just as we perceive motion only as isolated points and then infer it without ever actually seeing it. The suddenness with which many effects stand out misleads us; actually, it is sudden only for us. An intellect that could see cause and effect as a continuum and a flux and not, as we do, in terms of arbitrary division and dismemberment – would repudiate the concept of cause and effect and deny all conditionality.
>
> Friedrich Nietzsche, *The Gay Science*[1]

Introduction: Science as the new Metaphysics in Transcendental Philosophies of the Object

Whilst introducing Nietzsche as a political thinker, Keith Ansell Pearson explains that "one of the consequences of humanity's faith in morality is the cultivation of truthfulness, of a *will* to truth (think of the Christian confession, for example). Over time, this will to truth in Christianity is transmuted into the intellectual conscience which underlies modern scientific inquiry."[2] Science is the new metaphysics after the death of God: such is Nietzsche's diagnosis. To be sure, Nietzsche believes that European philosophy (and society?) since Plato has been infected by metaphysics – however, its recent evolution into 'science' is particularly cunning. On such basis Michel Foucault proceeded to analyse modern modes of metaphysical knowledge.

This chapter will be guided by the Nietzschean belief that modern scientific enquiry is characterised by a 'will to truth',[3] which takes the form of what

---

1 Nietzsche, *The Gay Science: With a Prelude of Rhymes and an Appendix of Songs*, 173.

2 Keith Ansell Pearson, *An Introduction to Nietzsche as a Political Thinker* (Cambridge: Cambridge University Press, 1994), 36. Equating modernity's quest for truth with modernity's craving for certainty is what allows Michael Dillon to translate such desire for certainty into a notion of security in modern political thought.

3 Babette Babich offers some related insights in her masterful analysis of *Nietzsche's Philosophy of Science*: "As the mechanism of contentment in the face of nothing, in the wake of nihilism, science is the 'latest and noblest form' of the ascetic ideal." Babette

Foucault described as transcendental philosophies of objects. Interestingly, the idea according to which there is no 'scientific truth' can be found in the works of both Nietzsche and Prigogine: as Babette Babich puts it:

> For Nietzsche, "Thinghood was invented by us from the first". Reality as we take it to be in itself and the understanding we have of reality necessarily correspond insofar as this is trivially insured by the reciprocity of any relational construction. This kind of interpretive correspondence is the communication or dialogue noted by Prigogine and Stengers: "Whatever we call reality, it is revealed to us only through the active construction in which we participate."[4]

Following this 'metaphysical will to truth' insight – which characterises two of the most fundamental axes of modernity – this chapter will unveil the epistemic configuration of contemporary IR theory and contemporary debates surrounding ethics, international law and universal human rights. Following the previous chapters, the two axes have been identified as historical linearity and the analytic of finitude. It is important to remember, however, that both factors are intertwined: in the last instance, according to Foucault, it is an analytic of finitude which produces fuzzy empirico-transcendental doublets, which in turn necessitate a concept of historical linearism in order to function. The present chapter will argue that the metaphysical nature of modern science – a nature that begins to dominate scientific epistemology from the Congress of Vienna onwards – characterises the formulation and deployment of knowledge in two important fields related to the Kosovo crisis: the evolution of academic IR and the characteristics of contemporary ethics in relation to humanitarian intervention.

The first section of the chapter will analyse the evolution of IR and unveil the inherent historical linearity present in its most dominant paradigms. A genesis of the discipline of IR will thus be elaborated and used to show how this discipline, as a modern empirical science, was formed on the bases of the epistemic rules identified by Foucault. The elaboration of such a genesis will allow a subsequent section to explain how the empirical formation of the discipline conditioned the discipline's understanding of the Kosovo crisis. In doing so, the work is consistent

---

Babich, *Nietzsche's Philosophy of Science: Reflecting Science on the Ground of Art and Life* (New York: State University of New York Press, 1994), 203. Also note the similarities between Nietzsche's definition of 'continuum and flux' and Bergson's views on the nature of real time (Chapter 1).

4 Ibid., 150. If the identification of Prigogine is the kernel that unites Foucault's and Bergson's definition of the limits of the modern episteme and the beginning of a new one, Babich's identification of Prigogine as a "Nietzschean" scientist only reinforces the arguments on the synergies between Complexity science and German philosophy outlined in the previous chapter.

with Rob Walker's approach to the analysis of academic IR, as an endeavour that is constitutive of IR practice.[5]

From this point of view any approach (such as Walker's) that tackles the issue of state sovereignty by analysing both its spatio-temporal assumptions and its fundamental dichotomy (particularity versus universality) – as the current study seeks to do through a Complexity-informed epistemic methodology – is particularly important. Thus, IR formations are not studied by virtue of what they *say*, rather, they are studied by virtue of what they (epistemically) *represent*.

Also, an understanding of how the modern episteme conditioned the formation of related understanding in IR will allow following chapters to discuss how Complexity's undermining of the modern episteme relates to a new challenge facing any analysis of crises that rely on such episteme. Considerations will also be made on how epistemic formations influence the discipline of geography (via geopolitics), and how this discipline challenges – through alternative conceptualisations of space – modern interpretations of the Kosovo conflict.

A second section will deal more specifically with the problem of an analytic of finitude in contemporary debates surrounding ethics, international law and human rights, areas in which the strains caused by the empirico-transcendental doublet are the most evident. Finally, the chapter will seek to re-introduce the ethos of Complexity as a philosophy of immanence in both instances. In sum, the current chapter seeks to apply the insights developed in the previous chapters to the development of theoretical knowledge, which, in turn, conditions the deployment of such knowledge in the context of the Kosovo crisis: the empirical consequences constitute, therefore, the focus of the final chapters of this book.

An Archaeology of International Relations (IR) Theory: From Raymond Aron to Kenneth Waltz

Following the archaeological method, it is important to proceed with an examination of the 'monuments' of IR theory in order to detect the traces of the modern episteme. The epistemic shift that characterised IR theory, which is identifiable

5 As Jorg Kustermans put it whilst reviewing a classical text in International Relations literature, "it is stated that the discipline of International Relations is not descriptive of the practice of international relations, but that it is rather *constitutive* of it. Walker speaks of theories 'demarcat[ing] and disciplin[ing] the horizons beyond which it is dangerous to pursue any political action […]' (p.6). A central aspect of this constituting power of International Relations Theory is its insistence on the principle of *state sovereignty*. This principle represents one particularly early modern spatio-temporal solution to the problem of *particularity versus universality*. The latter is a dichotomous tension that all people of all times have to deal with. The spatio-temporal construct 'state sovereignty' is at once elegant and problematic." Jorg Kustermans, "Walker, R.B.J. (1993), Inside/outside: International Relations as Political Theory, Cambridge/New York: Cambridge University Press" IPIS Book Review http://www.ipisresearch.be/download.php?id=125 (accessed 23 June 2008).

in the *documents* of the discipline, can help us to trace the evolution of such shift in other areas of international life. The Aron/Waltz shifts in not anachronistic: it illustrates the larger epistemic movement characterised by the establishment of transcendental philosophies of the object. The Aron/Waltz nexus is at the heart of recent and contemporary IR theory, for all the documents produced by the discipline ever since reflect one side or the other of the epistemic change. All IR theories are in one of the two sides of the same 'epistemic' coin. In fact, the Aron/Waltz debate is a clear correlation of the debates presented by Foucault in the discipline of economics as this discipline was trying to establish itself as a modern empirical science following the rules of the modern episteme. As following paragraphs hope to demonstrate, it is easy to see a Smith in Aron, and a Ricardo in Waltz.

Of course, many 'great debates' – which we could not possibly enumerate in a single book – have taken place, and continue to take place in academic IR since the Aron/Waltz split, but as this section hopes to make clear, such debates do not fundamentally alter the limits, the borderlines, within which knowledge is generated in IR. From a Foucauldian point of view, there is not much that is new under this particular epistemic sun in IR theory, and, for example, the rather obvious similarities between Aron's arguments in the 1960s and the Wendt-inspired 'sociological turn' far more recently is evidence of this.

The objective of Raymond Aron was, by his own account, to create a scientific theory of IR. He was not only one of those who advocated the introduction of a 'scientific' methodology in IR, he also was one of the first scholars who presented the enormous difficulties that this methodology implied, in order to reject it later in his career. This is largely the reason why his arguments and the reactions that these have caused, such as Waltz's formulation of neorealist theory, should constitute the starting point of a study concerned with the discontinuity that characterised much of the shift from a notion of scientific enquiry to another. In fact, the latest model of scientific research that emerged in IR is rooted in this discontinuity, which provides the justification for its claims. As the following paragraphs will argue, this epistemological rupture in IR is caused by the post-Vienna demise of empiricism in the philosophy of science and the subsequent triumph of the metaphysical approach that was described in detail by Foucault as he proceeded to unveil the nature of the modern episteme. In this epistemic context, and given the well documented relation between developments in the philosophy of science and in IR theory (and practice) it becomes particularly important to address questions related to the nature of such science (see Chapter 2).[6]

6 For the links between IR and scientific epistemology consider, for example, Smith, "Positivism and Beyond", Steve Smith and Martin Hollis, *Explaining and Understanding International Relations* (Cambridge: Cambridge University Press, 1996); Steve Smith and Ken Booth, eds, *International Relations Theory Today* (Polity Press, 1995), and, more importantly, Jim George, *Discourses of Global Politics: Critical (Re)Introduction to International Relations* (London: Palgrave Macmillan, 1994).

As Jean Jacques Roche explains, Aron's reference was the discipline of political economy, a discipline that had pushed forward its degree of theorisation.[7] Walras and Pareto had already noticed the reductionism that characterised this area, but it was thanks to this feature that political economy managed to give a simplified vision of a complex reality. This reductionism, however, did not adversely affect the utility of Keynes's 'General Theory', for example. This theory was possible because Keynes had identified a number of interdependent and dependent variables, which shaped the basis of his theoretical effort. This was also the underlying idea of Aron's *Paix et Guerre entre Nations*.[8] The purpose of this work was first to identify a field proper to 'IR' by elucidating its most obvious defining point: the ultimate legal and legitimate reliance on armed force by all of the actors involved in the field; in other words, the total lack of a common source of sovereignty. On this defining assumption, Aron began to identify categories within which generalities could be detected, and categories which were more 'anomalous'.[9] This categorisation required the detection of a certain number of dependent and interdependent data.

However, in a famous article published in 1967, Aron had to accept defeat by stating that a scientific theory of IR was illusionary for a number of reasons.[10] First, we should consider Aron's notion of 'theory'. According to Aron, there are two definitions of 'theory' in the Western philosophical tradition. The first equates a theory to a 'philosophy'. This definition places the word 'theory' at odds with the notion of practice: to have a particular theory about something is equivalent to making reference to a particular philosophy: thus, in this sense, the more something is 'theoretical' the least it is anchored to 'practice'. The second definition of theory is the one we find in 'scientific' practice: In this sense, "a theory represents a hypothetical-deductive system, that is constituted by a number of propositions in which the terms are rigorously defined and the relations between these terms (or variables) often take a mathematical form. *This system is elaborated from a conceptualisation of a perceived or observed reality…*"[11] This suggests that, according to Aron, a scientific theory must be grounded on empirical reality. This makes of Aron an empiricist, and, as such, it makes of Aron an intellectual who should have faced the challenges of empiricism as these were presented by the Vienna Circle.

---

7 Jean Jacques Roche, *Théories des Relations Internationales* (Paris: Montchrestien, 1999), 10–17.

8 Raymond Aron, *Peace and War: A Theory of International Relations* (New York: Praeger, 1966).

9 As explained by Stanley Hoffmann, "Théories et Relations Internationales," *Revue Française de Science Politique*, March (1961), 427.

10 Raymond Aron, "Qu'est-ce qu'une Théorie des Relations Internationales?," *Revue Française de Science Politique*, October (1967), 837–61.

11 Ibid., 838, my translation, emphasis added.

Aron knew that the relationship between theory and reality was more complicated than what the quote above suggests. For instance, Aron recognised that political economy must be founded on at least two presuppositions which cannot be qualified as being strictly empirically objective. These are the criteria of isolation and of idealisation: "…pure theory implies the creation of a well defined system (the economic system) within a more general system (global society) and the definition of a fictive actor (the homo economicus) which differs drastically from real actors."[12] Aron also states that economic theory "substitutes effective economic life with an artificial market, where it is not real men who interact, but subjects of whose characteristics are determined by the economist, who disposes of perfect information and who have a defined unique objective: the maximisation of any given quantity."[13]

Aron's interest in political economy, that is, for a modern empirical science, is interesting precisely because of the tensions between 'theory' (the metaphysical) and 'practice' (the empirical). Interestingly, Waltz's inspiration is also to be found within this empirical science, but while Aron is interested in macroeconomic Keynesianism, Waltz is interested in microeconomic theory. In Aron's reference to political economy, the tension is obvious: while, as the above quote suggests, pure theory forms conceptualisations from empirical reality, this reality must be limited and defined…by conceptualisations. Needless to say, we find in Aron's description of political economy all the features of the modern empirical sciences: the subject 'man' is analysed through the notion of interest which becomes, as Foucault describes it, the transcendental notion of desire (the experienced object). Moreover, it is the transcendental and eschatological notion of desire, that is the criteria of idealisation, which defines the analytic finitude of man as an object of enquiry for the organism 'political economy'.

Thus, Aron considers that "the progress of the economic sciences are due to a constant dialectic between theory and empirical reality."[14] The relationship between 'theory' (the formulation of transcendental notions) and empirical reality (the phenomenal world that is experienced by men) is qualified as being dialectical. This is so because in the relationship between the simplified models of economic theory and the reality they are supposed to explain, both factors are mutually constituted. Nonetheless, we cannot fail to acknowledge that in this tense relationship the 'empirical world' has the last word, and determines the validity of the criteria of isolation and of idealisation which, in turn, condition the study of the 'real' world. If we consider Aron's categorisation of the six main factors which characterise economic theory as a 'science', the above suggestion becomes evident. As to the first and second points, Aron explains that in order to isolate a sub-system, it is necessary to define it in terms of what makes it different and particular. Second, scientific progress is based on a continuous relationship

12 Ibid., 839.

13 Ibid.

14 Ibid., 840.

between simplified models and empirical observation. Third, idealisations are made, but these are rooted in the empirical world.[15]

The fact that even idealisations must remain anchored to the empirical world characterises what Aron means when he says that economic theory is 'scientific': such a theory can certainly be constituted by theoretical models, but such models are only possible once empirical research demonstrates what are the general 'essential phenomena' which can be eventually simplified through models that artificially isolate and idealise these phenomena.

Waltz summarised the reasons why *Paix et Guerre*, by the account of its author, had allegedly failed:[16]

1. There are a multitude of factors which do not allow the isolation of domestic politics from the area of international politics. The defining point of the discipline, anarchy, did not allow an effective separation of the field and the establishment of adequate parameters of study.
2. The State, as the principal actor, does not necessarily pursue a unique goal defined in terms of national interest or even security. In other words, it is extremely difficult to rationalise the main actors, while economic theory, for example, managed relative success by rationalising the consumer and turning it into homo economicus.
3. There is an impossibility to distinguish dependent variables from independent variables, which are supposed to provide the grounds for casual explanation.
4. There is an absence of quantitative data upon which researchers could rely.
5. There is an absence of an automatic restoration of equilibrium, which would suggest the presence of general patterns.
6. Finally, and partially because of the arguments exposed, the theoretical field of IR as defined by Aron does not offer the possibility to predict or act in the 'real' world of relations between state units.

As a consequence of all this, Aron concluded that it was only possible to study IR as some sort of *sociology* defined as an intermediary between theory and events (and is this not, after all, what the latest 'social turn' in IR seeks to do?

15 Consider: "During the last thirty years, the progress of scientific economic knowledge has been based mainly on empirical, statistical and descriptive studies. Empirical and statistical studies have allowed analysts to become conscious of essential phenomena... It is national accountancy, much more than theory, that has given governments the means to better master economic fluctuations." Ibid., 841.

16 Kenneth Waltz, "Realist Thought and Neorealist Theory", *Journal of International Affairs* Vol. 44, no. 1 (1990), 21–37. It is important to note that Waltz's formulation of Neorealism comes precisely as a reaction to Aron's argument on the impossibility of establishing a scientific theory of IR.

Are scholars such as Wendt simply picking up IR theory where Aron left it in the 1960s? And is constructivism not clearly based on what Foucault called 'Criticism', that is, approaches to study that begin from the experiencing subjects rather than experienced, transcendental, objects?).[17] Thus, "the field of IR does not allow the construction of a scientific theory, not because of the insufficient number of concepts but because the very nature of the field cannot be reduced to a unique approach."[18] This is a conviction that French political scientists have shared for quite a long time, and these show no signs of changing ideas.[19] Incidentally, this message also communicates the idea that IR can only be studied with interpretative (Weberian) methods, which could roughly fall within what Hollis and Smith defined as 'Understanding'.[20]

It is, therefore, probably correct to affirm that Aron's problems arise from the empirical world of IR. It is this empirical world that presents the six obstacles which have been enumerated. There is not, for instance, a strictly objective empirical factor that can differentiate the internal from the external. An 'internal' condition within France, for example, may trigger an 'external', or 'international', response by Germany, and vice-versa. The absence of quantitative data and of stability mechanisms further advance our reasons to believe that Aron is facing, as an empiricist, an empirical world which simply cannot be isolated, or quantified. Additionally, Aron makes it quite clear that the notion of 'anarchy' as the defining property of the system cannot account for the behaviour of states: the transcendental notion of anarchy does not make states unitary and rational actors as the notion of self interest turns humans into precisely that sort of unitary and rational actors.[21] Anarchy (or self help), unlike Interest or Desire, does not seem to be a functionally viable transcendental.

Opponents were quick to point out that Aron – and other 'backward positivists' like him – had missed the point. Vienna had already dealt with the issue of empiricism as a valid – and exclusive – ground for the formulation of scientific theories at length. It concluded that for knowledge to advance, it was necessary to

17 Roche, *Théories des Relations Internationales,* 9–17.

18 Ibid., 17, my translation.

19 Anecdotally, when a Professor of Political Science at the Institute for Political Studies in Lyon finished reading Wendt's *Social Theory of International Politics,* he came into the classroom the day after and solemnly declared "I am quite sure I have read the same book 40 years ago – Monsieur Wendt has forgotten our Aron".

20 Smith and Hollis, *Explaining and Understanding International Relations.*

21 As Aron put it: "Can this definition [absence of common source of sovereignty] serve as the foundation of a scientific theory…? There can be no scientific theory of international relations because we cannot assume that actors, under any historical period or within any system, pursue a unique objective: the conscious or unconscious will to maximise power. Those who suppose the actor's will to 'maximise power' do not even understand the basic mistake inherent in the terms they are using." Aron, "Qu'est-ce qu'une Théorie des Relations Internationales?", 846–47.

move beyond empirical positivism into logical positivism.[22] Backward positivists they were, so goes the argument, because they had not incorporated the lessons of great debates, like those provoked by the Vienna Circle, which precisely dealt with the problems that arise when we try to formulate what has been defined as non-empirical science. They failed to move IR from classical empirical positivism to some sort of 'logical positivism'.

Reconsider the arguments presented in Chapter 2: for realists, theory precedes any analysis, theory is a conceptual construct, these constructs are neither 'true' nor 'false', but simply useful or not. As Foucault explains, the irreducible notions that organise organisms in the modern episteme are not 'accessible', they are not really 'there', but they limit, and at the same time, ground the possibilities for understanding.[23] Theories explain laws. Here is when this reference to the philosophy of science becomes relevant for considerations on IR theory. Indeed, after an analysis of Waltz's arguments, it should become apparent that the discipline has moved from an 'anti realist' position to a 'realist' one. Or, in Foucault's triangle, there has been a shift from the positivist pole towards the metaphysical one (where modern scientific epistemology and the modern empirical sciences are located, and where the empirico-transcendental doublet exerts maximum authority), as metaphysical a posteriori constructs precede the analysis of the 'phenomenal world'. It could be argued that by posing metaphysical constructs at the core of the scientific enterprise, science elaborated a transcendental philosophy of the object, as the subjects of the scientific inquiry are analysed by their relation to these presuppositions, theoretical constructs...or transcendental objects. These also represent what Kuhn calls scientific paradigms. *Crucially, since metaphysical theorising is where the axes of modernity enjoy maximum authority, it will be argued that an analytic of finitude and historical linearity condition the way in which the modern empirical science of IR has been constructed. Thus, the following paragraphs will demonstrate that the immobilisation of time and the isolation of the discipline require each other, and that it is precisely this immobilisation of time, for example, that renders interpretations based on perennial 'ancient ethnic hatreds' in the Kosovo context possible.*

Neorealism is, in essence, an attempt to discredit empirical positivists and to update the discipline on the basis of logical positivism, which is itself reliant on metaphysical theorising, which in turn legitimises the positing of transcendental

---

22 As Smouts argues, "traditionalists close to the English School and those who assumed, like Raymond Aron, that the multitude of simultaneously pursued empirical objectives characterised state actors as being too un-determinist to formulate a proper theory, with premises, hypotheses and laws, these were categorised as backward positivists, unable to formulate Science." Marie-Claude Smouts, *Les Nouvelles Relations Internationales* (Paris: Presses de Science Politique, 1998): 16, my translation.

23 *"In their essence [Life, Will, Word] they are outside knowledge, but for this very reason, they are the condition to attain knowledge... "*, Foucault, *Les Mots et les Choses*, 257.

notions such as 'anarchy' at the heart of what is now proper 'scientific theorising'.[24] It should be evident from the six statements exposed above by Waltz that Aron rejected metaphysical theorising. For instance, if variables cannot be empirically detected and categorised, if a field of study cannot be inductively isolated, it is simply not possible to construct scientific theories on it. The single most important difference between realists and anti realists is based upon diverging ideas on whether or not it is possible to theorise on non-observable elements, or even on conceptual assumptions.[25]

Incidentally, Waltz's critique of Aron is entirely based on this aspect of realist philosophy. This critique could be seen as the IR equivalent of these debates that have taken place in the philosophy of sciences. This is where Foucault's archaeological method can prove to be useful: a precise shift within the modern episteme determines what it means to do 'science': different notions of 'science' are examined by the internal epistemic configuration they occupy. The shift from archaeology to genealogy would study in turn how these notions affect practice.

Why is this important? What does it have to do with either the Kosovo crisis or Complexity theory? In the answers to these questions lies much of the crux of the argument of the overall study. In a nutshell – and just to serve as a signpost leading to an argument that will be explored in much more detail in the last two chapters – the moment we accept that metaphysical theorising is not only a valid ground for the formulation and application of scientific knowledge, but that it represents, in fact, a more legitimate ground than empirical experience, we can start imagining and *justifying* all sorts of things – especially in an age that is characterised by the triumph of *techne* and by arguments which seek to emulate, and to justify themselves, on the basis of superior 'scientific theorising'. For example, Lord Carrington could imagine that Yugoslavia in 1991 was an 'artificial' construct whose dismantlement was both desirable and necessary to avoid conflict. Despite overwhelming evidence suggesting that the vast majority of Yugoslavs – except those very nationalist fanatics whose only hope to attract the attention of the masses was to generate as much havoc as possible – had no particular desire to start killing each other,[26] the Western intellectual and pseudo-scientific tradition

24 As Linklater put it, "Waltz's neorealism seeks to emulate developments in the philosophy of science and structural modes of social scientific explanation which are absent from classical realism. This quest for methodological rigour is central to the principal neorealist endeavour which is to delineate the main structural features of the system of state." Andrew Linklater, "Neoralism in Theory and Practice", in *International Relations Theory Today*, eds, Steve Smith and Ken Booth (Oxford: Polity Press, 1995), 46.

25 See an interesting example in Smith and Hollis, *Explaining and Understanding International Relations*, 208.

26 At this point it may be useful to remember David Campbell's important point about the real source of violence in Bosnia: "…the level of violence in Bosnia was brought on not by the clash of autonomous and settled identities but by the attempt to produce a society in which the divisions between people could be clearly seen and enforced. As one commentator remarked during the escalation of the war, 'those who now say that Bosnia is

meant that it was a lot easier to think that the region was cluttered with ancient ethnic hatreds whose pressures could only be kept at bay by the iron lid of a bi-polar world (Newtonian images of gravitational spheres of influence, political physics and balances of power seem to have been very much in fashion over the past few centuries).[27]

We could also imagine that the solution to the various crises could be solved on the bases of old census data containing rather flawed categorisations, and that the ethnic divisions allegedly characterising the region were more real than supposed. Paradoxically, such mechanisms for the generation and deployment of knowledge ended up by aiding the arguments of the very Yugoslav nationalists in whose interest it was to promote the idea that a nationalist solution for Yugoslavia was inevitable. Thus, the West's ideological imperative on the necessity of creating stable, tolerant and multi-ethnic states went strangely hand in hand with the West's preferred means of solving all Balkan crises since 1991: the partition of Yugoslavia (unilateral German recognition of Croatia and Lord Carrington's proposals), of Bosnia (at Dayton), and of Serbia (Kosovo). Such were the epistemic rules that characterised much of Western thinking: metaphysical theorising based on transcendental philosophies of objects (which are in turn characterised by the axes of modernity: an analytic of finitude enforced by historical linearity) – which is precisely what is being undermined by Complexity's focus on the realm of immanence and on the irreversibility of time. *From the moment the intellectual apparatus designed to understand crisis (IR) shifts towards the metaphysical pole – following the course traced by post-empiricist scientific epistemology – the two axes of the empirico-transcendental doublet begin to enforce contingency on the way in which knowledge on the Kosovo crisis was generated and deployed.*

But we have a duty to analyse how the metaphysical intellectual frameworks – which characterise much of practice – have been formed in order to outline how these can be dismantled by a Complexity ethic. Furthermore, this undertaking exposes the reason why it is so important to thoroughly analyse the genesis of contemporary philosophy of science: for all recent attempts at formulating 'scientific explanations' of conflicts are based on either Neorealism's attempt to emulate scientific epistemology after Vienna or by Neorealism's critics' refusal

---

being carved along its seams are wrong: Bosnia is being cut right through its living flesh, hence all the blood'". Campbell, *National Deconstruction*, 93, quoting Mensur Camo, "A Peacenik's Guide to 'The Other Bosnia,'" *War Report* 21 (August/September 1993), 16–17. In other words, the source of violence derived from a very flawed understanding according to which such violence had transcendental causes: another example of how flawed policy is very apt at generating self-fulfilling prophecies.

27 Interestingly, Kissinger notes with a discernible amount of frustration that there was absolutely no evidence supporting the Domino Theory which ultimately led the United States into the Vietnam quagmire. Evocative metaphysical images – based on sketchy representations of physical processes – seemed to be, however, more attractive than empirical facts. See Henry Kissinger, *Diplomacy* (New York: Simon and Schuster Paperbacks, 1994), 624.

to do so. Complexity – as the latest turn in scientific epistemology – also plays a crucial role in showing how IR theorists using 'scientific' explanations to justify their theories work on the bases of rather outdated scientific debates and thus fail, in their own terms, to bring the latest developments of scientific epistemology into any academic discipline related to the understanding of conflict.

Thus, Complexity represents a double failure for such theorists: the first failure relates to the fact that the scientific bases of their theories have been undermined by Complexity proper, the second, that such undermining has not been taken into consideration by them, meaning that – contrary to their claims – their own theories failed to account for the truly latest developments in scientific epistemology. As an illustration, consider that Kenneth Waltz was, in 1979, considering events that took place in 1922 (the Vienna Circle) as representing the latest developments in scientific epistemology, whilst in 1963, Edward Lorenz from the Massachusetts Institute for Technology was engaged in publishing the seminal work in which the Lorenz attractor – a precursor and a key element of the so called 'butterfly effect', and of subsequent formulations of Chaos and Complexity theories – was described for the first time. These are rather thin grounds for those who chose to argue that they were adapting the discipline of IR to the latest insights of scientific epistemology and to accuse others of being 'backward positivists'.

Indeed, Kenneth Waltz, by his own admission, sought to introduce logico-positivistic theorising in the analysis of conflicts. Metaphysical science was introduced in 'Scientific IR' by a theory which sought to shape the discipline as a modern empirical science and a transcendental philosophy of objects: it is for this reason that Kenneth Waltz can deploy Conant's quintessentially metaphysical definition of science in defence of his own theory: "science is a dynamic undertaking directed to lowering the degree of empiricism involved in solving problems."[28]

Since the study of how the philosophy of science, especially for what concerns positivism, has influenced the social sciences in general and IR in particular has been conducted elsewhere[29] it would be unfruitful to reproduce the same account here. However, it would be interesting to notice, on the bases of the arguments exposed above, the significance of the following statement:

> This view [the third 'variant' of logical positivism] was extremely important in the social sciences, where the orthodoxy of the 1950s and 1960s was one of trying to apply the ideas of the main proponents of this view, Carnap, Nagel, Hempel and Popper, to the fledgling social science disciplines. Particularly important was the work of Carl Hempel…because he developed an extremely influential account of what is involved in explaining an event.[30]

28 Kenneth Waltz, "Laws and Theories", in *Neorialism and its Critics* ed. Robert Keohane (New York: Columbia University Press, 1986), 34.

29 Smith, "Positivism and Beyond".

30 Barberousse. *La Philosophie Des Sciences Au Xxe Siècle*, 90, my translation.

Carnap had to give up the idea of irreducible propositions after the fierce criticism of Neurath, Popper can be considered as the champion of anti-foundationalism, Nagel (who Waltz quotes in his 1979 work against inductivists) criticises the empiricist stance, while Hempel formulated a famous paradox of empirical confirmation. All four took part in the debates within the Vienna Circle, and their refusal to consider empirical reality as a legitimate source of scientific propositions capable of explaining generalities, Waltz would argue, did not seem to be incorporated by behavioural 'data counters' in the social sciences.

Chapter 2 has illustrated how the Vienna Circle resulted in a profound schism within the philosophy of science. After these debates, empirical experience was no longer regarded as a legitimate source of scientific knowledge *di per se*. Within the triangle of knowledge designated by Foucault the consequences of this schism become evident. Any social science wanting to emulate normal science could take the path proposed by the likes of Popper and Nagel, which we can confidently designate as the metaphysical path (since, as stated above, metaphysical propositions must be elaborated in order to explain empirical generalities). In this path, empirical experience is relegated to testing propositions which do not necessarily originate from an observation of 'reality'. Therefore, the discontinuity rooted in the attempt at superseding empiricism entails some important consequences. This work will proceed to outline how Neorealism, as it floated towards the metaphysical epistemic pole by basing itself on a rejection of empiricism, was constituted according to the rules that framed those empirical sciences which adopted similar metaphysical theorising from the beginning of the modern epistemic configuration (economics and biology, for example).

Neorealist IR as a Modern Empirical Science

This work has so far sought to describe the modern organisation of knowledge, to demonstrate that the decline of empiricism in the philosophy of sciences pushed social disciplines claiming scientific status closer to the metaphysical pole, and exposed how the modern empirical sciences, situated in this metaphysical pole, were constituted through a transcendental philosophy of the object which was in turn characterised by an empirico-transcendental doublet composed by an analytic of finitude enforced by the creation of historical linearity. These sciences, moreover, were arranged according to the rules inherent to the metaphysical pole of the modern episteme: they structured and isolated knowledge around transcendental notions, and thus created what we can refer to as 'organic knowledge'. The isolation of fields of knowledge implied, among other things, the positioning of functionality as the main factor ordering elements, in temporal fashion, within these separate structures of knowledge. This section will proceed to explain how Neorealism, precisely because of its reference to the philosophy of sciences, was constituted as a modern empirical science, and therefore demonstrates striking conceptual similarities with the two disciplines analysed by Foucault (economics and biology).

This, it will be argued, characterised much of the intellectual grounds on which understandings of the Kosovo crisis were produced and deployed through a strict implementation of the two axes of modernity.

The belief that Neorealism's constitution resembles that of the modern empirical sciences, and that this is, in turn, due to the decline of empiricism in the scientific epistemology that Waltz sought to emulate, is reinforced by Foucault's arguments on the peculiar situation in which the human sciences find themselves. After reminding the reader of the triangular composition of the modern episteme, Foucault goes on to argue that the human sciences are to be found between these three poles, and that it is precisely this peculiarity that characterises the complexity of these disciplines. As was noted above, the modern composition of knowledge offers three answers to the decline of representation: the synthetic a priori of the mathematical sciences, the analytical a posteriori of empirical sciences, and the conceptualisation of man through philosophical reflection. Philosophy, in turn, deals with the appearance of man, which is the result of the collapse of representation and becomes, by definition, the object of the human sciences, in three ways: man can be questioned by that which he experiences or by his very capacity to experience, while the rejection of both conceptualisations, and the will to remain within the purely phenomenal world, gives birth to empirical positivism. According to Foucault, the main problem is that the human sciences find it difficult to locate themselves in this configuration of knowledge.[31]

Once empiricism declines in scientific and philosophical reflection, those human sciences that are aware of these developments can only shift within this modern triangle and approach the metaphysical pole. The nucleus of the argument is that, as we attempted to illustrate, the metaphysical pole (where the modern empirical sciences are situated) has been constructed upon the crucially necessary notion of finitude. This finitude is double: it is both historical and anthropological. And is this very notion of finitude understood as the contingent that Complexity science challenges? As Waltz discredits the empirical, the a priori mathematical formalisation, the inductive, and introduces a new discourse concerning the real nature of science, scientific IR can only float towards, and inspire itself from these empirical sciences that before it have conceptualised man, history and their finitude as that which enforces contingency, and that which really explains what happens at the empirical level. This framework of analysis provided by Foucault is much more useful to understand the present situation of IR theory than the fruitless

31 Consider: "From this epistemological trihedron the human sciences are excluded, at least in the sense that they cannot be found along any of its dimensions or on the surface of any of the planes thus defined…what explains the difficulty of the 'human sciences', their precariousness, their uncertainty…is *the complexity of the epistemological configuration in which they find themselves placed, their constant relation to the three dimensions that give them their space.*" Foucault, *Les Mots et les Choses*, 347–48, my translation, emphasis added.

and tiresome story of the 'great debates'.[32] It is also a more suitable apparatus for understanding how related, modernity-based understandings of the Kosovo crisis have been constructed.

Waltz's critique of Aron is entirely based on that aspect of realist philosophy that was exposed previously, which regards precisely the role of unobservaables and the validity of induction. This critique could be seen as the IR equivalent of these debates that have taken place in the philosophy of sciences. Waltz's work in 1979 begins with a powerful attack on empiricism and on induction. According to Waltz, realists (in the IR sense) such as Aron and others base their analysis on very problematic epistemological grounds. Adopting empiricist positions, they cannot conceptualise beyond what they describe. They analyse meticulously empirical data in the hope of accidentally finding regularities in the comparison of precise cases. In a sense, this is what Aron does when he draws categories (note how Aron seems to be adopting taximonic principles similar to those favoured by pre-modern epistemes) and differentiates general groups from anomalous ones (this is also why it takes 850 pages for Aron to complete a general theory of IR, while Waltz's account goes on for 251 pages only).

Unfortunately, 850 pages cannot account for much, because, as Waltz explains, the empirical world is potentially infinite. It is precisely this infinity which causes problems: in these circumstances, how could we possibly analyse man as an experiencing subject? Therefore, approaches that are based on induction will inevitably face failure: they don't tell us anything: that which is potentially infinite, that which consequently offers an infinite number of explanations, ends up by explaining nothing at all. Waltz agrees with Levi Strauss and describes this approach as 'inductive illusion'. Theory must precede inductive enquiry, because it is not 'the world out there' that can provide scientific explanations, but these explanations can be based only on scientific theoretical constructs, which explain reality:

> Rather than being mere collections of laws, theories are statements that explain them. Theories are qualitatively different from laws. Laws identify invariant or probable associations. Theories show why those associations obtain. Each descriptive term in a law is directly tied to observational or experimental tests. In addition to descriptive terms, theories contain theoretical notions. Theories cannot be constructed through induction alone, for theoretical notions can only be invented, not discovered.[33]

Here, Waltz quotes Nagel and Isaak. Waltz's notion of a scientific theory, thus, is rooted in a variant of logical positivism which advocates ideas first proposed by

32 See Yosef Lapid, "Through Dialogue to Engaged Pluralism: The Unfinished Business of the Third Debate", *International Studies Review* Vol. 5, no. 1 (2003), 128–31.

33 Waltz, "Laws and Theories", 32.

scientific realists in the Vienna Circle.[34] These concern the role of unobservables. That which cannot be observed, Waltz explains, is not only a legitimate ground for scientific enquiry, it constitutes the very factor that can hope to explain observables. Waltz proceeds in explaining how Newton based his laws of gravitation on theoretical constructs that were not only 'invented' for the purposes of scientific enquiry, but that were later proven to be completely inaccurate. Even so, Newton's theory of gravitation correctly predicts the movement of celestial and terrestrial bodies. Waltz deduces that theoretical constructs are neither true nor false, but simply useful or not. Moreover, these constructs are useful insofar as they allow us to aggregate otherwise dispersed empirical data around them (this is the criterion of aggregation): "...its power [Newton's Theory] lay in the number of previously disparate empirical generalisations and laws that could be subsumed in one explanatory system."[35]

Waltz's ideas, therefore, seem to be rooted in Nagel's conception of what a scientific theory is and on Conant's perception of what scientific theories are for: "science is a dynamic undertaking directed to lowering the degree of empiricism involved in solving problems."[36] Waltz explains quite well how the rupture from empiricism translates into a new scientific procedure for the study of IR: advances in logical positivism allow and require that a complex and potentially infinite empirical reality is analysed through the concepts of isolation, abstraction, aggregation and idealisation. These four criteria constitute, I suggest, Neorealism's 'Kuhnian paradigmatic box'.[37]

It becomes easy to understand how this shift determines the answers to Aron's six obstacles for scientific enquiry. For what concerns the complexity of our field, Waltz argues that the role of a scientific theory is precisely to simplify a complex reality. For what concerns the absence of quantitative data, Waltz reminds us that, for example, Adam Smith used very little empirical data in

34 Smith and Hollis argue that "...the attempt [to create a scientific study of society] was inspired by the works of logical positivists in the 1930s, notably Rudolph Carnap, Carl Hempel and Ernest Nagel". See *Explaining and Understanding International Relations*, 50.

35 Waltz, "Laws and Theories", 32.

36 Ibid., 34. As the quote defines the nature of the scientific enterprise after the collapse of empiricism it is useful to repeat it.

37 In Waltz's words, "The difficulty of moving from casual speculations based on factual studies to theoretical formulations that lead one to view facts in particular ways is experienced in any field. To cope with this difficulty, simplification is required. This is achieved mainly by following four ways: (1) by isolation, which requires viewing the actions and interactions of a small number of factors and forces as though in the meantime other things remain equal; (2) by abstraction, which requires leaving some things aside in order to concentrate on others; (3) by aggregation, which requires lumping disparate elements together according to criteria derived from a theoretical purpose; (4) by idealization, which requires proceeding as though perfection were attained or a limit reached even though neither can be." Ibid., 38.

his studies (and, following Foucault, we also know why). The identification of laws does not depend on their measurement. Waltz equally contests the notion that there is restoration of equilibrium within economics. For what concerns the capacity to predict, Waltz states that when economists fail in their predictions their approaches are no less scientific than when they don't. According to Waltz, a scientific theory does not predict but it establishes laws which are sufficiently constant for an eventual loose forecast.[38]

It is evident that Waltz bases his own thought on epistemological advances within the discipline of positive economics. On the other hand, Adam Smith's application of Newton to economics and Durkheim's sociology are fundamental for Waltz's thought.[39] Newtonianism can be discerned in both these classical theorists by the law of association. According to this law, units (planets, consumers, individuals or states), by their association create something that is more than the sum of their parts, something that therefore transcends units and something that thus dictates the behaviour of such units. Newtonianism in physics produces gravity, in economics it produces the invisible hand of the market, in sociology society's constraint on the actions of individuals, in IR the international system. We cannot see gravity, and we cannot see the invisible hand, but these are theoretical constructs, which make a number of assumptions that effectively allow the detection of regularities. These also represent the transcendental philosophies of the object described by Foucault.

Waltz's parallelisms with economics show that the international system becomes an IR version of the market, and, as Waltz explains, it should be studied accordingly. Microeconomic theory does not need a theory of the firm to detect market constraints just as an international theory does not need a theory of the state to detect the systemic constraint of the international system.[40] The scientific study of IR is no longer based on 'biological' models which attempt to discern regularities caused by the constant demands of human nature (Morgenthau), but on 'economic' models in which regularities are to be found within a system that transcends its component parts. This is one of the main consequences of the discontinuity between empiricism and post-empiricism.

Another important consequence is the reliance on theoretical constructs. While empiricism based scientific enquiry on sensory experience, thus allowing for broad parameters of study, post-empirical science relies on a set of assumptions which guide scientific endeavour. Waltz correctly points out that the empirical world is potentially infinite, but if this is true, we must deduce that the parameters of study under empiricism are very broad too. The paradox inherent in wanting to

38 Ibid.

39 Karl Manzer studies how Newtonianism is applied by both Adam Smith and Thomas Hobbes. See Karl Manzer, *Thinking in Complexity: The Complex Dynamics of Matter, Mind, and Mankind* (Berlin: Springer-Verlag, 2004), 257.

40 Waltz makes references to microeconomic theory all throughout chapters 2–5, in Keohane, *Neorealism and its Critics*.

synthesise a potentially infinite empirical reality into finite explanations based on finite sensorial bodies, characterises much of the analytic of finitude described by Foucault and many of the dilemmas of empiricism outlined by the Vienna Circle. On the other hand, the introduction of theoretical constructs limits research to what is permissible within the theory. In this sense, post-empirical science becomes paradigmatic. We can deduce a shift from Aron to Waltz in terms of a shift from a strictly empirical science to a science dominated by paradigms. It is the 'paradigmisation' of IR that serves as an intellectual filter, effectively dominating and reducing the number of alternative approaches that can be considered as 'scientific'. This filter also limits what can and cannot be considered when analysing the causes of the Kosovo conflict, and when designing adequate responses.

Unlike Carr and Morgenthau, for example, for whom the 'scientific' method meant different things at different times and established different dichotomies, paradigms, precisely because they are the result of metaphysical theorising and not of 'reality', abruptly determine what is scientific on a more exclusionary basis. To be sure, Kuhn argues that science has always been paradigmatic: scientists always relied on assumptions to make sense of their research. However, it can be argued, as Kuhn does, that the social sciences, including IR, were at a pre-paradigmatic stage. The adoption of paradigmatic science also implies the adoption of all its inconveniences (see Kuhn's definition of 'normal science' in Chapter 2).

Paradigmatic science involves the procedures elaborated by Waltz (abstraction, isolation, idealisation and aggregation) which are supposed to replace procedures based on induction. These are the limits of what Kuhn calls the 'preformed and relatively inflexible box'. The attempt to force social reality into it has not gone unchallenged. We can here note that Waltz's idea of the nature of scientific enquiry is extremely close to Kuhn's description of normal science. Indeed, Kuhn's *Structure of Scientific Revolutions* is dedicated to Conant, Kuhn's Professor, and key reference for Waltz when it comes to justify his anti-empiricist stance.[41]

Waltz wants to detect regularities, not change, and he is therefore not interested in alternative theories which could explain new phenomena. That which does not fit into the box is relegated to secondary importance, and this could be seen as the roots of the IR/International Political Economy (IPE) schism.[42] The critique of Neorealism, and the consequent fragmentation of IR theory, exposes substantial similarities with the description of paradigmatic science as exposed by Kuhn. Kuhn shows that, in the end, the acceptance of the implications of paradigmatic science depends on whether or not we accept 'paying the price' for depth in our analysis. Kuhn's descriptions of paradigms, which have become crucial within the modern philosophy of science, are what allows Waltz to construct the limits of IR

41 The 1983 edition of Kuhn's *Structure of Scientific Revolutions* includes a dedication to Conant: "To James B. Conant who is at the origin of this book". Waltz uses Conant's arguments about the purpose of scientific theory, see Waltz, "Laws and Theories", 34–6.

42 See Susan Strange, "International Relations and Political Economy, a Case of Mutual Neglect", *International Affairs* Vol. 46, no. 2 (1970), 204–315.

as a discipline, and to organise it around a transcendental notion based upon the four criteria of paradigmatic science. As with all other transcendental philosophies of the object, the new empirical science of IR necessitates a notion of analytical finitude and a notion of historical linearity (which is ultimately responsible for the popularity of interpretations based on perennial 'ancient ethnic hatreds') to enforce the contingency of the object on the subject. *Crucially, the criteria of isolation, abstraction and idealisation rely on an absolutely contingent notion of historical linearity (the "striking similarity in the quality of international life during the past millennia") in order to deploy the analytical finitude (particularly through the criterion of finitude) they are supposed to enforce.*

Isolation

John Gerard Ruggie argues that Waltz's intentions can be understood by analysing the analogous case of Durkheim.[43] Durkheim's objective was to establish sociology as an independent and 'scientific' field of enquiry. In the *Rules of the Sociological Method* Durkheim's first task is, thus, to isolate the discipline of sociology, to explain on what grounds this isolation is justified and to proceed the study according to the parameters established. One of the main ideas in Durkheim's thought was shaped by the law of association. By their interaction, individuals form something (society) which in turn determines the behaviour of the component parts. Sociology is thus defined as the scientific study of this system (society), and it finds itself isolated from other disciplines, for example, psychology, that study human behaviour but at a different level of analysis. As Weber said, "a discipline establishes itself by its method and not by its object of enquiry".

Waltz's objective is to establish IR as an independent field of enquiry. The justification of such isolation could already be found in *Man, the State, and War*,[44] where the third image (the international level) is identified as a legitimate source of explanation for the causes of war. *Theory of International Politics*[45] established the rules of the sociological method in IR. We are, thus, confronted with a double isolation: first, the isolation of IR from other disciplines, second, the isolation of the political. We should note how both isolations are based on exclusionary methods. Waltz defines the 'international' as that which is dominated by an anarchy and 'domestic' as that which is organised by hierarchic structures. As in Cuvier's biology, 'The Order of Things' is defined according to the functionality of the elements that compose them.

---

43 John Gerard Ruggie, "Continuity and Transformation in the World Polity: Toward a Neorealist Synthesis", in *Neorealism and its Critics*, ed. Robert Keohane (New York: Columbia University Press, 1985), 131–33.

44 Kenneth Waltz, *Man, the State, and War: A Theoretical Analysis* (New York: Columbia University Press, 2001).

45 Kenneth Waltz, *Theory of International Politics* (New York: McGraw-Hill, 1979).

Here, Waltz bases himself on the works of Nadel and Fortes to define the criteria of isolation. The system must be defined according to: 1) its principles of organisation; 2) the distinction between units and the detection of their functions; and 3) the distribution of capabilities between units which have the same functions. 1) is therefore characterised by anarchy. This has a very important impact on 2). The second point, in fact, defines states as the units of the international system according to their functions (survival and self-help). 3) consequently isolates IR as the study of units (nation-states) that interact in an anarchic system according to their functions: all units have similar functions but different capabilities to perform their tasks: "States are alike in the tasks that they face, though not in their abilities to perform them. The differences are of capability, not function."[46]

IR thus becomes the systemic study of capability distribution. The study of the distribution of power is more important than the study of the functions of the units. It matters more to know whether the system is bipolar or multipolar than it is to know whether or not welfare provision is a function of the French state, for it is the international system that places a structural constraint on the units. What is considered to be the major functional system is, thus, in anatomical fashion, isolated. The invisible hand of the system, the transcendental notion of Anarchy, becomes the focus of analysis as this is what determines behaviour. In microeconomic theory, it matters little how firms are organised internally as it is the invisible hand of the market that determines their behaviour.

In turn, this isolation of the international defines the political. A political theory of IR studies the structural constraint that the international system places on that kind of unit which is defined by self – help. Is 'political', therefore, that which deals with the pressure exercised by the international system formed by states and characterised by Anarchy on no other than its component parts. An anarchic system formed by firms would form the object of enquiry of another discipline. Naturally, states do change – but the analytical finitude inherent in the process of isolation is enforced, as argued below, by the concept of historical linearity.

Abstraction

Waltz introduces abstractionism with the idea that there are structural forces in operation in the international system, and that these can be seen only if we are willing to abstract. If the causes of state behaviour were to be found at the state level, the argument goes, a change in this level of analysis would necessarily alter the way states interact. However, despite all the changes that have occurred at the state level, regularities persist. Waltz explains that over the centuries states have changed their internal organisation, ideology, economic and social systems, but that 'regularities' still occurred. Therefore, despite all these changes, Waltz is keen to express the somewhat puzzling idea that the quality of international life has

46 Kenneth Waltz, "Political Structures", in *Neorealism and its Critics,* ed. Robert Keohane (New York: Columbia Press, 1986), 91.

been strikingly constant for the past millennia. Waltz does not deny the fact that the sources of some events are to be found at the level of states: "Causes at the level of units and of systems interact, and because they do so explanation at the level of units alone is bound to mislead."[47]

Waltz expresses the concept that a systemic science of IR looks at that system which is created by the association of units, and that, in turn, determines the behaviour of component parts, just like economic theory studies the market, and not the firm. If we want to study relations between states at the state level, as realists and behaviouralists alike did, we are dealing with the study of foreign policy. IR differs from the study of foreign policy Aron ultimately advocates precisely because it places its analysis at a different level. Here, Waltz is asking IR 'scientists' not only to ignore all that which has been left out by the principle of isolation, but to equally ignore that which studies the quality (ideology, internal organisation, economic system, religion, state society relations…) and to focus on the distribution of capabilities across the international system. A scientific study of IR is therefore focussed on the permanence of unit functions (self-help) to detect regularities that are derived from a system, which is, in turn, precisely characterised by these functions. The system is nonetheless more than the sum of its parts. At this point. the organic nature of IR and its similarity with the evolution of economics and biology is obvious – as far as a Complexity-based critique is concerned, however, the most important notion that links them together is the notion of historical linearity, for that is the very notion that has been undermined by Complexity science.

Waltz accepts that the visual range of his systems theory is quite limited: "Systems never tell us all we want to know. Instead they tell us a *small* number of big important things. They focus our attention on those components and forces that usually continue for long periods."[48] Or, in Kuhn's words, "the areas investigated by normal science are, of course, minuscule, but…". Once abstractionism becomes essential for the new self-image of scientific enquiry it becomes nearly nonsensical to accuse Waltz of reductionism. No more than Newton, quickly comes the reply. And where would we be without him now? All claims to scientific knowledge have always relied on a strong vision of science as a source of linear progress.[49] The implications of scientific research (such as reductionism) become in a sense the price to pay for such progress. The fact that most of Neorealism's critics failed to confront Neorealism on its own terms and on its own turf means that it has been relatively easy for Neorealists to dismiss critics as science-ignorant intellectuals who do not understand the purpose and nature of scientific theorising. The fact that no serious critic has been able to point out that Waltz's principles of isolation, abstraction and idealisation constituted conceptual dinosaurs in the epistemology of science and were largely outdated – even in 1979 – is quite surprising.

47 Waltz, *Theory of International Politics*, 68.

48 Kenneth Waltz, "A Response to my Critics", in *Neorialism and its Critics*, ed. Robert Keohane (New York, Columbia University Press, 1986), 329, emphasis added.

49 Ibid., 255–301.

Idealisation

The criteria of idealisation poses a threefold implication for the study of IR. As we understand it, it is probably the most controversial factor of Waltz's attempt to apply developments within the philosophy of science to IR. Waltz argues that: "We can freely admit that in fact states are not unitary, purposive actors. States pursue many goals, which are often vaguely formulated and inconsistent…we know that assumptions are neither true nor false and that they are essential for the construction of theory."[50] Equally, Prigogine reminds its readers the friction has to be ignored for a pendulum to work perennially.

Aron had attempted to define the realm of IR as that in which Anarchy prevails: however, he concluded that it was unfruitful to affirm that this defining property conferred a rational and unitary status on the actors. Above, Waltz is saying the same. But what is it, then, that allows Waltz, despite this agreement with Aron (there is no empirical evidence to suggest that states are unitary and rational actors…) to reinstate the notion of Anarchy as that which characterises the behaviour of units? We know that assumptions are neither true nor false and that they are essential for the construction of theory: we understand that post-empirical philosophy of science allows for this sort of argument. This is the essence of paradigmatic, post-empirical epistemology.

Anarchy becomes, thus, just the sort of transcendental notion that we associated with the modern empirical sciences: the hidden, unexplainable force that is outside of knowledge (for it does not really exist, it is neither true nor false) but grounds its possibility. This is an example of the sort of deadlock inherent in the empirico-transcendental doublet which again is being resolved through the transcendental. The argument is that, while we can say that units are not unitary and purposive actors, we have to assume that they are. Similarly, there are no strictly objective foundations for claims made by the 'homo economicus' model. The need to idealise is perhaps the most important theoretical construct which characterises Newtonian science. Here, Waltz is asking that not only a 'scientific' theory of IR should not question the unity and rationality of state actors (for the units are functionally alike and differ only in capabilities), but that such a theory should also develop a hypothesis precisely on the assumption that units will react as rational actors to structural constraints.

The first implication is then formulated in the rationality assumption. The second implication is to be found in the unitary character that is conferred on the units. Not only must we assume that units are rational, but also that they are unitary purposive actors. The most famous critique of this assumption is to be found in Allison's study of the Cuban missile crisis.[51] In this study, Allison shows that decisions made by the US were not the direct result of external pressures, but rather of a long bargaining process between American state bureaucracies, which all had different agendas.

---

50 Waltz, *Theory of International Politics*, 119.

51 Graham Allison, *The Essence of Decision: Explaining the Cuban Missile Crisis* (Boston: Little Brown, 1971).

Third, idealisation also means that we have to assume that the system has priority over the unit: we must, therefore, analyse the rational reactions of unitary states to systemic pressures. Here, idealisation means that we assume states act in response to systemic pressures. This has obvious implications for the structure and agency debate. Wendt, for instance, argues that units do not act in response to the logic of Anarchy, because 'anarchy is what states make out of it'. Smith argues, however, that Wendt's attempts to reconcile structure with agency ultimately lead his approach to fall on the 'explaining' side of the spectrum. It becomes obvious that if the study of IR is simply the study of the systemic constraint we assume that the capacity for autonomous action by agents is severely restricted.

Aggregation

Aggregation is the principle according to which apparently disparate elements can be analysed together if commonalities between them are detected through the processes of isolation, idealisation and abstraction.

The criteria here exposed have many implications for the notions of history and change. Waltz is very clear about this: "Within a system, a theory explains recurrences and repetitions, not change."[52] Incidentally, Foucault noted that all social science focussed on regularities rather than on change, was characterised by the exclusive attention paid to the functionality of the objects.[53] Idealisation, just like the other criterion, is embedded in a paradigm, and this is what allows for the detection of regularities. What is important to note, however, is that – just as Foucault predicted – *the only way in which Neorealism can successfully impose analytical finitude on the subject of enquiry is to dismiss any notion of change whilst focusing on historical linearity. Quite naturally, we will see continuity in the past few "millennia of international life" if that is the only thing we are allowed to look for by this 'scientific' paradigm, which has to assume the alleged permanence of the functions. This explains why time in IR has to adopt exactly the same linear stance it adopted in the modern empirical sciences of economics and biology. This linear history is what characterises, in turn, the 'Apprehensions of Time' Anderson argues lie at the centre of nationalist discourse (Chapter 6). Furthermore, this is the linear history that determines the way in which Kosovo was understood as yet another instance of perennial, ancient ethnic hatreds.*

All of the criteria exposed above imply the creation of a-historical science. Wallerstein remarks that the way in which forms of knowledge – especially those which greatly influenced the study of social organisation – can be fundamentally divided according to how they handle the concept of temporality. The so-called classical view of science relies on temporal linearity:

52 Waltz, *Theory of International Politics*, 69.

53 "…any analysis which seeks continuity is based on the alleged permanence of functions". Foucault, *Les Mots et les Choses*, 370, my translation.

> The so called classical view of science...was built on two premises. One was the Newtonian model, in which there exists *a symmetry between past and future*. This was a quasi-theological vision: like God, we can attain certitudes, and therefore *do not need to distinguish between past and future, since everything coexists in an eternal present*. The second premise was Cartesian dualism, the assumption that there is a fundamental distinction between nature and humans, between matter and mind, between the physical world and the social/spiritual world.[54]

The symmetry between past and future is, thus, one of the main characteristics of Newtonianism, and embodies perfectly Foucault's definition of the 'Age of History'.

In IR many have drawn attention to this main feature of the last scientific image in the discipline. Cox, for instance, categorises Neorealism as a 'problem-solving' theory.[55] These kinds of theories must, by definition, establish temporal parameters of study which allow the detection of regularities. Problem solving theories take the world as it is and try to make it work more smoothly. Within the latest version of 'scientific IR', history becomes little more than a ground where we can experiment theories, and not something which is constitutive of the very present 'reality' these theories are seeking to explain. Thus, we are faced with a scenario of ceaseless repetitions, in which regularities within the social field are seen not only as being separate from actors (the subject/object dichotomy) but also as separate from their own past. Overall, the implications of scientific enquiry can be summarised by reductionism (both spatial and temporal) and by the belief in an external reality independent from what constitutes it (the object/subject differentiation). Ashley summarises the implications of Neorealist positivism as follows:

> In general, positivist discourse holds to four expectations. The first is that scientific knowledge aims grasp a reality that exists in accord of human subjectivity (hence their objectivity) and internally harmonious or contradiction free (as if authored from a single point of view). The second is that science seeks to formulate technically useful knowledge, efficient action, and exert control in the service of given human values. The third is that sought-after knowledge is value-neutral. The fourth, consistent with the first three, holds that the truth of claims and concepts is to be tested by their correspondence to a field of external experience as read via (problematic) instruments or interpretative rules.[56]

54 Wallerstein, *Open the Social Sciences*, 2, emphasis added.

55 Cox, *Approaches to World Order*.

56 Richard Ashley, "The Poverty of Neorealism", in *Neorealism and its Critics*, ed. Robert Keohane (New York: Columbia University Press, 1986), 281.

Nonetheless, despite various categorisations of Neorealism as an 'a-historical' theory, could we not argue, with Foucault, that "paradoxically, Waltz's fixism can arise only against historical background: it defines the stability of things…"?[57] Whereas the anthropological finitude in Waltz's thought is clearly provided by non-empirical science, for that is what justifies the positing of (the object) Anarchy as the absolute through which (the subject) man will be studied, how is the empirico-transcendental doublet resolved in this newly formed modern human science that has just shifted towards the metaphysical pole, a pole which is embodied in modern empirical science?

The positing of Anarchy as that which produces man also introduces the question if, and to what extent, man produces Anarchy. Here, we realise that, for example, Wendt's maxim "anarchy is what states make out of it" does not, as such, represent a major epistemic shift from Neorealism, but simply chooses to deal with this empirico-transcendental notion from the opposite direction, just like when Foucault explained that a transcendental philosophy of the object does not break with Kantian transcendentalism (which, as we know, was posited in the subject), but simply operates from a different direction within the established architecture of knowledge. But how does Waltz limit the capacity of this man to go and build alternative worlds: is historical contingency not as necessary for Waltz, once the choice of developing a transcendental philosophy of object is taken, as it was for Ricardo and Cuvier? From a Foucauldian perspective the following represents the most striking representations of Neorealism as a modern empirical science: "*The enduring anarchic character of international politics accounts for the striking sameness in the quality of international life through the millennia.*"[58]

Thus, although it would require several pages to pin down this argument, one can readily imagine what an account of international history would be like once it becomes submitted to that Anarchy transcendental. We can readily see the world slowly, and linearly, being populated, somehow inexplicably organising itself into 'unit-like' elements, and once this process is complete, as the four corners of the globe are now filled and all units become aware of each other, just like when Ricardo predicted a permanent state of scarcity as a result of the spread of populations: we achieve a permanent state of Anarchy…at this point, history can only "*quiver for an instance upon its axis, and immobilise itself forever*".

It is, again, with an already cited sentence of Foucault that we believe we can show how the emerging transcendentalism of the object and the finitude of history in Waltz's thought need each other, for "it took the suspension, and, as it were, the placing between parentheses, of that kind of history to give the beings of nature and the products of labour [and, why not, the products of Anarchy], a historicity that would enable modern thought to encompass them, and subsequently to deploy

---

57 See Chapter 2 for Foucault's description of Cuvier's and Ricardo's historical fixism.

58 Waltz, *Theory of International Politics*, 66, emphasis added.

the discursive science of their succession…"[59] Waltz can offer a discursive science of the succession of events in international politics: by ensuring that Anarchy stops history, and that history limits men, Neorealism argues that successions of events are to be understood through the distribution of capabilities across functionally alike elements, because just as all men experience labour, it is their time and their pain; all units experience Anarchy. Here, too, we see how the anthropological versant of finitude, the fact that we can be allowed, contra Aron, to consider that, after all, Anarchy does determine what states can or cannot do, relates to an historical versant of finitude, *for anarchy, with its truth, is posited in time, and time is therefore finite.*

It is essential that we understand Neorealism's epistemic context if we are to criticise it in a constructive way. The real problem with arguments such as those presented in Ashley's critique[60] is that what the likes of Ashley regard as Neorealism's poverty is precisely what Neorealists regard as a strength: paradigmatic science (which is responsible for the principles of isolation, abstraction and idealisation Ashley is so keen on attacking). No wonder Waltz dismisses Ashley in just five pages.[61] Accusing Neorealism of idealising states is about as meaningful as blaming vegetarians for not recognising the merits of eating meat. On the other hand, understanding the epistemic genesis of Neorealism is crucial for it equates to understanding the epistemic context in which knowledge of the nature of crisis – including the Kosovo crisis – was generated and deployed. Complexity offers a mechanism for undermining such knowledge in its own terms. Incidentally, debates over the nature of Waltz's theory are all but dead. Ewan Harrison continued the legacy through a number of recent articles regarding Kant and systemic theories in the *Review of International Studies*.[62]

IR's Understanding of the Kosovo Crisis and the Role of Critical Geopolitics

Whereas the discipline of Critical Geopolitics seeks to examine social constructions of *space,*[63] *new turns in post-structuralist IR, anthropology and sociology seek to analyse the social construction of time.*[64] By reframing, questioning and exploring

59 See Chapter 2.

60 Ashley, "The Poverty of Neorealism".

61 Waltz, "A Response to my Critics", 337–41.

62 Ewan Harrison, "Waltz, Kant and Systemic Approaches to International Relations", *Review of International Studies* Vol. 28, no. 1 (2002), 143–62.

63 Consider: "Geography was not something already possessed by the earth but an active writing of the earth by an expanding, centralizing imperial state. It was not a noun but a verb, a geographing, an earth writing by ambitious endo-colonizing and exo-colonizing states who sought to seize space and organize it to fit their own cultural visions and material interests". Gearóid Ó Tuathail, *Critical Geopolitics* (London: Routledge, 1996), 2.

64 An evident example is Anderson's efforts in the section entitled "Apprehensions of Time" in *Imagined Communities*, 22–36.

the natures of time and space, these approaches resemble Prigogine's efforts in relation to time[65] and the efforts of countless others who sought to re-examine the nature of space in relation to the new discoveries of quantum mechanics and of Complexity science.[66] We also know that some of the pioneers of Complexity science can be found in German Natural Philosophy, we know that Bergson provides the bases of Prigoginian and Deleuzian arguments and we also know – thanks to Babette Babich – that Nietzschean perspectivism is very much in line with Complex understandings of time in space. Thus, it becomes possible to claim that post-structural approaches to international life – through their affinity with Complexity science – represent a more valid interpretation of 'scientific' IR than the Neorealist attempt to introduce logical positivism in the discipline. *Thus, the importance of understanding the genesis of Complexity (as Chapter 1 sought to do) – if Complexity understandings of Kosovo (see Chapters 5 and 6) are similar to post-structural accounts of the conflict, it is not because we may be attempting to present post-structural approaches as Complexity approaches in disguise: rather, this is so because both approaches share the same epistemic origin, which is rooted in their respective questionings of modernity's bases: the empirico-transcendental doublet (analytic of finitude and linear time).*

Neorealism does not fail because it is too 'scientific' – it fails because it is not 'scientific' enough, and because its incorporation of the 'latest scientific developments' stops in 1922. In other words, it fails in its own terms.

At this point, it would be interesting to outline how such different epistemic approaches to the issue of conflict generated alternative understandings of the Kosovo crisis. An interesting attempt to understand the Kosovo conflict through different theories – and to understand different theories through the Kosovo conflict – can be found in a volume edited by Jennifer Sterling-Folker.[67] Such volume constitutes a novel approach to the comparative analysis of different theories, which consists in applying such theories to a specific and common issue. In this context, it is interesting that Kosovo was chosen as the case study to be analysed. The reasons given for such choice are indicative of the importance of Kosovo for the very way in which we approach the issue of generating and deploying knowledge in the area of human conflict:

> These are elements that make Kosovo an event of interest to scholars of IR. It is an event that is ripe for multiple theoretical applications, since it involves a myriad of topics of interest to IR scholars, such as ethnic violence and war, identity politics, massive human rights violations, national sovereignty, cooperation among great powers, and international institutions, to name only a few of the

65 Consider again Babette Babich's quote of Prigogine: "Whatever we call reality, it is revealed to us only through the active construction in which we participate".

66 As an example, consider Manzer, *Thinking in Complexity*, 31–47.

67 Jennifer Sterling-Folker, *Making Sense of International Relations Theory* (Boulder: Lynne Rienner, 2006).

> more obvious. Because, as Sergei Medvedev and Peter van Ham have observed, *"Kosovo symbolizes and exemplifies the relevance of many 'end'-debates and 'post'-debates within the academic discipline."*[68]

It is, thus, that we should compare different understandings not only in relation to the subject at hand but also in relation to how such understandings de facto represent epistemic shifts that have been outlined up to now. Such interpretations of the crisis will allow the epistemic observer to gauge the epistemic shifts and changes within a specific configuration of knowledge in the first instance, and Complexity-like changes that represent genuine epistemic breaks in the second instance.

The epistemic approach – accompanied by a critical understanding of Complexity – allows us to immediately locate different approaches to the Kosovo crisis on the bases of where such approaches stand in the context of the epistemic fluctuations described throughout the current work. In particular, we can identify approaches which take the outside world as constituted – this is a world in which the actors (or, in Foucauldian terms, "Man") are analysed from the perspective of the objects that constitute them (in this case, the International System). As we have seen, this corresponds to the attempt at creating transcendental philosophies of objects. Adherents to this epistemic penchant often enjoy pointing out that their assumptions on the objective reality of the world equate to their ability in seeing things as they really are – they thus generally take pride in being described as realists.[69] On the other hand, we have Complexity-akin, critical geopolitical attempts to analyse how the subjects actually constitute the objects of study. Critical geopolitics thus looks at how practice generates normative discourse which, in turn, shapes the frameworks within which actors interact. As outlined by Jennifer Sterling-Folker, Kosovo represents a perfect case for contrasting the two approaches.

Kenneth Waltz's disciples often refer to the prophet's last attempt to update the Neorealist doctrine in a post-Cold War context.[70] This is the case with Neorealist approaches to the Kosovo conflict. Karen Ruth Adams, for example, concludes that:

> Neither Yugoslavia's disintegration nor US intervention in the Kosovo war was foreordained. Yugoslavia could have adopted policies more conducive to domestic harmony, and the United States could have been more mindful of Yugoslavia's dependence on US aid. *But due to the structural constraints of*

68 Ibid., 3, emphasis added.

69 Consider how Waltz responds to Ashley's and Cox's attempts to look at things from the other side of the epistemic spectrum: "Ashley and Cox would transcend the world as it is; meanwhile we have to live in it". Waltz, "A Response to my Critics", 338.

70 Kenneth Waltz, "Structural Realism after the Cold War", *International Security* Vol. 25, no. 1, 2000: 5–41.

> *international anarchy, polarity, relative capabilities, and the security dilemma, "patterns of behaviour nevertheless emerge"* (Waltz 1979: 92). The causes, conduct, and consequences of Yugoslavia's civil wars conform closely to structural realist expectations about these patterns. Yugoslavia, a weak state, experienced both civil and international war. Moreover, the United States, a state with unrivalled power, intervened in Yugoslavia's domestic problems and dominated international decisionmaking about how to respond to them.[71]

But what is Neorealism's explanation for the crisis, or for foreign intervention?

> Given the scope and scale of US dominance, much could change in Kosovo before a new balance of power emerges. Depending on how "the spirit moves it" (Waltz 2000: 29), the United States could take over the whole peacekeeping operation, walk away altogether, hold its position in the southeastern sector while the European sectors are consolidated, or even lead the way to a lasting settlement. None of these can be ruled out. In an anarchic realm, dominant power gives its possessor "wide latitude in making foreign policy choices" (Waltz 2000: 29).[72]

The paradox of these statements is, from an epistemic point of view, sublime. In a nutshell, Neorealism is telling us that nothing of what happened in the Kosovo crisis could have been predicted (or was foreordained), that because of the anarchic nature of the system anything could still happen, and that the unit 'United States' basically did what it did because it could. This basic and superficial description of reality is at odds with the promises of a theory that originated in opposition to Aron's descriptive sociologism devoid of any predictive – or scientific – power. Finally, the author in question manages to state that "patterns emerge" and that "nothing was foreordained" whilst "no options can be ruled out" within the same paragraph. The idea that "patterns emerge" refers to what Waltz was saying in 1979, whilst the idea that things go according to how "the spirit moves it" refers to what Waltz was saying in 2000.

But what was Waltz saying in 2000? Surprisingly, Waltz explains that Neorealism is not obsolete, whilst readily accepting that any change of system would indeed render Neorealism obsolete:

> True, if the conditions that a theory contemplated have changed, the theory no longer applies. But what sorts of changes would alter the international political

71 Karen Ruth Adams, "Structural Realism: The Consequences of Great Power Politics", in *Making Sense of International Relations Theory*, ed. Jennifer Sterling-Folker (Boulder: Lynne Rienner, 2006), 33, emphasis added. In this paragraph Adams is quoting Waltz, *Theory of International Politics*.

72 Ibid. In this paragraph Adams is quoting Waltz "Structural Realism after the Cold War".

> system so profoundly that old ways of thinking would no longer be relevant? *Changes of the system would do it, changes in the system would not.*[73]

Naturally, Waltz affirms that not much has changed because Anarchy and self-help still apply.

But then, why is it that Neorealism does not seem to have much to say about what was, arguably, one of the most important events in international life after the Cold War?

> Constancy of threat produces constancy of policy; absence of threat permits policy to become capricious. When few if any vital interests are endangered, a country's policy becomes sporadic and self-willed. The absence of serious threat to American security gives the United Sates wide latitude in making foreign policy choices. A dominant power acts internationally only when the spirit moves it. One example is enough to show this. When Yugoslavia's collapse was followed by genocidal war in successor states, the United States failed to respond until Senator Robert Dole moved to make Bosnia's peril an issue in the forthcoming presidential election; and acted not for the sake of its own security but to maintain its leadership position in Europe. *American policy was generated not by external security interests, but by internal political pressure and national ambition.*[74]

But then, Waltz concludes:

> Every time peace breaks out, people pop up to proclaim that realism is dead. That is another way of saying that international politics has been transformed. *The world, however, has not been transformed; the structure of international politics has simply been remade by the disappearance of the Soviet Union, and for a time we will live with unipolarity*. Moreover, international politics was not remade by the forces and factors that some believe are creating a new world order.[75]

These modern contradictions are crucial for our understanding of how a particular kind of knowledge was generated and deployed with regard to the Kosovo crisis. To sum up Waltz's points, we have the three following statements:

- Neorealism is a theory which states that anarchy and self-help condition the way in which units behave internationally. Anarchy is the transcendental object through which the subject is analysed in the context of what can be called, in Foucauldian terms, a transcendental philosophy of the object. Neorealism accepts that changes of structure would render it obsolete, but changes within structures would not.

---

73 Waltz, "Structural Realism after the Cold War", emphasis added.

74 Ibid., 29, emphasis added.

75 Ibid., 39, emphasis added.

- Self-help and Anarchy seem to have ceased enforcing constraints on the international activity of states. Indeed, Waltz openly states that American intervention in the Balkans was caused by internal factors rather than by systemic pressures. This alone would seem to constitute an acceptance of the fact that there has been a change of systems, rather than a change within systems, and that the theory no longer applies. It is safe to assume that the lack of systemic constraints is due to unipolarism (that is, lack of danger).
- However, Waltz concludes by stating that unipolarism constitutes an internal change within the system, rather than a change of systems, and that – despite everything Waltz states about the nature of American intervention in the Balkans – anarchical constraints still characterise international action, and that structural realism is therefore still relevant.

These paradoxes are crucial because they bring out the epistemic mechanism whereby knowledge is produced and applied in relation to international life, and prove the intrinsically modern nature of such knowledge. Indeed, it is easy to see how Waltz masters the two axes of the empirico-transcendental doublet to defend his claims. First, an analytic of finitude whereby inside/outside limitations are negotiated is applied. Thus, we can talk about changes within and without. Second, such analytic of finitude is enforced through a concept of historical linearity – but such claim only makes sense in the context of the empirico-transcendental doublet. The modern episteme is what allows Waltz to think and say that uniporalism does not constitute a change to the uninterrupted linear flow of time, but remains merely a change within a system that such linear time is de facto enforcing.

Thus, linear time becomes once again what provides meaning to the entire epistemic construct and prevents it from falling apart. It is only through the prism of linear time that all the paradoxes outlined above make, as it were, any sense at all. *The crucial point here is that, as the next chapters will demonstrate, it is exactly this mechanism of thought that allows the idea of Kosovo as a region frozen in time and filled with ancient ethnic hatreds to emerge.* Considering that Neorealism remains the dominant school of thought in academia and that – as the next chapter will argue – historically-linear accounts of the region have influenced key policy makers more than any other interpretation, the unveiling of the inner mechanisms of functional, linear time is of fundamental importance for understanding how related knowledge on the crisis was produced and enforced.

The Critical Geopolitical turn, on the other hand, offers an interpretation of social action that is far more closely aligned to the ethos of Complexity, especially in relation to the irreversibility of time and the social construction of the reality we examine. Three excellent examples of this, which all focus on the Kosovo crisis, can be found in the contributions of Alexandra Gheciu,[76] Vladimir Kolossov,[77] Virginie Mamadouh and Gertjan Dijkink.[78] The three contributions represent a geopolitical attempt at assessing the other side of the epistemic equation, that is, the way in which objects are constituted by subjects. This approach, for example, leads Gheciu to claim that "the international administration exercised significant power in the legal/institutional reconstruction of the province, and in its systematic attempts *to socialise Kosovars into accepting Western-based norms of liberal democracy as the only reasonable foundation of their polity.*"[79] Kolossov, on the other hand, examines how evolving factors influence the very way in which areas of research (in this case border studies) are framed:

> New *postmodern* approaches successfully complement traditional methods of border study, considering boundaries and cross-boundary interactions at different levels (from the global to the local) and as a single system. Moreover, recent publications show that the scale of analysis is not naturally determined, but represents a social construct and can be used to define the object and the scope of a conflict. Postmodern approaches help us to understand how a political discourse can define the position and role of articular boundaries and borders in foreign and domestic politics and thus enable critical thinking about political choices.[80]

Finally, Mamadouh and Dijkink provide insights into how shaping specific geopolitical areas according to normative cultural principle becomes embedded in the IR of some national states: "After the Kosovo war at the end of the 1990s, the Europeanisation of the Balkans became the key priority of the Greek government to stabilise the region and this process was naturalized and speeded up by consistently renaming the region South Eastern Europe."[81]

These constitute some hints of what sort of fundamental role Critical Geopolitics could play in the context of a Complexity-inspired epistemic configuration. However, the Foucauldian framework and the outline of Complexity's defining characteristics will allow the conclusion of the current work to better outline such

76 Alexandra Gheciu, "International Norms, Power and the Politics of International Administration: The Kosovo Case", *Geopolitics* Vol. 10, no. 1 (2005), 121–46.

77 Vladimir Kolossov, "Border Studies: Changing Perspectives and Theoretical Approaches", *Geopolitics Vol.* 10, no. 4 (2005), 606–32.

78 Virginie Mamadouh and Gertjan Dijkink, "Geopolitics, International Relations and Political Geography: The Politics of Geopolitical Discourse", *Geopolitics* Vol. 11, no. 3 (2006), 349–66.

79 Gheciu, "International Norms, Power and the Politics of International Administration: The Kosovo Case", 349, emphasis added.

80 Kolossov, "Border Studies: Changing Perspectives and Theoretical Approaches", 628.

81 Mamadouh and Dijkink, "Geopolitics, International Relations and Political Geography: The Politics of Geopolitical Discourse", 361.

role in relation to the dual functions that linear time and space play in knowledge-generating processes. In short, just as a linear notion of spatial and conceptual finitude and a notion of linear time require each other, it will be argued that non-linear approaches to space are essential to construct and understand the non-linear features of time which ultimately characterise both the Complexity approach and the approach of a new analysis of crisis, thus taking understanding beyond the constraints of the modern episteme.

Complexity, Ethics and the Analytic of Finitude

Whilst this chapter, so far, has sought to outline the epistemic background of contemporary mechanisms for the generation of knowledge in IR, the current section will apply such epistemic considerations to the issue of ethics. The final chapters of the book will reveal how the theoretical underpinnings exposed here have framed on the one hand, historically linear understandings of the Kosovo crisis and, on the other hand, analytically finite discourses on the ethics and legality of NATO's response. Hence, the two final chapters will show what the axes of modernity (historical linearity and analytical finitude) mean in practice.

The starting point for an epistemic consideration of the issues surrounding contemporary ethics is embodied in – following the nature of the modern episteme – the question of the transcendental. Furthermore, the Bergsonian link that unites Complexity science and post-structural philosophy will be outlined through a presentation of the Deleuzian understanding of the transcendental.

As Žižek re-discovers and presents Deleuze, the issue of ethics as a transcendental emerges with relation to virtually every issue. For instance, Žižek maintains that the most 'fundamental philosophical gesture' is not to attempt a closure of the gap between the empirical and the transcendental, but rather to open such gap to the point of rendering these fields irreducible to each other. Fundamentally, this is desirable because even what we refer to as 'the transcendental' is formulated within our very finite reality.[82] The appeal of Deleuze's philosophy, compounded by dilemmas in the sciences and the emergence of Complexity[83] is that the gap is

82 Žižek describes such fundamental gesture as thus: "Not to close the gap, but, on the contrary, to open up a radical gap in the very edifice of the universe, the 'ontological difference', the gap between the empirical and the transcendental, in which neither of the two levels can be reduced to the other (as we know from Kant, transcendental constitution is a mark of our – human – finitude and has nothing to do with 'creating reality'; on the other hand, reality appears to us only within the transcendental horizon, so we cannot generate the emergence of the transcendental horizon from the ontic self-development of reality)." Slavoj Žižek, *Organs without Bodies: On Deleuze and Consequences* (London: Routledge, 2004), 11.

83 Žižek himself elaborates on the connection between Deleuze's 'transcendental empiricism' and Complexity in ibid., 4. Note the similarity between Žižek's description of Deleuze's transcendental empiricism and Prigogine's transcendental-empirical account of the collapse of the wave function described in Chapter 1.

opened to the point that the empirical is embodied with an ethos of immanence, which in turn becomes transcendental:

> The genius of Deleuze resides in the notion of transcendental empiricism: in contrast to the standard notion of the transcendental as the formal conceptual network that structures the rich flow of empirical data, *the Deleuzian 'transcendental' is infinitely richer than reality* – it is the infinite potential field of virtualities out of which reality is actualised. The term 'transcendental' is used here in the strict philosophical sense of the a priori conditions of possibility of our experience of constituted reality. The paradoxical coupling of opposites (transcendental + empirical) points toward a field of experience beyond (or rather, beneath) the experience of constituted reality.[84]

This reading of Deleuze has a deep impact for the analysis of both axes of modernity, which are the object of this work. So far as the 'birth of History is concerned', Žižek argues that the process of becoming is the antithesis of history understood in the eschatological sense within the modern episteme. Thus, Žižek finds in Foucault the first attempt to produce an account of becoming, or to produce a history of history. Importantly, such attempt relies on analysing the immanent nature of such histories whilst disregarding (often distorting) the historical context.[85]

As will be argued below (Chapter 6), Žižek's understanding of this Foucauldian 'immanent history' informs his views on the Kosovo conflict – which resonate with a Complexity-based understanding – and on the flawed interpretations that were made. The Kosovo 'Event' has been understood in terms of the (not necessarily 'correct', or helpful) 'historical context' (ancient hatreds, ethnic divisions etc.) instead of being understood in terms of the very immanent political struggle. It is important to note how this notion of immanent history delineates the conceptual triangle Foucault – Bergson/Deleuze – Prigogine (Complexity). It is this triangle which, in many ways, substantiates the claim that Deleuzian post-structuralism equates to a Complex epistemology in the study of human affairs precisely because of its conceptualisation of time.

The analytic of finitude, on the other hand, is what really informs the inclusion and exclusion within an ethical analytic of 'rights'. Here, too, Žižek finds in Deleuze a way of not reducing the empirical and transcendental levels to each other:

84 Ibid.

85 In Žižek's words, "Foucault's discursive analysis studies *lekta*, utterances as pure events, focusing on the inherent conditions of their emergence and not on their inclusion in the context of historical reality. This is why the Foucault of *The Archaeology of Knowledge* is as far as possible from any form of historicism, of locating events in their historical contexts – on the contrary, Foucault *abstracts* them from their reality and its historical casualty and studies the *immanent* rules of their emergence." Ibid., 10.

> Deleuze is right in his magnificent attack on historicist 'contextualisation': *becoming means transcending the context of historical conditions out of which a phenomenon emerges*. This is what is missing in historicist anti-universalist multiculturalism: the explosion of the eternally New in/as the process of becoming. The standard opposition of the abstract Universal (say, *Human Rights*) and particular identities is to be replaced by a new tension between Singular and Universal: the Event of the New as a universal singularity.[86]

But what does this precisely mean for the concept of Human Rights? How can we understand Human Rights as a 'universal singularity'?

A 'Bergso-Deleuzian', Complexity-informed analysis of 'immanent transcendentalism' necessarily demands an exploration into the concept of the inside/outside: understood as that which remains inside or outside the classical transcendental realm. In what is possibly the most challenging work regarding the status of the modern episteme in relation to Complexity and Systems Theory, the question of Ethics is explored precisely through a Complexity-informed analysis of the inside/outside or immanent/transcendental. The collection of essays in *Observing Complexity: Systems Theory and Postmodernity*[87] represents a rare attempt at critically understanding the ethos of Complexity through the epistemic lenses provided by Foucault (for example, a whole section of the book is entitled *Systems Theory and the Postmodern Episteme*).

Rasch's important contribution regarding *Immanent Systems, Transcendental Temptations, and the Limits of Ethics*[88] begins with the recognition that "we have become distinctly suspicious of transcendental attempts to construct inviolate and panoramic levels of vision labelled God, Reason, or Truth."[89] Adorno and Horkheimer made the same point in Dialectic of Enlightenment, where they described how 'pure positivism', which is the end result of the Enlightenment, is driven by a fear of the outside: "Nothing at all may remain outside, because the mere idea of outsideness is the very source of fear."[90] Adorno and Horkheimer do not fear this as much as they fear the loss of the outside, understanding the outside as "an other of the all-pervasive administered society."[91]

The question of knowledge of the outside has been revitalised in the last century, precisely as a result of empirical research in all fields, as for example, the

86 Ibid., 14–15, emphasis added.

87 William Rasch and Cary Wolfe, eds, *Observing Complexity: Systems Theory and the Postmodern Episteme* (Minneapolis: University of Minnesota Press, 2000).

88 William Rasch and Cary Wolfe, "Immanent Systems, Transcendental Temptations, and the Limits of Ethics", in *Observing Complexity: Systems Theory and the Postmodern Episteme,* eds, William Rasch and Cary Wolfe (Minneapolis: University of Minnesota Press, 2000).

89 Ibid., 73.

90 Ibid.

91 Ibid.

inevitable self-referential aspects of quantum physics (the best known example), linguistics (the fact that research into language has to make use of language), the sociology of knowledge (which had demonstrated at least the influence of social factors on all knowledge), and, perhaps most significantly, cognitive science. Brain research has shown that the brain is not able to maintain any contact with the outer world on the level of its own operations, but – from the perspective of information – operates closed in upon itself. This is obviously also true for the brains of those engaged in brain research.[92]

This is the inescapable impasse of the modern episteme as described by Foucault: nothing remains outside: all explanations for the order of things originate from a mysterious source inside. Consider, for example, Maturana and Varela, who concluded that "the nervous system as such cannot distinguish between illusion, hallucination and perception. Such a distinction can only be made retrospectively, through the use of a different experience as a meta-experiential authoritative criterion of distinction."[93] On these bases, how can anyone possibly claim to have acquired any knowledge of the outside world? As Luhmann put it: "Knowing is only a self-referential process. Knowledge can only know itself, although it can – as out of the corner of its eye – determine that this is only possible if there is more than only cognition. Cognition deals with an external world that remains unknown and has to, as a result, come to see that it cannot see what it cannot see."[94]

Even the process of knowing is captured by the organic model of the modern episteme: the external as such remains unknown, but it grounds the possibility of knowledge in the inside. In the words of Rasch, "a living system has no access to its environment. What it presents to itself as the outside world are representations of its own internal states…There simply are no informational exchanges, no informational input-output relations between autopoietic living systems and their environments."[95]

Why is this relevant to a Complexity-based understanding of the ethics of the Kosovo crisis? The real point of the section is that a Complexity-based understanding (such as Luhmann's) reveals how the modern episteme places contingency on all ethical knowledge and necessarily reproduces paradoxes that are inherent within such episteme. All such paradoxes relate to an absolute impossibility of logically linking the transcendental to the empirical, despite the fact that the modern episteme requires a separation of the two fields through its empirico-transcendental doublet. *Chapter 5 will demonstrate how this essential paradox – which neatly translated into the Žižekian notion of Universal Exception – characterises the totality of ethical and legal discourses surrounding the Kosovo conflict.*

92 Ibid., 74.

93 Ibid.

94 Ibid.

95 Ibid., 75.

In the realm of ethics, it becomes difficult to see how the self-referential cycle can be broken. According to Luhmann, the key is to generate productive and meaningful knowledge within a *modern* system of thought which is aware of its own self-referential circularity. Indeed, the challenge is to understand "how the tautology of self-reference can be interrupted and unfolded in a productive manner. [Systems] are faced with the interesting and circular problem of generating meaningful external references where none exists. Luhmann considers *this loss of reference, or loss of the outside, to be a defining feature of the modernity we find ourselves in, and as such it makes no sense to condemn it*."[96]

The NATO intervention in Kosovo, as the following chapters will elucidate, was characterised by a deadlock. The very visible disjuncture between the reasons for intervention and that modus operandi of intervention (preventing ethnic cleansing on the ground with bombs from the skies only) is rooted in a very modern confusion regarding the status of transcendental notions 'outside'. Ultimately, the Universal that was constructed and deployed in relation to intervention proceeded through a system of exclusion: there was no meaningful relation with the 'outside'. A critical appraisal of Complexity, on the other hand, can show that "if moral codes…no longer deliver direct evidence of the transcendental realm, but rather become historicized and seen as socially constructed artefacts, the task of reclaiming authority must be negotiated within the domain of *immanence* that has been loosed from its transcendent anchorage."[97] The attempt to create an ethical relation at the level of immanence must, thus, be motivated by a desire to resolve the conflict that occurs in the realm of ethics, which is itself caused by the paradoxes inherent to the empirico-transcendental doublet.

It is in the context of self-referencing notions in language that Wittgenstein declared that "Ethics is transcendental".[98] Wittgenstein does put forward the most direct vision of the absolute inarticulateness of ethics. The world is, the argument goes, a closed system. In such system, all propositions are of equal value: therefore the world has neither sense nor value. Worse, if anything guaranteed non-contingency (that is, something that is of unequal value), that something must be outside the contingent world, and that exclusion alone would prevent it from exerting any influence in the contingent plane. Absolute transcendental value is impossible in a fully contingent world.[99] Of course, the implication of this is that "there can be no ethical propositions. Ethics cannot be articulated, cannot deal with the world, and cannot leave describable evidence of itself in the world; it serves as

96 Ibid., 76, emphasis added.

97 Ibid., strong emphasis added.

98 Ibid.

99 Or, as Rasch puts it, "Since everything in the world is contingent, nothing in the world can express lack of contingency. Whatever guarantees the non-contingency of the world, as opposed to the contingency of the facts within the world, must lie outside the world, or else it too would become contingent and incapable of guaranteeing non-contingency. Absolute value is absolutely different and distant from the world." Ibid., 77.

the unspeakable limit or condition of the world. Ethics is transcendental."[100] It is the closed nature of the system – *its very finitude* – that imposes full contingency on items within the system.

It would be difficult to find a more pertinent example of the modern episteme at work. In the self-referential universe of the organism, the 'outside', inaccessible and unspeakable 'limit' of the world grounds its 'condition' within the organic organisation of knowledge. The main difference from what Dillon would call the radical non-relational[101] and this organic (modern) organisation of knowledge is that in poetic endeavours the non-relational is seen precisely as that which cannot be attained (or 'the Sublime), whilst in the modern episteme we have non-relationals being incorporated in organisms of knowledge. In organic systems, the hidden, absolute values are determinants, whilst in poetic relationships they are precisely the opposite: that which prevents determinism from happening. Non-contingency is ensured precisely by the immanent actualisation of the virtual in time – *the crucial difference being that the virtual is potentially infinite, because it is a process of becoming.*

Wittgenstein, of course, describes the impossibility of ethics in terms of the contingency embodied in language: "a book on ethics would have to be a book outside of the world of language, since there is no language in which a book that could not be written otherwise could be written. But, of course, no book, in any meaningful sense of the word, could be written outside the world of language... [this] reveals the basic experience one has when confronted with the impossible task of ethics."[102] And, yet, the whole edifice is built on the problematic empirico-transcendental doublet: according to Wittgenstein "the entire project is fraught with a paradox" because "if ethics can only exist in the transcendental realm of necessity, then ethics can never be glimpsed from within the immanent world of contingency."[103] That is the crux of the paradox: how can we imagine something (ethics) that is, logically speaking, outside our possibility of knowledge?

Rasch identifies the typically modern problem regarding the contingent horizon from which we look at the transcendental (that is, the contingent horizon from which we aim at the transcendental notion of ethics).[104] On the basis of the impossibility inherent in fully grasping the transcendental from within the

100 Ibid.

101 Dillon, "Poststructuralism, Complexity and Poetics".

102 Rasch, "Immanent Systems, Transcendental Temptations, and the Limits of Ethics", 78.

103 Ibid.

104 In Rasch's words, "To wonder at the existence of the world is to attempt to place oneself outside of the world, but this attempt can only occur as a conceptualisation within the world and therefore becomes part of it...attempting to imagine ethics as absolute value is as noble and as futile as attempting to escape language by means of language...the attempt to escape the boundaries of our language, which are the boundaries of our world, is – ironically – perfectly hopeless." Ibid., 79.

empirical finitude in which we find ourselves Rasch concludes with a perfectly modern twist: “if it is to remain true to its own transcendence, ethics, it seems, must maintain the necessity of its own impossibility. In fact, ethics is identified *as* the necessity of its own impossibility.”[105]

The inherent modernity in these statements is something that has not gone unnoticed by Rasch. This is where the postmodern ethos, embedded in a culture of pure immanence within Complexity, informs the debate over ethics. Rasch’s basic argument corresponds to Žižek’s fundamental philosophical act, that is, “to open up the gap between the empirical and the transcendental, in which neither of the two levels can be reduced to the other”. In other words, to bring the transcendental back into the immanent, to operate the Deleuzian shift from the metaphysical to the virtual, to incorporate ethics into a philosophy of pure immanence, or of life.

Rasch thus argues that

> …Wittgenstein starts with a basic distinction – call it immanence/transcendence, inside/outside, relative/absolute, contingency/necessity, sense/nonsense – and attempts to think the possibility of crossing over from the left side of this distinction to the right. The world of language in which this attempt is made is radically immanent. It is a world in which sense is made, in which every proposition implies its own negation, i.e. the possibility of its own non-existence. The attempt to think ethics (defined as an absolute value) is an attempt, made from within the contingent world of sense-making, to transcend the contingent world of self making. *The inside stretches to become its own outside in order to see itself as and know itself as absolute necessity*. But the task is hopeless, necessarily doomed to failure.[106]

The sentence in italics encapsulates the status of the modern episteme. The paragraph that follows is its opposite, that is: an ethos of postmodernity embedded in Complexity. It could be regarded indeed as a manifesto of a postmodern (strictly in the Foucauldian sense) approach to ethics:

> The transcendental/immanent distinction, coupled with the impossibility of escaping the domain from which this distinction is made, results in a vast and oppressive immanence, the inescapability of which is guaranteed by the attributes given to that side of the distinction that cannot be reached. The world thus becomes absolutely contingent. It cannot be otherwise that the fact that the world can be otherwise. The impossibility of necessity is necessarily the case. Transcendence guarantees the conditions of the possibility of immanence by removing itself from the field of observation, for if observed, it would disappear into the vast immanence it calls forth. And so immanence becomes the closed system of the world whose contingency is *not* contingent. We are left with a

105 Ibid.
106 Ibid., 80.

> systemic solipsism. *The outside is acknowledged as the absolute condition for the existence of the inside, but it remains supremely unknowable*. It is the silence that delimits the world.[107]

This "silence of the world" is nothing other than what Foucault describes as the (modern) inner organic truth which finds itself outside all possibilities of knowledge but grounds – through its absence – all possibilities to attain knowledge. It is precisely the acceptance of this as a non-relational that turns the contingent into the non-contingent. The lesson here is that "the supreme power of transcendence, then, is its undoing. One cannot *evoke the outside and demand a radical change of the world, because the only change that could satisfy the claim of absolute ethics... [is] an ethical totalitarianism in all questions, a single-minded and painful preservation of the purity of the uncompromising demands of ethics*."[108] An aspect of this insight has been masterfully summarised by Peter Sloterdijk in the maxim "The question is not what is virtue without terror but what is terror other than consistent idealism."[109]

Intervention in Kosovo opened a new chapter in the collective imaginary, at least in the West, in which something legitimate (and legitimacy appeals to the transcendental 'outside') may not necessarily be something legal (legality being far more immanent, that is, what is or is not allowed by the rules as they are right here, right now). Yet, it is legitimate to ask whether this was not somehow framed in terms of an 'ethical totalitarianism' which pursued the construction of a Universal on the grounds of the exclusion of the particular. This is especially the case when one looks at the schism between intent and the way in which the intent was pursued. It is only in a context of flawed distinctions between the empirical and the transcendental, between the Universal and the particular, that it makes sense to bomb a TV station in the name of, amongst other things, freedom of speech. The moment we make differences between legality and legitimacy – the moment we allow statements such as "the intervention was legitimate but illegal" to be made (see Chapter 6) – we open up this irreducible ethical gap between the empirical and the transcendental.

The question of ethics as a transcendental necessarily develops into a question of the relationship between the self and the other. As Rasch puts it, "If...ethics is proclaimed to be a transcendental, then the domain of the ethical is simultaneously the domain of the other, and the question of the relationship of this ethical outside to the immanent inside becomes a meditation on the relationship of the self to the other."[110] Here is where concepts regarding the establishment of an ethical

---

107 Ibid.

108 Ibid., 81. The strong emphasis is justified by the relevance of this insight when applied to the notion of humanitarian intervention.

109 Peter Sloterdijk, *Critique of Cynical Reason* (Minneapolis: University of Minnesota Press, 1987), 102.

110 Ibid.

link with the other,[111] also in relation to the thoughts of Levinas and Derrida,[112] become relevant. It is, however, useful to bear in mind that "precisely because of the inescapability of violence and of language, Derrida resists in Levinas what we have seen in Wittgenstein's, the absolute transcendence of the other."[113]

With this in mind, we can now attempt to answer the question presented at the beginning of this section: how can we understand Human Rights as an example of Complex 'universal singularities'? According to Žižek:

> Often, we stumble on a particular case that does not fully 'fit' its universal species, that is 'atypical'; the next step is to acknowledge that *every* particular is 'atypical', that *the universal species exist only in exceptions*, that there is a structural tension between the Universal and the Particular. At this point, we become aware that the Universal is no longer just an empty neutral container of its subspecies but an entity in tension with each and every one of its species. The universal Notion thus acquires a dynamics of its own. More precisely, the true Universal is this very antagonistic dynamics between the Universal and the Particular. It is at this point that we pass from 'abstract' to 'concrete' Universal – at the point when we acknowledge that every Particular is an 'exception', and, consequently, that the Universal, far from 'containing' its particular content, *excludes* it (or is excluded *by* it). This exclusion renders the Universal itself particular (it is not truly universal, since it cannot grasp or contain the particular content), yet this very failure is its strength: the Universal is thus simultaneously posited as the Particular.[114]

Chapter 5 will demonstrate how virtually all legal cases surrounding the Kosovo conflict failed to 'fit the Universal species', which were, in turn, constructed precisely on the bases of the exclusions they generated. In the case of the European Court of Human Rights, for example, these exclusions were formed through the notion of 'territory', or rather, through social construction of such notion. Incidentally, this Deleuze-inspired discussion on the Universal brings us back to...Complexity, for Žižek – after outlining this relationship between the Universal and the Particular – states: "no wonder one of Deleuze's references here is Ilya Prigogine..."[115] So, Prigogine talks about Bergson when outlining the ethos of Complexity, whilst the Bergsonian Deleuze talks about Prigogine when outlining his views on ethics. As should be clear from the epistemic lenses provided by our study this is not a

111 See, for example, David Campbell, "Justice and the International Order: the Case of Bosnia and Kosovo", in *Ethics and International Affairs: Extents and Limits* eds, Jean Marc Coicaud and Daniel Warner (Tokyo: The United Nations University Press, 2001).

112 Campbell, *National Deconstruction.*

113 Rasch, *Immanent Systems, Transcendental Temptations, and the Limits of Ethics*, 83.

114 Žižek, *Organs without Bodies*, 50–51.

115 Ibid., 51.

coincidence: both approaches have something very important in common, and that is, an attempt to overcome the modern episteme.

Deleuze's reliance on Prigogine for the formulation of his own approach to transcendental empiricism is evident, and Prigogine's own reliance on Bergson – arguably Deleuze's starting point – closes the Complexity-Post-structuralism circle. This is the circle that will allow the rest of the current work to treat a Deleuzian understanding of ethics as a Complexity-based understanding of ethics, which will be used to elucidate the practical implications for the way in which ethics were deployed in the legal context of the Kosovo crisis in Chapter 5.

The crux of the argument is that a post-structural approach to ethics would seek to eliminate the outside transcendental as a determinant whilst bringing the ethical relation to the other on the 'inside'. As such, the 'Universal Human Rights' would become, simply, the 'rights of humans': by removing the outer, transcendental notion of Human, it is necessary to operate after what Foucault termed the 'death of Man'. Fundamentally, the idea that Universal Human Rights should be applied to particular ethnic groups (which are themselves determined and constructed within particular discourses) is essentially and 'epistemically' a modern idea. Such an application results in a construction of the Universal in terms of exclusions.[116]

Rasch explains how Drucilla Cornell attempts to create this Derridean approach to the other by recognising the other's otherness while bringing it into the system of the self: Cornell's transcendental other must have a way of entering into the system while still retaining its status as 'outsider'.[117] The result is the creation of a semi-transcendental other, which does not accept the absolute transcendence of the other but remains the 'outside' within the self that allows for the self to engage in ethical relations. Indeed, Cornell's objective is "to establish a hierarchical relationship between ethics and morality. Morality, which is to be subordinated to ethics, is equated with the enunciation of behavioural norms and the generation of a system of rules. The *ethical relation*, on the other hand, does not manifest itself as discourse. Rather, it is embodied by a carefully semi-specified way of being that allows it to sit in judgement on moral systems."[118]

---

116 This debate goes back a long way. Scholars have, for example, identified similar notions of cosmopolitanism in Diogenes of Sinope: when Diogenes proclaims to belong to the 'cosmos', rather than the 'world' or to any other location, the message is that the Cynic regards other men and women as members of a 'cosmos' which, in its very immanence, transcends local cultures, religions, historical periods, etc. That is how, despite its inherent immanence and disregard for metaphysics, Cynic cosmopolitanism was inherently ethical: its relation was based on the belief that the 'other', despite its 'otherness', was an integral part of our 'self'. Thus, the construction of ethical arguments on the basis of ethnicity would have been meaningless for Diogenes and other Cynics. The construction of Universals on the exclusionary basis of the 'other' is, nonetheless, a defining characteristic of the two axes of modernity under scrutiny.

117 Rasch, *Immanent Systems, Transcendental Temptations, and the Limits of Ethics*, 85.

118 Ibid., 84, emphasis added.

Because ethics cannot express itself through discourse, it is equivalent to the radical non relational, thus giving a 'poetic' character to the ethical relation. This bringing of the 'outside' into the self differs radically from the modern approach to ethics which sees ethics as the transcendental 'outside', which, nonetheless, imperfectly characterises organic systems from within as our (Kantian) gaze on transcendental imagination – as Žižek explains – is emphatically always limited by our own finitude. This role of ethics is also present in Luhmann's thought. According to Rasch:

> The distinction between morality and ethics is historically conditioned. Ethics as the reflection theory of morality becomes necessary when castle-based moral codes of conduct, defined by Luhmann as *the unity of morality and manners*, gives way, along with the stratified ('feudal') social organisation in which it flourished, to increasingly complex, differentiated modernity. In both its utilitarian (Bentham) and Kantian varieties, this new emphasis on ethical reflection is registered as the necessity for establishing criteria for choice. In other words, ethics becomes formalised, moved from a consideration of the moral 'fibre' or substance of an individual to a consideration of action on the face of competing alternatives. *The Kantian solution, as is well known, relies on the validity of the transcendental/empirical distinction and therefore, in Luhmann's view, is no longer tenable.*[119]

What is crucial here is the idea of ethics understood, as a reflection of morality emerges when the moral ethos – understood as the unity between itself and manners – is dissolved. This dissolution causes a fragmentation between the goals of morality and the means of achieving these, and it is only here that ethics emerge as the 'self-consciousness' of morality. It is because of this 'modern' dissolution that we can conclude with Luhmann: "By acting as a mediator between morality and society, ethics is charged with minimizing the devastation morality is capable of unleashing."[120]

Whilst most critiques of intervention in Kosovo are concerned with the legality and morality of intervention, few of these ask whether the modus operandi of intervention was compatible with its own, 'ethical' goals. As the next case studies will seek to demonstrate, this is because the Universal at the heart of the moral argument was based on its own exclusions. The very actors of the conflict were constructed following the rules inherent to the modern episteme and on the basis of a Kantian ethical model. The conceptualisation of the conflict in terms of imagined communities (the 'ethnic Albanian') impeded an analysis of the immanent political struggle at the root of the crisis. At this immanent level, it is much more difficult to reduce the multitude to such an imagined community: to the 'ethnic Albanians', for example. By following a classical modern pattern of

119 Ibid., 93, emphasis added.

120 Ibid.

thought, the actors had to be defined according to an analytic of finitude, which equally entailed a very contingent historical linearity. *In the case of Kosovo, historical linearity was enforced through a notion of ancient ethnic hatreds, whilst ethical analytical finitude was deployed in the legal and ethical understanding of the conflict (Chapters 6–7).* Thus, the multitude was stratified and personalised into a (finite) body, to which the logic of Universal Human rights – itself operating through a logic of exclusion – was applied. A more immanent approach would have warranted a reflection in terms of the ethical relation to others, preceded by an immanent analysis of a political problem.

The construction of the other – perceived as something outside – lies at the heart of the problem embedded in moral arguments regarding Human Rights and intervention. When the dissolution between morality and its manners occurs, the problem becomes more evident, and calls for an ethical approach to make judgements on its own morality. It is only after an (exclusionary) construction of the other has taken place that it makes sense for an institution to refer to a multitude as the 'ethnic Albanians'.

Metaphysical Law and Ethical Categorisations

An interesting categorisation of approaches to the problem of ethics has been conducted by Holzgrefe in the collective work *Humanitarian Intervention: Ethical, Legal and Political Dilemmas.*[121] The categorisation of ethical approaches perfectly illustrates the essentially Kantian divide present in all arguments. According to Holzgrefe, we could design an ethical chart with four axes or dimensions, each with two extreme poles. The first ethical divide would consist of concerns over the source of moral concern. Here, we would find that "*Naturalist* theories of international justice contend that morally binding international norms are an inherent feature of the world" whilst "*Consensualist* theories…claim that moral authority of any given international norm derives from the explicit or tacit consent of the agents subject to that norm".[122]

The second ethical divide deals with the appropriate objects of moral concern. Here, we find that "*Individualist* theories of international justice are concerned ultimately with the welfare of individual human beings" while "collectivist theories…maintain that groups – typically ethnic groups, races, nations, or states – are the proper objects of moral concern".[123] The third ethical divide is related to the appropriate weight of moral concern. Here, "*Egalitarian* theories of international justice claim that the objects of moral concern must be treated equally" whilst

121 J.L. Holzgrefe, "The Humanitarian Intervention Debate", in *Humanitarian Intervention: Ethical, Legal and Political Dilemmas*, eds, Robert Keohane and J.L. Holzgrefe (Cambridge: Cambridge University Press, 2003).

122 Ibid., 19.

123 Ibid.

"*Inegalitarian* theories...require or permit them to be treated unequally".[124] Finally, the fourth ethical divide regards the proper width of moral concern. Here, "Universalist theories assert that all relevant agents – wherever they exist – are the proper objects of moral concern". On the contrary, "Particularist theories...hold that only certain agents...are the proper objects of moral concern".[125]

The fact that Holzgrefe is able to devise such a *taxinomia* and to classify utilitarianism, natural law, social contractarianism, communitarianism and legal positivism according to its principles is telling. In the end, it is simple to discern the different approaches to the empirico-transcendental doublet inherent in the modern episteme. The problem inherent in approaching such 'divides' from one extreme or the other is not a concern of contemporary ethical theory: it is just assumed that positions and the extremes of such divides are irreconcilable. Interpretations of specific events can thus always be preceded by qualifications such as 'under X approach'. A telling example: supporters of 'act-utilitarianism' claim that any military action is justified if it saves more lives than it loses: "Thus, for example, NATO's killing of 10 civilian employees of Radio Television Serbia (RTS) in Belgrade during Operation Allied Force could be justified on act-utilitarian grounds if destroying 'a source of propaganda that is prolonging this war and causing untold new suffering to the people of Kosovo' [quote by Claire Short] saved more lives than it cost."[126]

Presumably, it would be safe to assume that Claire Short, Madeleine Albright (we believe that the price is worth it...) and Tony Blair (I cannot apologise for removing a brutal dictator...) are all act-utilitarians. Is it not the case that ultimately the arguments of this group represent a classical example of morality, understood as Luhmann does, as a concern emanating from the vision of the outside which relies on the construction of 'the people of Kosovo'? Is the ethical relation here not absent in the sense that those 10 RTS employees have already, anyway, been constructed as the 'other' and excluded by a Universal constructed according to the processes Žižek describes above? Do they count in the calculation aiming to reduce 'untold new suffering'? Is the job of ethics in this case to 'minimize the devastation morality is capable of unleashing'? Is the terror unleashed here nothing other than a case of consistent idealism?

As Kratochwil puts it, "there is in law itself always a tension between positive law and those transcendental standards, which – according to the natural law approach – provides positive prescriptions with the character of 'true law'."[127] With Kratochwil we have an attempt to surpass the Kantian deadlock, and in a

124 Ibid., 20.

125 Ibid.

126 Ibid., 22.

127 Friedrich Kratochwil, "International law as an approach to international ethics: A plea for a jurisprudential diagnostics", in *Ethics and International Affairs: Extents and Limits*, eds, Jean Marc Coicaud and Daniel Warner (Tokyo: The United Nations University Press, 2001).

sense the modern episteme itself, in law. It is an approach guided by the same principles that inform Prigogine's attempt to remove the metaphysical and to act on immanent populations, or what Deleuze would call the manifold. The crux of the argument is that contemporary ethics – following Kant – are placed under the aegis of what we would call Foucault's 'analytical' strand in the modern episteme. This approach, it is argued, has failed on its own terms.

According to Kratochwil, the analytical-transcendental approach to ethics poses a number of dilemmas:

> Beginning with abstract principles rather than concrete practices and institutions leads not only to a devaluation of the 'state' as an institution…but it also reinforces the tendency to conceive of ethics as an analytical enterprise, concerned with the elaboration of standards to which every rational being has to consent. But then, such an approach reduces ethical reflection to a largely cognitivist enterprise that can be tackled through the demonstration and application of the right principles to a specific 'subsumed' situation. On the other hand, since abstract principles do not come with their own specification for application, we are often at a loss when a situation can be described from two different perspectives and can be subsumed under two different principles, or even when the same principle leads to entirely different prescriptions in a concrete case, depending on the level of generality one applies…[128]

These are the dilemmas of the empirico-transcendental doublet all over again. Kratochwil recognises that this analytical ethical enterprise is founded on Kantian deontology which, when applied to the immanent reality "quickly becomes incoherent."[129] In this field, Kratochwil advocates a renaissance of jurisprudence since according to this approach "a rule has a definite meaning if its terms clearly correspond to the factual circumstances selected as relevant by the rule."[130] In the end, Kratochwil states that "what we primarily need is an appropriate heuristics for helping us in our perplexities rather than abstract principles from which we can elegantly and parsimoniously derive our more particular action-guiding prescriptions, ranging from nuclear war to animal rights."[131] A Complexity, postmodern approach to the Kosovo conflict would take into account these attempts to depart from the transcendental in the realm of international law (see Chapter 5).

128 Ibid., 17.
129 Ibid., 20.
130 Ibid., 32.
131 Ibid., 33.

Conclusion

This chapter has sought to trace evidence of the modern nature of our understanding of contemporary conflict, ranging from the way in which we have constructed a 'modern social science' primarily concerned with the study of war (IR theory) to the ethics surrounding arguments related to humanitarian intervention. The final chapters of the study will deconstruct the arguments related to the Kosovo conflict to show how this intrinsically modern way of thinking conditions practice, and will also seek to reveal how an understanding of the conflict based on a Complexity inspired, postmodern approach may have warranted different outcomes. The main findings of the chapter reflect the presentation of the modern episteme and an outline of Complexity as a challenge to such episteme in Chapters 1 and 2. In particular, this chapter has sought to reveal how:

1. The academic discipline of IR has followed the path of other empirical sciences which were constituted as transcendental philosophies of objects. Such formation is characterised by the two axes of modernity embodied in the empirico-transcendental doublet: the isolation of an organic body of knowledge whose finitude is enforced by the linearity of time. It will be argued that such a perspective influenced the way in which the Kosovo crisis was understood and acted upon.
2. Critical Geopolitics and new approaches to IR which question, respectively, the social nature of space and time can – and should – be understood as Complexity-based approaches to understanding the reality of conflicts. Such approaches thus constitute a valid application of 'Complexity science' to the field, and the fact that leading in different areas refer to each other to argue their points in evidence of this (the Prigogine–Bergson–Deleuze triangle constituting the most obvious example).
3. Such triangle also forms the basis of an understanding of the modern episteme's formulation of transcendental ethics. Rasch's interpretation of Luhmann's Complexity-based systemic approach is a particularly relevant attempt at surpassing the paradoxes inherent within modern ethics and at bringing the issue of ethics to the level of Deleuze's transcendental empiricism. Finally, the ensemble of paradoxes inherent in the modern approach to ethics (paradoxes which have been carefully located within the two axes of modernity and within the empirico-transcendental doublet) have been described in the context of what Žižek calls the principle of Universal Exclusion. Finally, such paradoxes have been brought to light in the context of contemporary debates regarding the role of the ethical link in the context of moral responsibilities, the categorisation of ethical approaches to humanitarian intervention and the role of jurisprudence in deploying legal constraints on issues surrounding humanitarian intervention.

4. By bringing down meta-theoretical concepts to the level of theory it has been possible to see how the two axes of modernity translated into a notion of historical linearity in academic IR and a notion of Universal Exclusion in contemporary ethical thought. The rest of the study will bring such notions down a further level by showing that in the case of Kosovo historical linearity was enforced through a notion of perpetual 'ancient ethnic hatreds', that Universal Exclusion characterised legal and ethical debates surrounding the intervention.

Such conclusions will be applied to the specific case of the Kosovo conflict in the coming chapters, allowing this work to address the three research questions outlined in the Introduction.

Intermezzo
A Roadmap to an Argument

The final chapters of this book will synthesise the theoretical perspectives outlined so far and indicate how a Complexity-informed epistemic approach would account for the events that unfolded in Kosovo, and for alternative understandings in IR theory. At this point it may be useful to summarise what the theoretical insights exposed so far entail:

1. Foucault argues that the modern episteme is essentially characterised by an empirico-transcendental doublet, which is enforced in all modern attempts to generate knowledge through transcendental philosophies of objects. The doublet is implemented through the two axes of modernity, namely, an analytic of finitude and a concept of historical linearity. The construction of modern scientific epistemology – which greatly conditioned the formation of academic IR – followed these modern epistemic rules from Vienna on, adopting what Dupré calls a metaphysical stance,[1] and what Kuhn refers to as paradigmatic science.[2] According to Foucault, the modern episteme opens what here refers to as the 'age of History', as the newly born subject 'man' can only be isolated and thought of because of a concept of historical linearity. Foucault also believed that Bergson – and consequently Deleuze – were philosophers who transcended the modern episteme precisely because they recognised the role that linear temporality played in the generation of modern knowledge and created alternative conceptualisations of time that radically differed from the modern concept: whereas linear time serves the modern purpose of enforcing contingency, Bergson's and Deleuze's virtual time serves the purpose of guaranteeing novelty.
2. Complexity theorists such as Prigogine recognise that the defining feature of the new science is its alternative conceptualisation of time and the recognition that time is irreversible – what Prigogine calls the 'arrow of time' is therefore at the heart of his new science of uncertainty. Incidentally, Prigogine also uses Bergson as a starting point for his own science, reinforcing the idea that Complexity represents an epistemic break. Considering that recent research has unveiled the influence that German Natural Philosophy and Romanticism exerted on the early precursors of Complexity, and the consequent similarities that have been noted between philosophers such as Nietzsche and these precursors, a number of

1 Dupré, *The Disorder of Things.*
2 Kuhn, *The Structure of Scientific Revolutions.*

commentators have proceeded to outline the idea according to which post-structuralism represents one side of the Complexity coin in philosophy. Overall, the roots of Complexity call for a re-opening of ancient debates on the role of reasons after the Enlightenment: whereas the modern episteme has sought to ensure that Reason was tasked with the mission of providing certainty (through the generation of metaphysical thought and science), Complexity in a postmodern episteme would rather have Reason serving the purpose of ensuring that we can cope with an uncertainty which – far from being the consequence of inadequate human understanding – is a defining feature of nature.

3. Following a detailed analysis of the nature of the modern episteme it has been possible to thoroughly examine how the rules inherent within such episteme have conditioned the generation and application of knowledge in IR and in the field of ethics. The whole of Chapter 3 sought to descend the theoretical ladder and to show how the insights presented in the previous two chapters influence the way in which two specific areas of knowledge (IR and ethics) are affected by the constraints imposed by the modern episteme.
4. The last two chapters of the study seek to demonstrate that notions of historical linearity translated into assumptions on the existence of ancient ethnic hatreds, whilst analytical finitude enforced contingency through Universal Exclusions in ethical and legal discourse. The identification of the axes of modernity in Kosovo-related discourse allows for an epistemic understanding of how Complexity challenges the very grounds upon which these understandings of the Kosovo crisis were constructed.

From now on, our task is to relate what has been explored so far to the specific incident of the Kosovo crisis, in order to provide an answer to the two questions that motivate this exercise: In what way can the emergence of what we loosely refer to as "Complexity Theory" enhance our understanding of social affairs generally, and of human conflict in particular? And why is the Kosovo conflict a particularly good example to illustrate the role that Complexity can have in enhancing such understanding?

Following the arguments above, the following chapters will seek to answer questions that can be found across all disciplines that sought to understand various aspects of the Kosovo crisis through Complexity-informed epistemic lenses. For each argument above, the remaining two chapters will use such lenses to identify what sort of questions and knowledge would really be regarded as being crucial for a Complex understanding of the crisis, and in particular to demonstrate that:

1. The ethnic conflict in Kosovo is essentially a modern conflict brought about by very modern attempts to enforce authority. As such, and contrary to many claims, the ethnic conflict was not the product of ancient ethnic hatreds which remained constant (linear history) but the product of very

immanent political struggles. Such a vision is Complexity-based insofar as history is regarded as a non-linear process and this is far more akin to the Deleuzo-Bergsonian notion of 'actualisation of the virtual in time' (and the virtual comprises an infinite number of possibilities) rather than the modern notion of 'realisation of the (limited) possible'. In other words, Chapter 6 will seek *to demonstrate that the ethnic conflict was itself generated by the actualisation of virtual myths which served the purposes of immanent political struggles*. Furthermore, Chapter 6 will demonstrate that the creation of the ethno-nationalist discourse depends on a successful deployment of the two axes of modernity, namely an analytic of finitude, and – especially – a concept of linear time.

2. The modern episteme equally characterised the way in which ethical and legal knowledge was generated and deployed in the aftermath of the crisis. *Therefore Chapter 5 will seek to demonstrate how the two axes of modernity were applied in the context of ethic and legal discourse in the Kosovo crisis.*

In each case, it will be argued that a Complexity-ethic guides the analysis. In this context, the conclusion of the work – apart from summarising the findings – will seek to explain how the disciplines of Critical Geopolitics and Critical IR can successfully constitute a new Complexity paradigm in the study of conflict.

PART 2
The Kosovo Crisis and its Contradictions

Chapter 4
International Relations and Modern Interpretations of the Kosovo Crisis

> History is a battlefield. It's constantly being fought over because the past controls the present. History is the present. That's why every generation writes it anew. But what most people think of as history is its end product, myth.
>
> Edgar Lawrence, *Doctorow*[1]

The purpose of this chapter is to analyse to what extent existing scholarship on the Kosovo crisis addresses the underlying epistemic constraints that characterise the production of knowledge on this topic in specific and relevant disciplines. As such, the works that appear in this chapter have been selected with the purpose of illustrating the main debates in the main disciplines related to the Kosovo crisis in order to outline how such debates can be synthesised through an epistemic approach – this is, thus, not a 'literature review' or a 'state of the art' in the classical sense, but an attempt to distil developments in various disciplines in order to get to the essence of various, relevant debates – and to put these in an epistemic context. As outlined in the introduction, the current work's claims relate to the idea that an epistemic approach applied to different disciplines affected by the Kosovo crisis would reveal the commonality of specific constraints and consequent debates that characterised the ways in which the crisis was framed, understood and acted upon. Such claims can be mainly summarised as follows:

1. A modern approach to knowledge characterised our understanding of the Kosovo conflict as a mainly ethno-historical struggle despite overwhelming evidence to the contrary. An approach informed by the ethos of Complexity would, on the other hand, instinctively address the immanent political struggle, which is responsible for the construction of the past in the present.
2. This understanding of the conflict, coupled with the metaphysical contradictions intrinsic within the modern episteme, conditioned the armed intervention. For example, confusion over the practicalities of the war is reminiscent of the confusion present in a particular approach to knowledge that characterised the intervention.

1 Quoted in Sam Girgus, "The New Covenant and the Dilemma of Dissensus: Bercovitch, Roth and Doctorow" in *Summoning: Ideas of the Covenant and Interpretative Theory*, ed. Ellen Spolsky (New York: State University of New York Press, 1993), 258.

These two points represent a Foucauldian understanding of the modern episteme, as such an episteme is characterised by an 'empirico-transcendental doublet'. The two axes of this doublet are an analytic of finitude (which characterises point 2 above, that is, the concept of humanitarian intervention and its practical application) and the concept of historical linearity (which characterises point 1). These two concepts are strictly related: they are, as it were, two sides of the same coin, the coin being the empirico-transcendental doublet. The work will also claim that this Foucauldian understanding of knowledge allows a critical appraisal of Complexity as a knowledge practice that radically departs from the modern episteme, and addresses how this complex, 'postmodern' episteme affects our understanding of ethno-political conflicts and humanitarian interventions in general, and of the Kosovo crisis in particular.

In order to fully make these claims, and in order to show how epistemic constraints condition the establishment of particular debates in all related branches of knowledge, four broad strands of literature have to be reviewed. First, we have scholarship regarding the nature of the conflict itself, which frames the crisis along ethno-historical lines, and analyses the conflict from an academic IR point of view (nature of war, national interest, national sovereignty and so on). To this we can add a specific line of analysis aimed at understanding the geostrategic, geocritical and geopolitical dimension of the conflict. Second, we have abundant scholarship on the conduct of the war, which reveals the confused practicalities related to the contradicting needs of conducting a 'humanitarian war'. Third, we have an abundant amount of scholarship on the concept of 'humanitarian intervention' itself, and of its legal implications. This is important with regard to the second claim of the current work enumerated above, as the objective is to demonstrate that the concept of 'humanitarian intervention', both at the legal and ethical level, is in itself a consequence of the modern episteme. Fourth, we have official institutional documents emanating from national parliaments, multilateral organisations etc., which crystallise a specific understanding of the Kosovo conflict, both as an ethno-historical war and as a case of legitimate humanitarian intervention. Since these constitute primary sources when outlining the overall narrative of the conflict, the bulk of these sources will be scrutinised in the relevant chapters (5 and 6) – this current section will simply outline the most relevant material in the context of the issue at hand (that is, the epistemic commonalities that characterise key debates across disciplines on this subject).

In short, the four strands of literature regarding the Kosovo conflict that will be approached from an epistemic perspective in this section can be summarised as follows: 1) International Relations, History/Diplomatic History, Geopolitics; 2) Conflict Resolution, Military and Defence Studies, and to a certain extent Peace-keeping studies; 3) International Law, International Humanitarian Law (the crucial difference being that whilst the former addresses the legality of intervention *per se*, the second investigates the intervention from the point of view of the requirements imposed by human rights law, for example), Ethics; and 4) official documentation, primary sources.

Finally, this chapter will conclude with an analysis and summary of key debates within existing scholarship, and address how the apparent contradictions and paradoxes in such scholarship can be synthesised through an epistemic approach. The works outlined below are not supposed to represent a comprehensive review of the state of the art in all relevant disciplines: rather, they have been selected because they represent the most emblematic expositions of key debates and paradoxes in each discipline. As such, this should not be regarded as an attempt to produce a comprehensive summary of developments in each area, but as an exposition of how all the relevant disciplines face debates that – as it will be argued throughout the current work – can be adequately synthesised through our epistemic approach. It is hoped that by outlining the key questions in each discipline and by outlining the merits of the epistemic approach to such questions, the value-added of the current effort will become more explicit. Specific chapters will proceed to refer to relevant key works in specific disciplines according to the focus of each chapter.

Ethno-Diplomacy and International Relations

A vast amount of scholarship has been developed in relation to the history of the Balkans and the allegedly related conflicts in Bosnia and Kosovo. As a norm, most serious academic research on the issue tends to dismiss the idea that events in the region are caused by 'ancient ethnic hatreds' and proceed to meticulously analyse how present power struggles determine interpretations of the historical record, thus shaping a collective imaginary.[2] What most works fail to do, however, is to address the philosophical question beyond the recognition of the fact that conflict is not historically determined: these consequently fail to investigate how and whether such techniques of building the past into the present work – in other words, they fail to ask the question "Why interpretations based on the ancient ethnic hatreds idea so popular despite evidence suggesting these are fundamentally flawed?". Outlining the historical evidence is not a satisfactory way of explaining why and how – precisely contrary to such overwhelming evidence – the collective imaginary, both in the region and beyond, continues to be captured by such distorted historical notions, both in the media and in debates taking place at the political level within relevant legislative processes. On the other (policy-making) hand, the dividing line between those who interpret the conflict in terms of 'ancient ethnic hatreds' and those who refuse to do so by focusing exclusively on the immanent political struggle can be found across the whole political spectrum: from debates in the media to debates in national parliaments.

2 See, for example, Robert Thomas, *Serbia under Milošević* (London: Hurst and Co. Publishers, 1999).

Amongst the key studies in the academic context we can find works by Noel Malcom,[3] Miranda Vickers[4] and Thanos Veremis and Evangelos Kofos.[5] These three volumes represent an impressive and detailed historical account of 'ethnic' conflicts in the region – Vicker's account does not outline the history with the same amount of erudition as does Malcom's, but she devotes 10 out of 14 chapters to the last century, especially the second half of it. This makes both works highly complementary. Interestingly, they both justify these monumental efforts in academic history by arguing that history is constantly being trawled by those on both sides in Kosovo who are looking for arguments in support of current policy. For example, both books analyse and dismiss the claim according to which a depopulated post-1690 Kosovo was abusively occupied and settled by Albanians, who took advantage of the Hapsburgs' (the Serbs' allies) defeat at the hands of the Ottomans. This claim was used as a justification for the notorious policy of forced Albanian emigration from Kosovo to Turkey in the 1920s and 1930s. Malcom famously claims that the outcome in Kosovo will depend to a large extent on "the ability of ordinary Serbs to challenge the fixed pattern of thought which has held them in its grip for so long."[6] Indeed, according to Malcom, both sides in the conflict have developed blinkered views of the history of Kosovo, but Serbia holds the key to change, for the time being at least, because it has the power to make change or block it. These statements reveal how well documented historical analysis can, nevertheless, lack adequate philosophical frameworks to interpret the historiographic evidence. From Malcom's account it is difficult to understand how the author himself can reach such conclusions from his own data, and the work lacks an analysis of how mechanisms of historical revisionism work. In other words, the study fails to show how the subject of analysis could be more helpfully located in the study of a phenomenon, that is, the rise and rise of an intellectually contingent notion of ethno-nationalism, which operates in fundamentally the same way across the imagined 'ethnic' divides. Furthermore, the question of whether the Serbian side really holds the key to change in a situation of open conflict is dubious – unfortunately, the gap between the Albanian and the Serbian visions for Kosovo has widened, not narrowed, since the escalation of the armed conflict. Indeed, this alarming absence of common ground between the two sides in Kosovo is analysed in detail by contributors to the excellent volume edited by two Greek scholars, Evangelos Kofos and Thanos Veremis. Finally, other research has demonstrated how the fiction of 'Greater Albania' has been successfully developed and presented by politicians within Kosovo as a means of mobilising the masses. This parallel

3 Noel Malcom, *Kosovo: A Short History* (Basingstoke: Macmillan, 1998).

4 Miranda Vickers, *Between Serbs and Albanians: A History of Kosovo* (London: Hurst, 1998).

5 Thanos Veremis and Evangelos Kofos, *Kosovo: Avoiding another Balkan War* (Athens: Hellenic Foundation for European Foreign Policy and University of Athens, 1998).

6 Malcom, *Kosovo: A Short History*, 355–6.

development has been particularly well researched by the likes of Paulin Kola[7] and Dobriaca Cosic.[8]

One of the objectives of the current effort is to go beyond the analysis of the historical record and question the reasons why and how such record is seen as being meaningful at all. In a sense, this is about borrowing Benedict Anderson's conceptualisation of nationalism as an ideology that depends on a 'modern' (strictly in a Foucauldian sense) notion of historical linearity and exploring how such a notion underpins all historical interpretations of the conflict, from Washington all the way to Moscow, via Priština and Belgrade (see Chapter 6). These fundamental notions of historically-contingent development are being fundamentally challenged by the rise of Complexity Science.[9] It should be noted that the idea of applying the insights of Complexity to the study of history is not new. In *A Thousand Years of Nonlinear History* Manuel De Landa addresses that very question, and outlines how an alternative, Complexity-based understanding of history would differ from more traditional approaches.[10] The specific issue of ethnic conflict, or the rise of nationalisms, is however not treated.

Another impressive collection and analysis of documents can be found in Marc Weller's *The Crisis in Kosovo 1989–1999: From the Dissolution of Yugoslavia to Rambouillet and the Outbreak of Hostilities*.[11] Tim Judah, author of *Kosovo: War and Revenge* refers to Weller's work as the "sine qua non of all future studies of Kosovo and the war."[12] It is not difficult to see why: in terms of sheer scope, this collection contains a mixture of legal documents, official communiqués, letters and informal notes, press conference transcripts, and internal reports and documents produced by a varied array of international organisations. Its scope is only matched by Auerswald's *The Kosovo Conflict, a Diplomatic History through Documents*, which covers a shorter historical period (Weller traces the constitutional development of Kosovo back to 1944, whilst the evidence collected

7 Paulin Kola, *The Search for the Greater Albania* (London: Hurst, 2003).

8 Dobrica Cosic, *Kosovo* (Belgrade: Novosti, 2004).

9 The issue of whether and to what extent history, or time, places contingency on the development of phenomena is at the heart of the Complexity epistemic revolution. Complexity theorists such as Ilya Prigogine have gone as far as arguing that all the differences between alternative approaches to scientific epistemology boil down to whether one chooses to assume that time is irreversible. This issue is explored in great detail in Chapter 1.

10 Manuel De Landa, *A Thousand Years of Nonlinear History* (New York: Zone Books, 1997).

11 Marc Weller, *The Crisis in Kosovo 1989–1999: from the Dissolution of Yugoslavia to Rambouillet and the Outbreak of Hostilities* (Cambridge: Documents and Analysis Publishing, 1999).

12 Tim Judah, *Kosovo: War and Revenge* (London, New Haven: Yale University Press, 2000).

by Auerswald goes back to 1987).[13] What transpires from these collections of historical documents is the difference of opinion between state leaders and mediators before 1998: State leaders tended to regard the problem as primarily one of self determination, whilst groups working on the ground in Kosovo, such as the Organization for Security and Co-operation in Europe (OSCE), tended to frame the issue in terms of human rights – these differing views (that is, a view based on the notion of self-determination and a view based on the notion of Human Rights) lead to a very interesting paradox that will be presented below. Indeed, whereas the notion of Human Rights is necessarily Universalistic the notion of self-determination relates necessarily to the particular.

Tim Judah's contribution is often presented as the most authoritative account of what happened 'behind the scenes' in the Kosovo conflict.[14] The basic argument of the book is that there were no conspiracy theories, no overriding ethical imperatives, but that, quite simply – to put it in the author's succinct prose – "they all got it wrong."[15] In other words, everybody was drawn towards a conflict that they did not understand, and in the case of NATO, which they did not particularly care about in the first instance. This argument is virtually identical to Hobwsbawm's[16] and Kissinger's.[17] Although this is probably the most plausible interpretation of the conflict – and indeed, the one that more closely matches the notion of 'emergence' in Complexity theory, as a phenomenon that grows out of complex systems to determine its own rules of development – the interpretation lacks an analysis of why exactly, at the intellectual level, all of us did indeed get it all wrong. It certainly was not due to lack of first hand information – it would have been a lot more helpful if Judah had asked why information, which was indeed readily available (note the presence and excellent work of the Kosovo Verification Mission), was interpreted in such a clumsy way. In short, were there any constraints that limited the understanding of the Kosovo crisis despite the availability of abundant information? However, this view is controversial for another obvious reason: if the whole affair was a mistake, there is not really much left to explain – this is naturally a view that many IR analysts are not too keen to share.

13 Philip Auerswald and David Auerswald, *The Kosovo Conflict, a Diplomatic History through Documents* (The Hague: Kluwer Law International, 2000).

14 Judah, *Kosovo: War and Revenge.*

15 Ibid., 311.

16 Eric Hobsbawm, "Guerra Umanitaria? No, e solo un pasticcio" in *L'Ultima Crociata? Ragioni e Torti di una Guerra Giusta*, eds, Ulrich Beck and Norberto Bobbio (Rome: Libri di Reset, 1999), 58–67.

17 Henry Kissinger, "New World Disorder: The ill-considered war in Kosovo has undermined relations with China and Russia and put NATO at risk," *Newsweek*, 31 May 1999.

Robert Thomas'[18] excellent account of the political struggle within Serbia, which pointed towards the need for manipulating Kosovo for political reasons, is a lot more helpful in enhancing our understanding of the relevant actors' alleged motivations. Thomas has the merit of revealing the inner workings of Milošević's nationalist strategy, which did precipitate the conflict – in this context we are presented with an analysis of how this specific environment was formed (that is, an environment in which others could make 'mistakes'). The understanding of this environment is crucial regardless of how one perceives the alleged motivations of those who eventually decided that an air campaign was a suitable solution to the problem.

David Bruce MacDonald's impressive study on the representation of the Holocaust in the Balkans wonderfully illustrates how such motivations are translated in revisions of history.[19] In a similar way, Julie Mertus' *Kosovo: How Myths and Truths Started a War*, concentrates on unveiling the many misunderstandings, but fails to provide a comprehensive explanation of why and how the myths could be successfully deployed for political reasons, and how they progressively started to be perceived as truths.[20] In this context, Auerswald's game-theory based explanation has at least the merit of defining its assumptions, without apparently being concerned by the extraordinary nature of such assumptions.[21] Works mainly focusing on the historical dimension also include a collection edited by Serbian academics, *The Road to War in Serbia: Trauma and Catharsis*,[22] where the issue of political manipulation of history also features prominently, as

18 Thomas, *Serbia under Milošević.*

19 David Bruce MacDonald, *Balkan Holocaust? Serbian and Croatian Victim-Centred Propaganda and the War in Yugoslavia* (Manchester: Manchester University Press, 2002).

20 Julie Mertus, *Kosovo: How Myths and Truths Started a War* (London, Berkeley: University of California Press, 1999).

21 David Auerswald, "Explaining Wars of Choice: An Integrated Decision Model of NATO Policy in Kosovo", *International Studies Quarterly* no. 48 (2004), 631–62 wants to convince his readers that institutional analysis alone can settle the question of why and how some states can decide to act on wars of choice in order to defend crucial geo-strategic interests (the author seems happy to state that the idea according to which states follow their geo-strategic interests when they can is the 'only' assumption of his model). The author, however, forgets to explain what those interests are, and how they were served by armed intervention. Worse, the conclusions do not explain past or present behaviour. Thus, the theory goes, countries such as Italy and Germany intervene less because of the nature of their institutions, yet, this did not seem to matter too much when Germany took the arguably extraordinary decision to unilaterally recognise Croatia and when Italy unilaterally decided to intervene in Albania a few years later.

22 Nebojša Popov, *The Road to War in Serbia: Trauma and Catharsis* (Budapest: Central University Press, 2000).

it does in Branimir Anzulovic's *Heavenly Serbia: from Myth to Genocide*,[23] and in Thomas Benedikter's *Il Dramma del Kosovo: dall'Origine fra Serbi e Albanesi agli Scontri di Oggi*[24] (The Drama of Kosovo: from the origins to today's conflict between Serbs and Albanians). Again, the generic problem persists: whilst both the Serb and the Italian academics insist on stating that the historical record is often manipulated, they fail to account for how such manipulation is either possible or successful, or both. Reviewing both works, Christopher Cviic, thus, adequately repeats the standard mantra: "In 1991 Milošević converted to the concept of the Greater Serbia that had previously been the preserve of nationalists like Vuk Draskovic and Vojislav Šešelj. This was a political master stroke because it completed the process of Milošević's transformation into a national icon." But even more pertinently, Cviic asks – with evident frustration, which is shared by this author – the question that is not addressed by these works: *"But what made this possible? Why did the Serbs respond to him so well?"*[25] This is really the crucial question. Again, the lack of philosophical analysis leaves all of this 'historical record' in a conceptual vacuum from which it is difficult to understand the nature of the knowledge frameworks that allowed such approaches to history to emerge. The works on the issue of ethnic nationalism in the region that were published prior to the NATO intervention at least have the merit of situating the rise of such phenomena in a broad historical context, thus examining the complex relationship between the issue and wider considerations over the nature of European Modernity and its uneven spread across the continent. Such works include Ivo Banac's *The National Question in Yugoslavia: Origins, History, Politics*[26] and Tom Winnifrith's *Shattered Eagles, Balkan Fragments*.[27]

Finally, Michael MccgWire provides another interesting example of the way in which a linear understanding of history (in itself responsible for the framing of the conflict in terms of 'ancient ethnic hatreds') seems to have handicapped the way in which the conflict was handled by the relevant actors. In an article simply entitled, *Why did We Bomb Belgrade?*[28] MccgWire notes how NATO failed to grasp the *immanent* political struggle at the heart of the struggle, opting instead for a sketchy historically-based understanding of the conflict:

---

23 Branimir Anzulovic, *Heavenly Serbia: from Myth to Genocide* (London: Hurst, 1999).

24 Thomas Benedikter, *Il Dramma del Kosovo: dall'Origine fra Serbi e Albanesi agli Scontri di Oggi* (Rome: Datanews Publications, 1998).

25 Christopher Cviic, "The Serbian Exception", *International Affairs* Vol. 75, no. 3 (1999), 639, emphasis added.

26 Ivo Banac, *The National Question in Yugoslavia: Origins, History, Politics* (Ithaca, London: Cornell University Press, 1984).

27 Tom Winnifrith, *Shattered Eagles, Balkan Fragments* (London: Duckworth, 1995).

28 Michael MccgWire, "Why did We Bomb Belgrade?," *International Affairs* Vol. 76, no. 1 (2000), 1–24.

> There are other lessons to be drawn from the Balkan tragedy, including the tendency to define complex conflicts in oversimplified and moralistic terms, labels which then drove policy and shaped public expectations. In part, this reflected our damaging *ignorance of the convoluted politics* of the situation, a debility compounded by our slow learning curve. Reacting to each conflict in turn, the *West applied undigested lessons from the previous one, whereas the underlying causes of the 'four successive wars' were qualitatively different, each requiring a particular set of responses.*[29]

Thus, MccgWire concludes that there is an underlying assumption according to which history – including recent history – is something that we have something to 'learn from' and that this assumption determined the West's clumsy approach to the Kosovo crisis and its lack of understanding regarding the immanent, particular political struggles that actually underpinned the crisis and specific aspects of the conflict. The surprise with which Albright reacted to the fact that the Kosovar delegation did not seem at all convinced about the Rambouillet agreements at first, shows a striking ignorance of the internal politics characterising the delegation's deliberations.[30]

The disciplines of Critical Geopolitics and IR have examined the Kosovo crisis and generated their own particular debates. From a geopolitical perspective, the most indicative contributions include John O'Loughlin's and Vladimir Kolossov's reflections on the geopolitics of the Kosovo war,[31] Alexandra Gheciu's study on the interactions between norms, power and politics in a specific geopolitical context[32] and Mark Corson's and Clemson Turregano's analysis of the unintended consequences resulting from a failure of thinking geopolitically.[33] O'Loughlin outlines how 'geopolitical' wars are becoming more and more dependent on public opinion and shows how such public opinion allowed for NATO intervention. Interestingly, the argument overlooks the question of which variable (public opinion and geostrategic considerations) ultimately carried more weight: presumably, given the context presented by the article, the conclusion is that geostrategic goals are now being shaped by public opinion, which ultimately has the last say on what is strategically important and what is not. However, there seems to be a lack of consensus on the variables or set of variables (if any) that decisively led NATO to the decision of waging its first war.

---

29 Ibid., 22, emphasis added.

30 Wesley Clark, *Waging Modern War* (New York: Public Affairs, 2002), 163–89.

31 John O'Loughlin and Vladimir Kolossov, "Still Not Worth the Bones of a Single Pomeranian Grenadier: the Geopolitics of the Kosovo War 1999." *Political Geography* 21 (2002), 573–99.

32 Gheciu, "International Norms, Power and the Politics of International Administration: The Kosovo Case".

33 Mark Corson and Clemson Turregano, "Spaces of unintended consequences: The Ground Safety Zone in Kosovo," *GeoJournal* Vol. 57, no. 4 (2002), 273–82.

In analysing institutions that have been set up in Kosovo after the conflict Gheciu invites the reader to consider the role played by such institutions in great debates in International Relations,[34] outlining the differences between Kantian-inspired liberal theorists (the new institutions represent a positive development in the context of an evolving enforcement of human rights) and the take of critical theorists (such institutions represent Western hegemonic values, which are not, strictly speaking, Universal).[35]

The debate is interesting insofar as it presents a curious paradox: if humanitarian war is indeed waged, at least to some extent, to defend self-determination (or at least the cultural characteristics of populations that are threatened simply because of their ethno-cultural nature), how can it do so in the name of Universal principles? Indeed, how can particularity and diversity be upheld through Universalism? Gheciu's own take on the matter is particularly revealing. After arguing that scholars on both sides tend to under-analyse the relationship between the nature of governance and the nature of subjects upon which governance is enforced, Gheciu suggests that practices of governance are implemented precisely to provoke a subjective change in the nature of individuals. Thus, "the international administration has sought to establish new institutions around Western-defined norms of liberal democracy, and, at the same time, to socialize Kosovars into taking such norms for granted, and (re)producing them – at the expense of alternative (e.g. socialist and/or nationalist) norms – in their province."[36] In other words, Gheciu seems to be arguing that in the struggle to defend diversity, such diversity must be replaced by a system that eliminates its defining feature, which in this case seems to be nationalism.

The most apparent paradox addressed by existing scholarship in this first strand of literature relates to the tendency of framing the conflict in terms of 'ancient ethnic hatreds' despite substantial evidence to the contrary and despite the views expressed by key actors. On the other hand, recurring debates in Geopolitics and IR often relate to questions on the exact relationship between geostrategic ('material') and other proclaimed motives in the Kosovo crisis and to questions on the relationship between the Universal and the particular, or, more exactly, on how a particular issue can be defended through a Universal approach.

34 Again, Kosovo has had an enormous impact on the discipline of International Relations: so much so that some standard textbooks take this crisis as a starting point when outlining different approaches within the discipline: see, for example Sterling-Folker *Making Sense of International Relations Theory*.

35 Gheciu, "International Norms, Power and the Politics of International Administration: The Kosovo Case," 123.

36 Ibid.

Fighting Ugly: Doing Good by Doing Evil

Probably the most significant account and assessment of the operational details of the conflict were presented by the Independent International Commission on Kosovo.[37] The Report makes, predictably, a number of references to the historical circumstances affecting the crisis in the region, and famously concludes that the NATO intervention was 'illegal but legitimate', without apparently realising that such a statement quite simply does away with the legalist approach to international law (or with the UN Charter, which has been trying to impose the legalist approach on IR in the post war period). Such approach relies on the idea that what is legal in a democratic collective security system must necessarily be legitimate, but the same does not necessarily apply vice-versa: this is the essence of Francis Boyle's appropriately named *Foundations of World Order: The Legalist Approach to International Relations (1898–1922)*.[38] It is particularly interesting in this context that the Report does not address the dislocation between the illegality of the war and its intentions with the word 'moral or 'ethical', choosing instead to deploy the word 'legitimate', thus undermining the very body of law that is supposed to determine what is legal and therefore necessarily legitimate. This paradox is addressed in Chapter 5.

The paradoxical approach of 'ultimate causes and minimum risk' is one of the cornerstones of our work, as it is argued that such dislocation is always necessarily caused by a metaphysical approach to the notion of Human Rights. Countless books and articles address this obvious paradox, and yet fail to address the conceptual reasons why such 'ultimate causes' could even be presented without the relevant bodies of public opinion questioning the nature of 'minimum risks' in a context of such transcendental importance. Such works include Pierre Martin's and Mark Brawley's *Alliance Politics, Kosovo and NATO's War: Alliance or Forced Allies?*;[39] Michael Waller's, Kyril Drezov's and Bulent Gokay's *Kosovo: The Politics of Delusion*,[40] but especially Albrecht Schnabel's and Ramesh Thakur's *Kosovo and the Challenge of Humanitarian Intervention: Selective Indignation, Collective Action, and International Citizenship*.[41] This last work in particular does a great

37 Independent International Commission on Kosovo. *The Kosovo Report: Conflict, International Response, Lessons Learned* (Oxford: Oxford University Press, 2000).

38 Francis Boyle, *Foundations of World Order: The Legalist Approach to International Relations (1898–1922)* (London and Durham: Duke University Press, 1999).

39 Pierre Martin and Mark Brawley, *Alliance Politics, Kosovo and NATO's War: Alliance or Forced Allies?* (London: Palgrave, 2001).

40 Michael Waller, Kyril Drezov, and Bulent Gokay, *Kosovo: The Politics of Delusion* (London, Portland: Frank Cass, 2001).

41 Albrecht Schnabel and Ramesh Thakur, *Kosovo and the Challenge of Humanitarian Intervention: Selective Indignation, Collective Action, and International Citizenship* (Tokyo: United Nations Press, 2000).

job in identifying a good number of contradictions between words and actions in relation to the way in which the air campaign was conducted.

A very interesting source of analysis of the paradox between the humanitarian concerns of the campaign and the actual practice covering the selection of targets is to be found in a legal study conducted by the Australian Aerospace Centre.[42] Amongst other things, the study notes that NATO members decided to ignore the legal constraints of Humanitarian Law (and not simply the UN Charter, but also humanitarian law covering the laws of war, that is, additional Protocols to the Geneva Conventions, agreed in 1977, and especially Protocol 1 in order to be able to conduct this particular humanitarian war: "it is significant that the UK, as a party to Protocol 1, holds that it was a political rather than legal obligation to avoid collateral damage to civilians by the positive identification of the target by NATO strike pilots."[43]

The study clearly indicates that Australian law may be incompatible with NATO's targeting practice, and that this may have consequences in terms of the interoperability of possible future US – Australian operations. The nature of such incompatibility is revealing. Indeed, Protocol 1 does require combatants to carry greater risks than civilians, meaning that "Australia may have to insist on Rules of Engagement that expose its forces to a more than minimal risk, and an obligation to protect civilians and civilian objects to a higher degree than may have been required of the US whose Rules of Engagement reflect the less constrained pre-1977 customary international law."[44] According to Cochrane, Protocol 1 makes the talk of ultimate aims (human rights) incompatible with the notion of 'minimum risk'.

The Australian study clearly shows that the humanitarian principle was dropped when NATO decided to disregard the legal consequences of Protocol 1. This was possible because the US was the only NATO party that was not a signatory to the 1977 addendum to the Protocol, and it was the US that conducted most of the bombing: "the US is not a party to the 1977 First Additional Protocol to the Geneva Conventions…it is largely because Protocol 1 binds the US only to the extent that it reflects customary international law that the US carried the bulk of the bombing sorties in the Kosovo campaign – a campaign much criticized for its targeting decisions."[45]

The situation is, thus, that a Humanitarian War could be conducted without violating US domestic law (for Protocol 1 is necessarily incorporated into the domestic legislation of all signatory parties) precisely because the US refused to

42 Kathryn Cochrane, "Kosovo Targeting: A Bureaucratic and Legal Nightmare: The Implications for US/Australian Interoperability", *Australian Aerospace Center*, June 2001. http://www.defence.gov.au/raaf/airpower/html/publications/papers/apdc/apdc_03_kosovo_targeting.pdf (accessed 23 April 2008).

43 Ibid., 14.

44 Ibid., 18.

45 Ibid., 4.

sign a treaty obliging combatants to assume the greater risk in war situations, a treaty that was designed precisely to protect civilian populations, thus turning it into a major piece of humanitarian law within *jus ad bellum*. Thus, humanitarian wars occur as a result of countries not adhering to law treaties designed to defend humanitarian principles. As Chapter 5 will demonstrate, this is but one of the many paradoxes that emerge out of a metaphysical understanding of humanitarian war, caused by the conceptual impossibility to reconcile the phenomenal imperatives of conflict with the declared noumenal maxims of transcendental values. This study will seek to demonstrate how this is caused by the nature of the modern episteme.

Other works have attempted to ask the question of why NATO decided to intervene in Kosovo. Tariq Ali's edited volume is probably the most emblematic attempt from the Left.[46] Here, we read that there are a number of reasons why NATO decided to intervene, ranging from the (allegedly) strategic importance of Kosovo as a transit point for natural resources coming from the Caspian Sea to an American desire to weaken Europe by flooding it with refugees. Then we have, of course, Chomsky. Although Chomsky does his usual great job in pointing out the discrepancies between intentions and actions, the reader can be excused for feeling at a loss when trying to understand the logic of Chomsky's militant 'imperialist' approach. In 200 pages of *The New Military Humanism: Lessons from Kosovo*[47] we are presented with a devastating account revealing the hidden motives of intervention, without ever being told what those motives were. The closest we come to a motive is encapsulated in the mysterious claim according to which NATO's intervention was intended to remove "an unwelcome impediment to Washington's efforts to complete its substantial takeover of Europe."[48]

A rather more interesting attempt at reconciling words with deeds can be found in Michael Ignatieff's *Virtual War: Kosovo and Beyond*.[49] Here, the author laments the fact that "we had talked the language of ultimate causes and practiced the art of minimum risk", a critique very similar, if not identical, to Michael Walzer's.[50] However, the work fails to critically assess the reasons why such paradoxes are apparently so recurrent, and does not analyse the conceptual confusions that lie behind this failure to act out the full consequences of one's words. This evident dislocation between the proclaimed objectives and the methods that were adopted to implement them is not to be found in Ivo Daalder's

46 Tariq Ali, ed., *Masters of the Universe? NATO's Balkan Crusade* (London: Verso, 2000).

47 Noam Chomsky, *The New Military Humanism: Lessons from Kosovo* (London, Pluto Press, 1999).

48 Ibid., 137.

49 Michael Ignatieff, *Virtual War: Kosovo and Beyond* (London: Chatto and Windus, 2000).

50 Brian Orend, "Michael Walzer on Resorting to Force," *Canadian Journal of Political Science* Vol. 33, no. 3 (2000), 523–47.

and Michael O'Hanlon's *Winning Ugly: NATO's War to Save Kosovo*.[51] In this work, the Powell Doctrine is vigorously defended and the intervention is classed as a total success, albeit an 'ugly' one – however, the authors fail to analyse the nature of this ugliness or to reconcile such ugliness (which, as stated above, included the deliberate and systematic undermining of Humanitarian Law *ad bellum*) with the aims of the war.

When looking at accounts of how the bombing campaign was conducted the relevant literature seems to unveil another key debate that relates to another relevant paradox: why was there such a clear dislocation, or incompatibility, between the proclaimed objectives of the intervention and the means adopted to attain them? The current effort suggests that the paradoxes that inevitably arise in such contexts (dislocation between aims and means to achieve them) are caused by the very nature of the modern episteme, which undermines all related actions: these are the inevitable gaps that we find between the transcendental notion of human rights and the phenomenal nature related to their implementation. As the final part of this study will suggest, such paradoxes are characterised by the two axes of the modern episteme, which in the case of Kosovo mutated into a concept of 'ancient ethnic hatreds' (historical linearity) and into Universal Exclusions in the legal and ethical discourse (analytical finitude).

The Evolution of Humanitarian Intervention

By far the largest body of literature on the Kosovo crisis revolves around the practice, legality and morality of humanitarian intervention. From an ethical perspective, J.L. Holzgrefe's and Robert Keohane's *Humanitarian Intervention: Ethical, Legal and Political Dilemmas* represents the most interesting attempt at presenting the various strands of the debate in a coherent manner.[52] However, the work fails to recognise the underlying epistemic characteristics of all different positions, and does not address the context in which such ethical concerns are formed.[53]

On the notion of humanitarian intervention, four recent works in particular have sought to analyse and trace the development of such phenomenon: Simon Chesterman's *Just War or Just Peace?*;[54] Christine Gray's *International Law*

---

51 Ivo Daalder and Michael O'Hanlon, *Winning Ugly: NATO's War to Save Kosovo* (Washington DC: Brookings Institution Press, 2000).

52 Robert Keohane and J.L. Holzgrefe, eds, *Humanitarian Intervention: Ethical, Legal and Political Dilemmas* (Cambridge: Cambridge University Press, 2003).

53 Aspects of this work will be addressed in Chapter 5.

54 Simon Chesterman, *Just War or Just Peace? Humanitarian Intervention and International Law* (Oxford, New York: Oxford University Press, 2001).

and the Use of Force,[55] Nikolaos Tsagourias's *Jurisprudence of International Law*[56] and Nicholas Wheeler's *Saving Strangers*.[57] Overall, these four works on humanitarian intervention focus on five broad topics: the nature of the law, its relationship with the notion of legitimacy, the divide between the legality and morality of humanitarian intervention, the role of institutions, the role of alliances and the cautionary principle – but they all fail to identify the underlying epistemic axes that characterise and determine the evolution of ideas within those different strands. Out of these topics, the most interesting debate in the context of the current effort relates to the relationship between the notions of legality and morality. Reviewing these works, Nico Krisch identified this debate as playing a crucial role: "it seems – and much of the public debate on Kosovo focussed on this issue – that the main problem of humanitarian intervention consists in the divergence of law and morality: while considerations of justice and human rights demand the recognition of a right to intervention, international law prevents this by anachronistically relying on order and on state sovereignty."[58]

The solutions to these debates are particularly revealing in the context of the epistemic analysis that will be conducted in the following chapters, which explore the difficulties inherent in reducing a metaphysical principle into immanent action. This also concerns debates on foundationalism in the philosophy of science. Indeed, as Krisch argues, those who argue in favour of intervention regard humanitarian concerns as being more important than maintaining a foundational reference in Treaty-based law, whilst detractors are more concerned by the possibilities of abuse emanating from this relativistic approach to the law.

The considerations above were based on the assumption that morality demands a right to unilateral humanitarian intervention, as claimed by Tsagourias and Wheeler. But does morality indeed warrant such a clear answer? According to the usual claim, the problem of humanitarian intervention highlights the tension between human rights and state sovereignty and the resulting argument suggests that whilst human rights are based on moral grounds state sovereignty is not.[59] This is how the whole debate is framed in the context of a conflict between sovereignty

55 Christine Gray, *International Law and the Use of Force* (Oxford, New York: Oxford University Press, 2000).

56 Nikolaos Tsagourias, *Jurisprudence of International Law: The Humanitarian Dimension* (Manchester: Manchester University Press, 2000).

57 Nicholas Wheeler, *Saving Strangers: Humanitarian Intervention in International Society* (Oxford, New York: Oxford University Press, 2000).

58 Nico Krisch, "Legality, Morality and the Dilemma of Humanitarian Intervention After Kosovo", *European Journal of International Law* Vol. 13, no. 1 (2002), 323–27.

59 The debate between Idealism and Realism in International Relations is an old one. What the moralistic approach seems to ignore, however, is that the entire post-war settlement is supposed to represent and enforce a 'moralistic' (or 'legalistic', which is precisely the reason why morality and legality are equivalent in such system) approach to international relations, and the United Nations was set up precisely to police this principle. See footnote 66 above but also Kissinger, *Diplomacy*.

and morality: since sovereignty is not regarded as having strong foundations in justice, the conclusion is drawn that human rights should, in a moral perspective, prevail. Yet, a question remains: how and why can we even think in terms of opposition between the morals and the law of humanitarian intervention when the latter is supposed to be the instrument through which the former is applied? In the question "what should be more important: the absolute value of the law or the reality of victims on the ground?" we can discern all the paradoxes inherent within the modern episteme, related to the vicissitudes of linking the noumenal and phenomenal realms. These interesting paradoxes will be examined in the penultimate chapter of our analysis.

This leads to an important observation related to Nikolaos Tsagourias' contribution. Tsagourias, in *Jurisprudence of International Law*, approaches the issue of humanitarian intervention from a jurisprudential angle. For most of the book, however, he merely describes different strands of thought in international law and their approach to humanitarian intervention. He eventually opts for a 'discursive model of human dignity', which is based on critical reflections on international law. The book is theoretically deficient, and fails to tackle the otherwise interesting question of whether the notion of human rights is better served by a system of customary law based on jurisprudence than by a deficient system of Treaty-based meta-law. In reality, the issue of whether state practice, case-law and a jurisprudence-based approach (as opposed to a Treaty-based meta-law) constitute a legitimate way of looking at the issue of humanitarian intervention represents a central preoccupation within the discipline of international humanitarian law (see Chapter 5).

An interesting observation on the tension between jurisprudence and meta-law in the context of humanitarian intervention can be found in Michael Glennon's *Limits of Law, Prerogatives of Power: Interventionism After Kosovo*.[60] Glennon argues that: "[The UN] Charter failed for the same reason that the League Covenant failed: Member States declined to accept an automatic commitment to use force in response to an armed attack, leaving victim states to fend for themselves."[61] In other words, Treaty-based law failed precisely because Member States did not want to be bound by it – this makes the argument of whether humanitarian intervention should draw its legitimacy from customary case law and jurisprudence or meta-law rather interesting. Indeed, we have a situation in which Treaty law fails precisely because States do not want to be bound by it, and, yet, such law exists precisely to defend States from each other. To enhance the paradox, the alternative to Treaty law is jurisprudence based on customary law, that is, law based on actual practice and precedents: precedents that are hard to come by, precisely because States tend to refuse any automatic responsibility when it comes to humanitarian emergencies – which is precisely the reason why treaty-based law exists. How can we replace a system that did not function precisely because States refused to

60 Michael Glennon, *Limits of Law, Prerogatives of Power: Intervention After Kosovo* (New York: Palgrave, 2001).

61 Glennon, *Limits of Law*, 9.

make it function by a system that works on the basis of precedents in the context of the very same issues (humanitarian disasters), to be established by the very same actors – who refuse to be bound by automatic responsibility? In other words, is the jurisprudence route not simply justifying an *ad hoc* approach to humanitarian law (in itself a paradox, since humanitarianism implies Universality), and if so, to what extent is this *ad hoc* approach consonant with traditional ideals of justice?

The three paradoxes and debates that can be encountered in this context relate to; 1) the anachronistic[62] juxtaposition of legality and morality (or legitimacy), 2) what kind of legal practice ought to be considered when regulating humanitarian intervention, and 3) the paradox inherent in treaty-law as a set of practices that are meant to defend States from each other and, yet, falls out of favour as such States see the related binding resolutions as being potentially more dangerous than the dangers these are meant to prevent. As the penultimate chapter of the current work will demonstrate, metaphysical notions of human rights are precisely what allow for a related law system to be extremely contingent, and it is the failure of the relevant actors to accept the full consequences of breaches that undermine the very nature of the system. In other words, it is precisely because the meta-law is conceptualised in metaphysical terms that relevant actors can pick and choose when to accept responsibility for breaches to humanitarian law and then argue in favour of an approach based on jurisprudence: it is the dislocation between the nominal and the phenomenal (again, a dislocation that is allowed for by the nature of the modern episteme) that allows for the fragmentary interpretation of the law.

Conclusion: Epistemic Considerations on the Key Debates

The accounts of individuals who played a key role in shaping the conflict can be also used to broadly reflect all the paradoxes identified in the relevant disciplines outlined above. When reading accounts written by some of the key actors in the Kosovo crisis it becomes immediately apparent that the paradoxes and debates outlined and categorised above played a crucial role in the policy-makers' minds. Consider, for example, the following contradicting statements in relation to the historical nature of the struggle. First, John Norris, Communications Director for Deputy Secretary of State Strobe Talbott:

> While many of the disputes in the Balkans have been mislabelled as "ancient ethnic hatreds", Kosovo probably comes closest to living up to the title. Disputes between Serbs and Albanians over control of the territory stretch back centuries. The region has deep symbolic importance to both ethnic communities, and the twentieth century was marked by a disturbing series of violent ethnic

62 Anachronistic because such juxtaposition was meant to have been solved by the Wilsonian legacy and by the establishment of a legalist approach to international relations, embedded in the UN.

> expulsions and counterexplulsions by both Serbs and Albanians in an effort to demographically dominate the region. These tensions also often took on religious overtones...[63]

Second, Wesley Clark, NATO's Supreme Allied Commander for Europe:

> And throughout the process of negotiations, I had learned the region and its personalities. Above all, I recognized that fundamentally, quarrels in the region were not really about age-old religious differences but rather the result of many unscrupulous and manipulative leaders seeking their own power and wealth at the expense of ordinary people in their countries.[64]

The generic point according to which those famous 'ancient ethnic hatreds' were more a product of actual political needs than a permanent feature of the region is expressed by Richard Holbrooke in the Bosnian context:

> Thus arose an idea that 'ancient hatreds', a vague but useful term for a history too complicated (or trivial) for outsiders to master, made it impossible (or pointless) for anyone outside the region to try to prevent the conflict.[65]

Finally, this view seems to be corroborated precisely by one of the region's 'unscrupulous and manipulative leaders' during a remark he made in the earlier parts of his career (early visits to Kosovo):

> Orthodox priests held aloft icons of Milošević and Lazar, while thousands of men and women crowded around the podium. Arguably, this was Milošević's finest hour. Secretly, however, he admitted that most of this was nothing more than 'bullshit'.[66]

Yet, the 'ancient ethnic hatred' theory was extremely popular in the policy circles of relevant capitals. Going through the literature, one cannot help concluding that the propensity that relevant actors had to give this theory any credit was inversely proportional to the amount of time they had spent in the region, or the amount of time they had spent conducting 'hands-on' policy in this context. It is telling that diplomats and policy makers who spent a substantial amount of time on the ground

63 John Norris, *Collision Course* (London: Praeger, 2005), 19. Note how Norris states that the 'ancient ethnic conflict' label applies to Kosovo more than to any other conflict in the Balkans and proceeds to justify such statement by listing a number of reasons why this is so without apparently realising that all the factors he enumerates are applicable to the 'imagined history' of virtually all other conflicts in the former Yugoslavia.

64 Clark, *Waging Modern War*, 68.

65 Holbrooke, *To End a War*, 22.

66 MacDonald, *Balkan Holocaust?*, 71.

(for example Holbrooke and Clark) seem to have been more likely to conclude that the conflict had in fact very little to do with those alleged ancient hatreds.

In sum, the paradoxes and key debates that have been outlined throughout this section and which will constitute the key pillars of follow-up chapters include:

1. In terms of history and IR, the most obvious debates relate to the following questions:
   1.1 Was the conflict characterised by ancient ethnic hatreds or by immanent political developments in the region, which sought to reconstitute the past in the present in order to sustain related political claims?
   1.2 Why did NATO decide to intervene, and to what extent were considerations genuinely based on humanitarian concerns, rather than on political (NATO's credibility, for example) and geopolitical (new balance of power, access or transit for key raw materials) factors? Alternatively, if the whole affair was a huge 'mistake', was such mistake simply characterised by the relative competence of relevant administrators (as Kissinger suggests) or by a deeper, psychological – not to say epistemic – framework which led to a specific understanding of the conflict and consequently to specific 'solutions'? Or was it just a genuine mistake characterised by a simple…coincidence (Hobsbawm)?

2. When it comes to the technicalities of the conflict, the key debates relate to the following issues:
   2.1 The nature of the relationship that exists or ought to exist between the notions of 'legality' and 'legitimacy'.
   2.2 The contradiction inherent in fighting a war in the name of ultimate causes with minimum risks.
   2.3 The contradiction inherent in side-stepping Humanitarian Law in order to fight a Humanitarian War.
   2.4 The contradiction inherent in adopting a strategy reliant on the principle of 'diplomacy backed by force' whilst restricting that strategy by openly limiting the extent and nature of the force factor (note the explicit announcements that no ground forces would be used at the outset of the conflict).

3. When it comes to legal approaches to the conflict, key debates involve the following issues:
   3.1 The nature of the relationship that exists or ought to exist between the notions of 'legality' and 'morality'.
   3.2 The issue of whether moral and ethical imperatives are better served by a treaty-based or a jurisprudence approach to humanitarian intervention.

So, why exactly should all of these debates be framed and understood through an epistemic approach? All of the debates outlined above fall into one of the two following categories: 1) the relationship between temporality and causality; 2) the relationship between transcendental principles and their (finite) implementation. In other words, these are all debates that can be approached and explained through an epistemic approach, and through an understanding of the modern episteme's empirico-transcendental doublet in particular. Crucially, an epistemic approach will inform how the two categories above depend on each other: that is, an understanding of an analytic of finitude (category 2 above, or that which determines how transcendental principles are framed and implemented) relies on a linear and contingent interpretation of temporality (category 1 above).

The current work has dissected the debates outlined above and placed them in their respective epistemic contexts. For instance, the anatomy of the empirico-transcendental doublet (which is composed of the two axes exposed here, that is, historical linearity and the analytic of finitude) has been discussed in Chapter 2. The role of historical contingency – and the way in which such role is being challenged by Complexity – has been explored in Chapter 1. The analytic of finitude, and its consequences for debates on humanitarian intervention, has been debated in Chapter 3, which has also looked at how the knowledge and practice of IR and ethics has evolved according to these two axes. Chapters 5 and 6 will reveal how they operated in framing understanding and action in the context of the Kosovo crisis.

Chapter 5
Legal-Ethical Frameworks on Kosovo, Modern Analytical Finitude at Work

> I hope the distress of the public will, must undermine support for the authorities in Belgrade…I think no power to your refrigerator, no gas to your stove, you can't get to work because the bridge is down – the bridge on which you held your rock concerts and you all stood with targets on your heads. That needs to disappear at three o'clock in the morning.
>
> General Michael Short in "Belgrade people must suffer", *International Herald Tribune*, 16 May 1999[1]

Introduction

This chapter is an attempt to apply the arguments presented above – in particular, those presented by Žižek on the notion of Universal Exclusion, by Rasch on a Complexity-ethic, and by Kratochwil on the nature of a jurisprudence-based approach to law and ethics – to specific law cases that followed the Kosovo crisis. It is very important to bear such conceptual framework in mind when approaching the specific cases outlined below. For example, when Kratochwil states that a new form of jurisprudence must be based on heuristic principles, to what extent is it possible to claim that such a knowledge practice would be consonant with a Complexity ethos, and indeed with a Complexity-*ethic*? The refusal to depart from a metaphysical ground in itself would cover jurisprudence with a level of immanence that is hard to find in the modern age. Heuristic jurisprudence would be a continuation of the epistemic revolution outlined above in the realm of law, it would necessitate a flat ontology and it would be – strictly in the Foucauldian meaning of the word – absolutely positivist (i.e. Foucault describes positivism simply as the rejection of all transcendentalisms, that is why he described himself as one). Could we not say of modern jurisprudence what Davidson said of empirical positivism before the advent of the Vienna Circle? *The foundations of knowledge must be simultaneously objective and subjective, that is, certain but, nevertheless, subject to eventual refutation.* Is the problem of foundationalism in science and in law, and throughout the modern episteme, not strictly *the same thing*? A trial is supposed to be an enquiry into the Truth, and the Truth must be

---

1 Michael Gordon, "Crisis in the Balkans: The Overview", *The New York Times/ International Herald Tribune*, 13 May 1999.

absolute. One cannot be guilty only in part (curiously, Foucault detects the rise of the concept of 'absolute guilt' in *Discipline and Punish*, where the birth of Man is shown to correspond to the emergence of the modern episteme, and, thus, with the modern concept of law).[2] In other words, is the modern episteme not throwing at us the same potential schism in the law that has already occurred in other fields of knowledge?

One can perfectly imagine a re-conceptualisation of the dilemmas faced by the likes of Carnap and Popper in law: the paradox of simultaneous objectivity and subjectivity would encourage some scholars *á la* Carnap and Neurath to argue that it is more adequate to renounce the idea of an absolute foundation of knowledge in order to maintain the objectivity of *justice* (relativism), while those in the mould of Schlick would consider an absolute foundation of justice as indispensable, thus rejecting the idea that foundations must necessarily be objective. The idea of a relative notion of justice may sound odd at first, and, yet, there are a number of examples that demonstrate quite clearly how, ultimately, justice is *undecidable* and contextual. If the European Court of Human Rights determines that the death penalty is inhumane, does this mean that normatively speaking the Court would regard some American practices as 'inhuman'? So, is the essence of 'American humanity' different from its European counterpart? Yet, anything that speaks in the name of Humanity must, by definition, refer to a Universal.

Ultimately, a Complexity approach would not be troubled by these dilemmas, because it would have surpassed them. Just like in scientific epistemology it no longer makes any sense to speak of 'foundational causality' – due to the fact that we have understood that there is no such thing as essentialist causality as all matter is about *process* – an understanding of 'humane' laws and Human Rights as such can only take place when we have a concept of a human being as something which is essentially defined. When Foucault identifies the 'birth of Man' and encourages us to overcome it, that is, to reach an age in which Man is dead: is he not in reality advocating the same move away from *transcendental metaphysics* that can be found in Nietzsche's death of God? However, Nietzsche had a lot of reasons to be worried about the death of God – as he saw perfectly well that God would have to be replaced by something else after men became engulfed by the most profound nihilism: "God is dead, but given the way of men, there may still be caves for thousands of years in which his shadow will be shown. And we – we still have to vanquish his shadow, too".[3] In prophetic fashion, Nietzsche saw the shadows of a defunct God in the rise of pan-germanic nationalism, as well as in the evolution of the scientific method. But what would a notion of justice after the death of Man entail? Could we still speak of Humanitarian intervention?

This chapter will limit itself to demonstrating that the legal discourse surrounding the Kosovo incident is conditioned by the contradictions inherent in the modern episteme. In particular, it will be argued that as NATO faced the

2 Michel Foucault, *Surveiller et Punir* (Saint-Amand: Editions Gallimard, 1993).

3 Nietzsche, *The Gay Science*, 167 aphorism 108.

challenge of the law, this law had to deploy a characteristically modern analytic of finitude that enabled the exclusionary principle to take place, or what Žižek calls the 'Universal Exclusion'. This principle, moreover, has to operate in tandem with a concept of historical linearity. A conclusion will seek to envisage what a flat ontology in law would look like, and to what extent a Complexity-ethic may take us from a 'Universal Exclusion' to an 'Exclusive Universality'.

NATO and the International Court of Justice

On 2 June 1999, the International Court of Justice (ICJ) reached a decision regarding a request from the Government of the Federal Yugoslav Republic demanding the indication of provisional measures in the case concerning the legality of the use of force (*Yugoslavia v. United States*). The decision went against Yugoslavia, and was adopted by 12 votes to three. The application instituting proceedings against the United States of America "for violation of the obligation not to use force" was filed by Yugoslavia on 29 April 1999.[4] What was the reasoning of the Court, and how does this reasoning relate to the arguments presented in previous chapters regarding the analytic of finitude and the presence of the empirico-transcendental doublet in contemporary international law?

Yugoslavia filed the application under Article IX of the Convention on the Prevention and Punishment of the Crime of Genocide – the Genocide Convention. Yugoslavia was effectively accusing the United States of participating in genocide committed in its own territory. The grounds for such an allegation were summarised as follows in the Yugoslav request:

> The subject-matter of the dispute are acts of the United States of America by which it has violated its international obligation banning the use of force against another State, the obligation not to intervene in the internal affairs of another State, the obligation not to violate the sovereignty of another State, the obligation to protect the civilian population and civilian objects in wartime, the obligation to protect the environment, the obligation relating to free navigation of international rivers, the obligation regarding fundamental human rights and freedoms, the obligation not to use prohibited weapons, the obligation not to deliberately inflict conditions of life calculated to cause physical destruction of a national group.[5]

4 International Court of Justice (ICJ), "Decision by the International Court of Justice on the Case Concerning the Legality of Use of Force (*Yugoslavia v United States of America*), 2 June 1999" in *The Kosovo Conflict, a Diplomatic History through Documents*, eds, Philip Auerswald and David Auerswald (The Hague: Kluwer Law International, 2000).

5 Ibid., 1061.

According to the Yugoslav statement, all such actions, including the use of depleted uranium, the destruction of radio and television stations, of roads and bridges, of hospitals, oil refineries and chemical plants correspond to a "deliberate creation of conditions calculated at the physical destruction of an ethnic group, in whole or in part."[6] Interestingly, the statement does not indicate what 'ethnic group' is suffering from acts of genocide, simply impersonating the victim in the institutions of Yugoslavia: "*In bombing the Federal Republic of Yugoslavia* military and civil targets were attacked. Great numbers of people were killed…the above-mentioned facts are deliberately creating conditions calculated at the physical destruction of an ethnic group, in whole or in part."[7] The statement would have us conclude that the ethnic group in question is the 'Yugoslav', and that such an ethnic group is embodied in the territory and government of the Federal Republic of Yugoslavia. The analytic of finitude and the delimitation of the inside/outside is already present in this legal reasoning.

The argument of genocide was only part of the Yugoslav request, which also cited numerous pieces of international legislation (including: the Genocide Convention, The Geneva Convention of 1949 and its Additional Protocol No. 1 of 1977 on the protection of civilians and civilian objects in time of war, Article 1 of the 1948 Convention on the Free Navigation of the Danube, several provisions of the International Covenant on Economic, Social and Cultural Rights and the International Covenant on Civil and Political Rights of 1966, but more importantly, perhaps, Article 53 of the Charter of the United Nations).

The Yugoslav request demanded a declaration by the ICJ, consisting of the following, "The Court is asked to indicate the following provisional measure: The United States of America shall cease immediately the acts of use of force and shall refrain from any act of threat or use of force against the Federal Republic of Yugoslavia." The American response simply requested "that the Court rejects the request of the Federal Republic of Yugoslavia for the indication of provisional measures."[8]

In its decision the Court declared itself

> …deeply concerned with the human tragedy, the loss of life, and the enormous suffering in Kosovo which form the background of the present dispute, and with the continuing loss of life and human suffering in all parts of Yugoslavia…the Court is profoundly concerned with the use of force in Yugoslavia, whereas under the present circumstances such use raises very serious issues of international law.[9]

---

6 Ibid.

7 Ibid.

8 Ibid., 1065.

9 Ibid.

Nonetheless, there were more serious issues that the Court had to deal with, which included considerations over jurisdiction. The controversy here is caused by what kind of jurisdiction is necessary to enact a provisional measure. The Court's reasoning explains:

> Whereas the Court, under its Statute, does not automatically have jurisdiction over legal disputes between States parties to that Statute or between other States to whom access to the Court has been granted; Whereas the Court has repeatedly stated "that one of the fundamental principles of its Statute is that it cannot decide a dispute between States without the consent of those States to its jurisdiction" (East Timor, Judgment, ICJ Reports 1995, p. 101, para. 26); and Whereas the Court can therefore exercise jurisdiction only between States parties to a dispute who not only have access to the Court but also have accepted the jurisdiction of the Court, either in general form or for the individual dispute concerned.[10]

In essence, for a State to be subject to the ICJ's jurisdiction it has to both have access to the Court (i.e. to be a recognised sovereign entity and member of the UN) and accept ICJ's authority for each particular case. Nonetheless, when it comes to provisional measures,

> ...whereas on a request for provisional measures the Court need not, before deciding whether or not to indicate them, finally satisfy itself that it has jurisdiction on the merits of the case, yet it ought not to indicate such measures unless the provisions invoked by the applicant appear, prima facie, to afford a basis on which the jurisdiction of the Court might be established.[11]

In other words, jurisdiction does not need to be established a priori for the Court to issue a provisional measure, but the Court does need to have indications that it will be able to eventually establish jurisdiction before issuing such measures. The issue thus becomes, did the Court have such indications? We can proceed to examine the arguments:

> Whereas in its Application Yugoslavia claims, in the first place, to found the jurisdiction of the Court upon Article IX of the Genocide Convention, which provides:
>
> "Disputes between the Contracting Parties relating to the interpretation, application or fulfilment of the present Convention, including those relating to the responsibility of a State for genocide or for any of the other acts enumerated in Article III, shall be submitted to the International Court of Justice at the request of any of the parties to the dispute".

10 Ibid., 1066.
11 Ibid.

> Whereas it is not disputed that both Yugoslavia and the United States are parties to the Genocide Convention; but whereas, when the United States ratified the Convention on 25 November 1988, it made the following reservation:
>
> "That with reference to Article IX of the Convention, before any dispute to which the United States is a party may be submitted to the jurisdiction of the International Court of Justice under this Article, the specific consent of the United States is required in each case."[12]

In these paragraphs of the Court's reasoning it becomes evident that the key issue becomes the reservation made by the United States in 1988. Such reservation specifically requires that *any* dispute (thus including preliminary requests for temporary measures) which is presented on the basis of the Genocide Convention (Article IX) must obtain the consent of the United States before *any* jurisdiction is established. It follows that,

> ...whereas the United States contends that "[its] reservation [to Article IX] is clear and unambiguous"; that "the United States has not given the specific consent [that reservation] requires [and]...will not do so"; and that Article IX of the Convention cannot in consequence found the jurisdiction of the Court in this case, even prima facie; whereas the United States also observed that reservations to the Genocide Convention are generally permitted; that its reservation to Article IX is not contrary to the Convention's object and purpose; and that, "since... Yugoslavia did not object to the...reservation, it is bound by it"; and whereas the United States further contends that there is no "legally sufficient...connection between the charges against the United States contained in the Application and the supposed jurisdictional basis under the Genocide Convention"; and whereas the United States further asserts that Yugoslavia has failed to make any credible allegation of violation of the Genocide Convention, by failing to demonstrate the existence of the specific intent required by the Convention to "destroy, in whole or in part, a national, ethnical, racial or religious group, as such", which intent could not be inferred from the conduct of conventional military operations against another State.[13]

The refusal to grant jurisdiction is accompanied by statements according to which there is not enough evidence linking the acts listed by the Yugoslav request and the notion of intent – this is of course normally for the Court to decide, but given the special reservations made under Article IX such Court lacks any jurisdiction, even *prima facie*. In any case, disputes over the interpretation of the Genocide Convention are irrelevant as the issue of jurisdiction is paramount in determining whether the Court can act:

---

12 Ibid.

13 Ibid., 1066–67.

> Whereas Yugoslavia disputed the United States' interpretation of the Genocide Convention, but submitted no argument concerning the United States reservation to Article IX of the Convention; whereas the Genocide Convention does not prohibit reservations; whereas Yugoslavia did not object to the United States reservation to Article IX; and whereas the said reservation had the effect of excluding that Article from the provisions of the Convention in force between the Parties; whereas in consequence Article IX of the Genocide Convention cannot found the jurisdiction of the Court to entertain a dispute between Yugoslavia and the United States alleged to fall within its provisions; and whereas that Article manifestly does not constitute a basis of jurisdiction in the present case, even prima facie.

Thus, a piece of legislation on (Universal) Human Rights finds itself contextualised within a very particular reality of juridical finitude. The rest of the text, however, reveals one peculiar issue – apparently any State that does not accept the ICJ's jurisdiction remains, nonetheless, responsible for violations of international law. But responsible to whom?

> Whereas there is a fundamental distinction between the question of the acceptance by a State of the Court's jurisdiction and the compatibility of particular acts with international law, the former requires consent; the latter question can only be reached when the Court deals with the merits after having established its jurisdiction and having heard full legal arguments by both parties.
>
> Whereas, whether or not States accept the jurisdiction of the Court, they remain in any event responsible for acts attributable to them that violate international law, including humanitarian law; whereas any disputes relating to the legality of such acts are required to be resolved by peaceful means, the choice of which, pursuant to Article 33 of the Charter, is left to the parties; whereas in this context the parties should take care not to aggravate or extend the dispute; whereas, when such a dispute gives rise to a threat to the peace, breach of the peace or act of aggression, the Security Council has special responsibilities under Chapter VII of the Charter.[14]

This bizarre statement indicates that the ICJ cannot issue a temporary measure calling for the cessation of armed intervention, that such a measure cannot be issued because the ICJ manifestly lacks jurisdiction, that, nonetheless, this does not make a violation of international law less of a violation and consequently the ICJ is effectively calling for the parties to resolve a dispute by peaceful means – which is precisely what the temporary measure (which could not be enunciated because of lack of jurisdiction) was supposed to do. But this 'call' is both legal and

14 Ibid., 1067–68.

illegal, and a violation of international law remains so, even when international law has no jurisdiction. How can this be?

The issue at hand is the concept of sovereignty. Is the notion of sovereignty ultimately not a representation of the famous analytic of finitude, the limit, the notion that grounds all possibility of knowledge but lies outside that very knowledge? In other words, is sovereignty – understood as a legal concept – at the basis of the empirico-transcendental doublet in law, whereby the application of its principle at the metaphysical level must necessarily be contradictory in the realm of immanence (i.e. responsibility for a violation is adjudicated by an authority which recognises that it has no authority)?

To be sure, there was a dissenting opinion from one of the judges. Inevitably, this opinion had to make references to legal precedents.[15] In other words, the challenge to the particular analytic of finitude that was deployed took the form of historical arguments, which were supposed to better represent the essence of the law in a particular situation. References to precedents naturally included previous statements of the ICJ such as "...the protection of human rights, a strictly humanitarian objective, cannot be compatible with the mining of ports, the destruction of oil installations, or again with the training, arming and equipping of the contras."[16]

In any case, what is important to note is that, ultimately, when the issue of whether NATO's humanitarian intervention was justifiable and legal under customary international law, the argument deployed by the interested parties did not include references to the ethics of intervention, did not make references to the (rather limited) body of intellectual-legal opinion according to which the intervention was both legal and justifiable: but it had to appeal to the principle of exclusion due to jurisdiction. In other words, the metaphysical argument was implemented through technicalities at the level of immanence which manifestly contradicted such argument, and had to boil down to the notion that in order to save the human rights of some, the Genocide Convention cannot apply to others. The whole episode has been masterfully summarised by Mark Littman, QC as follows:

> On 29 April 1999 Yugoslavia brought proceedings against several members of NATO, including the UK, before the International Court of Justice alleging that the NATO intervention was unlawful....A response to these submissions was made on behalf of the UK by a distinguished team of lawyers consisting of Sir Franklin Berman QC, HM Attorney-General John Morris QC and Professor Christopher Greenwood, Professor of International Law at the LSE. However,

15 See International Court of Justice, "Dissenting opinion of Judge Kreca", http://www.icj-cij.org/docket/index.php?pr=371&code=yus&p1=3&p3=6&case=114&k=25 (accessed 20 April 2008).

16 Ruling of the International Court of Justice, *Nicaragua v. United States*, 1985, cited in ibid.

> no member of the UK team addressed any of the propositions or legal authorities cited on behalf of the complainant. They concentrated entirely on a jurisdictional issue: a caveat to the UK's acceptance of the Court's compulsory jurisdiction where the other party had made the complaint less than 12 months after accepting the Court's jurisdiction. The Yugoslav case fell within this exception to the UK's general acceptance and so it fell on this technicality. The Court was bound to sustain this objection since, as Judge Rosalyn Higgins, the British judge at the ICJ, put it: "...the jurisdiction of the Court – even if one might regret this state of affairs as we approach the 21st century – is based on consent". However, the UK could have waived this objection and accepted the Yugoslav challenge to have the legality of the bombing tested before the Court. It chose not to do so. *By resort to a legal technicality, the Government thus deprived the British public of the opportunity of an authoritative decision on this crucial matter.* In his speech, the Attorney General said: "I say very firmly that the UK has acted and will continue to act, in accordance with international law". Why then did the Attorney General not welcome the opportunity to gain the support of the Court for the UK position?[17]

According to the British Foreign Office, the UK Government was not willing to participate in what it regarded as a misguided use of international justice by the Federal Republic of Yugoslavia, and, thus, decided that holding up to technicalities was the best way to send the signal that it had no case to answer.

The problem here is not so much that one ought to be scandalised because the intervention may have been illegal. The problem, rather, is that the Kosovo conflict, for the first time in the post-war legalist world order, catalysed some of the most visible contradictions inherent to the modern episteme insofar as it put into question the notion that *what is legal must necessarily be legitimate.*[18] Once this notion is superseded, we find ourselves dwelling again in the empirico-transcendental doublet: how do we deal with the ethical imperative at the level of immanence? In effect, the transcendental principle in itself remains unquestioned (i.e. the notion of human rights). In other words, the main reason for concern should simply be that positions such as "the intervention was illegal but legitimate"

17 Mark Littman, *Kosovo: Law and Diplomacy*, Paper published by Chamaleon Press: Centre for Policy Studies, November 1999.

18 Does that mean that what is illegal is therefore, by definition, illegitimate? If we accept Francis Boyle's argument (see *Foundations of World Order*) that the legalist approach was set up precisely to 'illegitimise' the illegal use of force for the resolution of conflict it would be difficult not to reach such conclusion. If we do not accept that, it can still be argued that any illegal action which is subsequently presented as being legitimate simply weakens the system as a whole, which means that illegality is 'indirectly' tied in with illegitimacy, for it attacks the legitimacy of the system.

even become possible.[19] This is precisely when the contradictions caused by transcendental theorising translate in 'Universal Exclusions' and the proverbial 'engine for universal relativism'. By contrast, the task of the postmodern (again, in Foucauldian), immanent, Complexity ethic is of resolving the issue of universality by eliminating the transcendental realm as such – in other words, this is about the creation of what we may call an 'Exclusive Universal'.

NATO and the International Criminal Tribunal for the Former Yugoslavia

The issue of how the International Criminal Tribunal for the Former Yugoslavia (ICTY) proceeded to examine accusations against NATO needs to be studied, not so much because it may be a case of partisan justice (i.e. the proverbial 'victor's justice'), but because it is an extraordinary example of how the contradictions inherent within the modern episteme *allow* for an exclusionary discourse of international humanitarian law to even take place. The difficulties related to the need of articulating the transcendental notion of human rights at the level of human practices very quickly transform themselves in 'Universal Exclusions' which, at least at the level of normative arguments, are allowed to make sense due to the present epistemic configuration of knowledge. This section will proceed to analyse ICTY's reasoning in the context of such an analytic of finitude.[20]

On 13 June 2000, the ICTY published its Final Report to the Prosecutor by the Committee Established to Review the NATO Bombing Campaign Against the Federal Republic of Yugoslavia.[21] This was done in response to several requests for the ICTY to investigate potential breaches of International Humanitarian Law (IHL) committed by NATO. In what was an unusual step, the Prosecutor decided to set up an ad hoc Committee to advise the Tribunal on whether NATO actions ought to be investigated. The main conclusions of the report indicate that "in all cases either the law is not sufficiently clear or investigations are unlikely to result in the acquisition of sufficient evidence to substantiate charges against high level accused or against lower level accused for particularly heinous offences."[22] But how did the Committee reach this decision? More importantly, how did it – or rather, what kind of discourse allowed it to – interpret current IHL and existing case law (much of which the ICTY had a great role in establishing) in such a fashion?

19 This is the conclusion reached by the Independent International Commission on Kosovo. See The Independent International Commission on Kosovo, *Kosovo Report.*

20 There has been much scholarly debate regarding ICTY's reaction to a request regarding the investigations of alleged NATO war crimes. In particular, see a special issue of the *European Journal of International Law* 12 (2001).

21 International Criminal Tribunal for the Former Yugoslavia (ICTY). "Final Report to the Prosecutor by the Committee Established to Review the NATO Bombing Campaign Against the Federal Republic of Yugoslavia", http://www.un.org/icty/pressreal/nato061300.htm (accessed 8 April 2008).

22 Ibid., paragraph 90.

On 2 June 2000, the Prosecutor made statements that went beyond the report by the Committee by stating that "although NATO had made some mistakes, it had not deliberately targeted civilians" (the Committee never reached that conclusion, it merely stated that the law was not sufficiently clear and that the acquisition of further evidence was unlikely to help the investigation in that context).[23] In either case, the question arises as to whether IHL only covers 'intentional' breaches, or whether a war crime remains a war crime despite the original intentions of the perpetrators.[24] Moreover, the murky issue of whether journalists and factory workers can be considered as civilians or not does not seem to have influenced the Prosecutor's deliberations.

The legal scholar' Paolo Benvenuti has analysed the case put forward by the Committee in some detail.[25] Benvenuti identifies a number of important features:

- The unbalanced evidence on which the review committee made its findings,
- The relevance given exclusively to civilian casualties in evaluating the legality of the bombing campaign with regard to specific incidents,
- The assessment of damage to the environment,
- The assessment on the legality of use of dubious weapons (cluster bombs and depleted uranium),
- Target selection,
- The principle of proportionality,
- The assessment of specific incidents: the attack on the Grdelica Gorge bridge, the attack on the Djakovica Convoy, the attack on the Serbian TV and radio station, the attack on Korisa village, the attack on the Chinese Embassy.

In each case, Benvenuti proceeds to examine the arguments of the Committee in the context of its generic claims (i.e. that the law is not sufficiently clear and that the gathering of further evidence was unlikely to make it any clearer). For each one of these cases, it becomes easy to identify the notion of analytical finitude and the confusion caused by metaphysical interpretations of the law. It will be argued that such confusion provides the epistemic underpinning of Universal Exclusions and the background in which such arguments at the phenomenal level take place. In particular, all the contradictions intrinsic within the modern episteme come out rather clearly in discussions surrounding the issues of target selection/level of analysis (that is, the aggregate level at which responsibility can be attributed)

23 United Nations Security Council. Press Release, SC/6870, 2 June 2000. http://www.un.org/News/Press/docs/2000/20000602.sc6870.doc.html (accessed 8 April 2008).

24 Similarly, see Ted Hondrich's criticism of arguments relying on intentionality only in Chapter 5.

25 Paolo Benvenuti, "The ICTY Prosecutor and the Review of the NATO Bombing Campaign against the Federal Republic of Yugoslavia". *European Journal of International Law* Vol. 12, no. 3 (2001), 503–29.

and the principle of proportionality. In reality, the level of analysis problem (that is, to what degree within the phenomenal world a transcendental principle can be applied) cuts across all the issues identified below. The conclusion of our analysis is that Universal Exclusions are created by a system of thought whereby the aggregate level of responsibility is shifted precisely because of the flexibility with which the limits of analysis are applied (that is, through a differential use of analytical finitude). Paradoxically, within different analytics of finitude the case still looks as though it reflects the transcendental: in reality the transcendental has already been defined once analytic limits are imposed on it. As it outlined in Chapter 3, the transcendental can be gazed, but only within the limits of our rather phenomenal world. On the other hand, it will be suggested that a Complexity approach to the matter would have focussed on the emergence of events in their own right, and that, as such, it is possible to see similarities between a Complexity ethos in the philosophy of science and a jurisprudence-based approach to the issue of human rights.

If we turn to the first of the bullet points above, we can easily identify the designation (or rather, analytical delimitation) of relevant actors as legitimate players in law processes as the principle problem of the Committee. Indeed, the Committee states that it relied heavily on evidence forwarded by NATO because it had no 'official channels' with the FRY. In the first case, it should be noted that the Committee sent a detailed set of questions to NATO for which it only obtained "generic responses".[26] The second claim also seems to be plagued by an absurdity:

> Why was it impossible for an international institution – furthermore, one claiming primacy over national jurisdictions – to solicit information through a letter addressed to the FRY authorities? What kind of official channel is needed? One may observe that, in the same period, on 22 May 1999, the ICTY issued an indictment and an arrest warrant against Slobodan Milošević and four other high officials of the FRY and that the indictment and warrant were sent to the Federal Ministry of Justice of the FRY without raising any problem whatsoever of there being no official channel.[27]

Thus, we have a first Universal Exclusion – the exclusion of evidence coming from the FRY on the grounds that the FRY falls outside the limits of institutions allowed to participate in the analysis of the events. Again, this contradiction is allowed for by the metaphysical approach of the Court – it is only by attempting to apply a transcendental principle to the phenomenal realm that we can find flaws in such realm, thus allowing for the non-application of the Universal principle at the transcendental level. But what is really surprising is the affirmation of the fact that exclusive attention would be given to NATO responses – on the basis that the

26 Ibid., 506.
27 Ibid., 507.

Committee had no reason to doubt that such responses were honest – even though such responses had been judged to be inadequate and circumstantial:

> The Committee has conducted its review relying essentially upon public documents, including statements made by NATO and NATO countries at press conferences and public documents produced by the FRY. *It has tended to assume that the NATO and the NATO countries' press statements are generically reliable and that explanations have been honestly given.* The blind trust by the Review Committee in NATO's reliability is undiminished despite the Committee's own acknowledgement of the inadequacy of some of the replies from NATO. The Committee states: "The Committee must note, however, that when the Office of the Prosecutor requested NATO to answer specific questions about specific incidents, *the NATO reply was couched in general terms and failed to address the specific incidents*.[28]

So, why is it that in these circumstances generic answers are accepted in the context of *specific* questions? To what extent does the generality of the issue exclude issues that fall within particular scopes? Finally, why can we even think in terms of such dichotomies (specific/generic) in the context of case law, whose primary objective is precisely to investigate case-by-case specific violations of IHL? In other words, why is a different level of analysis being applied to both parties in the context of the same investigation? Indeed, as it will become evident below, the main tactic of the ICTY has been to apply a very generic level of responsibility to NATO countries whilst FRY officials were investigated for their specific involvement in precise incidents.

A second controversial decision of the Commission related to the exclusive relevance given to civilian casualties in evaluating the legality of the bombing campaign with regard to *specific* incidents (and the casualty threshold applied to evaluate such incidents). Benvenuti focuses on how the Committee explained that, in conducting its review, it

> "...has focussed primarily on incidents in which civilian deaths were alleged or confirmed", while "the Committee's review of incidents in which it is alleged that fewer than three civilians were killed has been hampered by a lack of reliable information." In other words, the attitude of the Committee was to carry out a legal evaluation of the facts taking into account only civilian deaths, while damage to civilian property was deliberately not considered. In fact, very deleterious consequences may result for civilians for material damage caused by an attack: therefore it was essential to take such damage into account. Summing up, it is unsatisfactory to assess the lawfulness of an attack with regard to the principle of proportionality if damage to civilian property is not evaluated.[29]

28 Ibid.

29 Ibid., 508.

In reality, this is a very serious matter as there is ample evidence suggesting that damage to property was indeed meant to undermine the morale of the population and was, therefore, precisely targeting civilians – such strategy has been openly defended by NATO commanders, including, amongst others, Wesley Clark himself (consider the statement of General Short at the beginning of this chapter: "I hope the distress of the public will, must undermine support for the authorities in Belgrade…I think no power to your refrigerator, no gas to your stove, you can't get to work because the bridge is down – the bridge on which you held your rock concerts and you all stood with targets on your heads. That needs to disappear at three o'clock in the morning"). Besides, is the limitation of the number of casualties to three not another evident imposition of an analytic of finitude to the subject matter? How can a Universal Human Right be assessed on the bases of artificial delimitations? Is the message here that violations to IHL can indeed occur, as long as they occur in pairs only?

Targeting civilian infrastructure exclusively or in part, but in any case deliberately, to cause unnecessary harm to civilians is of course illegal, both in absolute terms (Article 57 of Additional Protocol 1 to the Geneva Convention) and in relative terms (the principle of proportionality). Again, the analytical lenses applied to the investigation excluded – through Universal principles – precisely its constituent parts. The notion becomes even more worrying when one considers that some doubts had already been advanced on this topic by the fourteenth report of the Defence Select Committee of the UK House of Commons issued on 24 October 2000 (of which the ICTY had a copy):

> An examination of the choice of strategic targets during…the campaign does not readily reveal a clear pattern of a graduated strategy of coercion or evidence of increasing coercive effectiveness. Some targets appear difficult to justify. No clear explanation of the decision to bomb the Danube bridges at Novi Sad yet appears to be given.[30]

Is the lawfulness of the systematic targeting of power stations, industries and factories beyond any doubt? The fourteenth report went on to state:

> As the air campaign moved into 'Phase 2A', UK and NATO targeteers made some efforts to identify and strike targets that were not just of military value to Serbian air defences military command and control and the field forces in Kosovo, but would also influence perceptions. There appear to have been two target audiences for this. The first was the Serbian people as a whole. There was a belief – or hope – in the UK and in the wider alliance that Serbian morale 'would crack' and that the Serbian population would be encouraged by the air campaign to protest against the policies of the Milošević government.[31]

30 House of Commons, Defence Select Committee, Fourteenth Report, 24 October 2000, paragraph 124.

31 Ibid., paragraph 99.

In this context, it is not reassuring to read the following in the report – which reflects the reasoning of the ICTY Review Committee: "however, air strikes targeted at the Serbian population in general were never at the heart of Alliance Strategy".[32] The Universal Exclusion has now determined that specific events will not be evaluated in their own right, but in relation to how they stand within a broader strategy. This effectively means that the level of responsibility has been lifted from the particular incident to the generic strategy, and that through the application of Universal IHL such particulars are *de facto* excluded. Furthermore, this equally indicates that IHL violations – even deliberate ones – cannot be considered if such actions are not 'at the heart' of relevant military strategies. Victims can rest assured that their deaths were not 'at the heart' of what was being done there.

This rather staggering principle is reinforced – explicitly – when one looks at the Court's reasoning on target selection. In this case, it is merely sufficient to let the Committee speak for itself:

> In combat, military commanders are required: (a) to direct their operations against military objectives and (b) when directing operations against military objectives, to ensure that the losses to the civilian population and the damage to civilian property are not disproportionate to the concrete and direct military advantage anticipated…The commanders deciding on an attack have the duties: (a) to do everything practicable to verify that the objectives to be attacked are military objectives (b) to take all practicable precautions in the choice of methods and means of warfare with a view to avoiding or, in any event minimizing incidental civilian casualties or civilian property damage [the same damage that was not considered in relation to further investigations in specific cases by the Committee itself!] and (c) to refrain from launching attacks which may be expected to cause disproportionate civilian casualties or civilian property damage.[33]

To note that the Court is referring to *requirements* without dwelling on the details of when such requirements must be observed (as in, always, most of the time, intentionally, unintentionally…). This presumably means that such requirements must be respected at all times, in all cases. But then the Committee starts introducing doubts on the automatic applicability of relevant sanctions:

> …attacks which are not directed against military objectives (particularly attacks directed against civilian population) and attacks which cause disproportionate civilian casualties or civilian property damage *may constitute* the *actus reus* for the offence of unlawful attack under Article 3 of the ICTY Statute.[34]

32 Ibid., paragraph 100.

33 International Criminal Tribunal for the Former Yugoslavia, "Final Report to the Prosecutor by the Committee Established to Review the NATO Bombing Campaign Against the Federal Republic of Yugoslavia", supra note 1 in paragraph 28.

34 Ibid., emphasis added.

The above quotes leave no doubt that such attacks are committed wilfully: if we agree that the law is more than mere opinion, we have to say that the Committee should rather have affirmed very clearly that such attacks *must* (rather than *may*) be regarded as war crimes. The reader's confusion grows when the Committee subsequently explains:

> A determination that inadequate efforts have been made to distinguish between military objectives and civilians and civilian objects *should not necessarily focus exclusively on a specific incident.* If precautionary methods have worked adequately in a very high percentage [note: no percentage given] of cases then the fact that they have not worked well in a small number of cases [note: no number given] does not necessarily mean they are generally inadequate.[35]

The reader must conclude that the Court is saying that violations to IHL are not violations if they occur in a 'small number of cases'. As Benvenuti puts it: "One could be induced to think that war crimes occur and should be prosecuted only if committed in the context of a plan or of a large scale commission, when the inadequacy of precautionary measures is deliberate on the part of the warring party. This approach is inconsistent with the case law of the ICTY itself."[36] One is tempted to argue that the statements above leave no space for induction, as Benvenuti affirms: for that is precisely what the ICTY statements actually say. The Universal Exclusion has now introduced the notion of 'probability' in IHL – those falling outside cannot be considered to be the victims of war crimes. We have witnessed the birth of the notion of 'War Crimes *Lite*', undeserving of the attention of an international Court of Law. It is again through a generality, or through a vertically differential application of Universal principles, that constituents have been excluded.

Another exquisite paradox emanating from the contradictions inherent within the modern legal episteme can be found in the Committee's reasoning on the legality of the use of dubious weapons. Apart from the omission of some serious legal criteria when evaluating the evidence (the principle of unnecessary suffering and the principle of distinction) we have a curious interpretation of the ICJ's advisory report on the legality of nuclear weapons. We are referring, of course, to the fuzzy classification of weapons containing depleted uranium. As Benvenuti puts it:

> The Committee appears to have been afraid of widening its inquiry and, because of such fears, it had no qualms about misinterpreting to the point of absurdity the Advisory Opinion of the ICJ in the *Legality of Nuclear Weapons* case. 'Indeed', the Committee observes, relying on the ICJ Advisory Opinion, 'even in the case of warheads and other weapons of mass destruction – those which are universally

35 Ibid., paragraph 29, strong emphasis and comments added.

36 Benvenuti, "The ICTY Prosecutor and the Review of the NATO Bombing Campaign against the Federal Republic of Yugoslavia", 515.

> acknowledged to have the most deleterious environmental consequences – it is difficult to argue that the prohibition of their use is in all cases absolute'. This could even be understood to mean that according to the Committee's view the humanitarian problems of Kosovo could have been solved through the use of nuclear warheads against the FRY.[37]

Is there really anything we need to add to outline the inconsistencies caused by the adoption of a metaphysical approach to the issue of IHL? The Universal Exclusions have been presented, and the mechanisms through which these operate have been identified. Importantly, we can conclude that such exclusion will take place every time we attempt to apply transcendental principles to phenomenal realms. It is through the imposition of this analytical finitude that 'others' are created, and that corresponding identities are formed. In our case, the most staggering example refers to the differential identification of aggregate responsibility. In this context, it is important to thoroughly consider Benvenuti's final remarks, as these crucially address the level of analysis issue – although without realising that such an issue is precisely the fruit of a modern episteme which causes all subsequent paradoxes:

> Having completed an examination of the report, for which the Prosecutor has accepted full responsibility, I do not have a specific final comment to add. One-sided attitudes, the vague use of legal concepts, the disregard for ICTY case law, the shortcomings in legal reasoning and in selecting relevant facts, and the reluctance to start in-depth investigations of its own, are the preamble for a document which is largely inadequate to its task. But I have to make a final criticism, to myself also: in fact, in coming to the end of my analysis, I have a feeling of dissatisfaction with it. I am aware that my comments are characterised by a regrettable move away from the proper ground of the conduct of the individual allegedly responsible for the commission of war crimes, to the ground of the conduct of the state allegedly responsible, at the international level, for violations of IHL: there is no clear-cut distinction between the two levels in my comments, and perhaps the second level is prevalent. I confess, it is a quite embarrassing confusion, because my comments relate to a report prepared by a committee working in the framework of an international criminal tribunal, that is to say an international body with the task of assessing individual positions, not in the framework of an inter-state tribunal (such as the ICJ) evaluating state positions. I apologize for this approach, but I realise that I have been led in this direction by the approach of the Review Committee itself and I have not been able to avoid this unwanted consequence while I was following its reasoning… the Committee has done its best to deny the international responsibility of the state as such, in order to achieve an a priori *exclusion* of the role of the ICTY in evaluating the positions of individuals.[38]

37 Ibid., 512.

38 Ibid., 526–7, emphasis added.

It is difficult to find a more apt concretisation of Žižek's Universal Exclusions – here, the ICTY is excluding itself from its Universal role precisely by opposing its remit to the particular nature of the issues at hand.

Thus, what is for Benvenuti and for the legal scholar an anecdote and passing remark at the end of a thorough analytical examination, is for us the crux of the argument. It is, in fact, the nucleus of our reasoning. The legal scholar does not ask why the Court chose – or rather, why it was in an epistemic position to even choose – to adopt this particular 'level of analysis' (for lack of a better expression). But we can relate it to the nature of the modern episteme, and that is how we understand the knowledge formation processes behind the technique.

Another Failed Jurisdiction: The European Court of Human Rights

Proceedings at the European Court of Human Rights (ECHR) followed similar patterns. On 20 October 1999 an application was lodged in relation to attacks on the RTS by six applicants, five of whom applied on behalf of relatives killed during the bombing, whilst a sixth applied in her own capacity as an alleged victim. In response:

> The European Court of Human Rights decided that the applications were inadmissible against Belgium and sixteen other contracting parties to the European Convention on the Protection of Human Rights and Fundamental freedom; the extraterritorial acts in question did not bring the applicants and their deceased relatives under the "jurisdiction" of the respondent states as required by Convention Article 1. With respect to the "ordinary meaning" of the phrase "within their jurisdiction" in public international law, the Court observed that the jurisdictional competence of a state, *while not excluding extraterritorial acts per se, is essentially territorial in nature and hence limited by the sovereign territorial rights of other states*. In its view, "Article 1 of the Convention must be considered to reflect this ordinary and essentially territorial notion of jurisdiction, other bases of jurisdiction being exceptional and requiring special justification in the particular circumstances of *each case*."[39]

This time, the finitude, or jurisdiction, of legal action is not determined by reservations (ICJ) or by dubious assessments on validity (ICTY), but by the notion of sovereignty embedded in a notion of territory. Note, however, such notion of jurisdiction, despite being 'essentially territorial' does not exclude extraterritorial acts – nevertheless such extraterritorial acts are exceptions (another exclusion) and require 'special justification'. Once again, a Court tasked with defending Universal

39 Alexandra Rüth and Mirja Trilsch, "*Bancovič v Belgium*, Admissibility, Application No. 52207/99", *The American Journal of International Law* 97, no. 1 (2003), 168–72, 168, emphasis added.

Human Rights at the transcendental level needs to negotiate and limit its action in the phenomenal world through exclusive analysis on case-by-case bases. What was then ECHR's reasoning?:

> The Court then examined the special circumstances under which extraterritorial acts could be recognized as constituting an exercise of "jurisdiction" under Article 1of the Convention…It concluded that it had recognized the exercise of extraterritorial jurisdiction: "when the respondent State, through the effective control of the relevant territory and its inhabitants abroad as a consequence of military occupation or through the consent, invitation, or acquiescence of the Government of that territory, exercises all or some of the public powers normally to be exercised by that Government."[40]

In other words, the ECHR will consider jurisdiction over extraterritorial acts when respondent states fulfil the functions they normally fulfil within their territories extraterritorially. This seems to mean that, paradoxically, the ECHR will claim jurisdiction over extraterritorial acts once respondent states have de facto imposed their full sovereignty on foreign territory and territorialised such sovereignty. The paradox emerges out of the fact that imposing sovereignty of foreign territories de facto equates to incorporating such territories into existing constituencies, and, yet, the Court insists on using the adjective "extraterritorial" to characterise its own jurisdiction in such circumstances.

The Court, however, and despite all objections on recognition, conceded that if it was not for the *specific circumstances* of the case such case would have been an object of the Court's concern, indeed, in the context of its *ordre public* obligations:

> Finally, the Court also rejected the argument that any failure to accept the jurisdiction of the respondent states for the impugned acts would defeat the Convention's *ordre public* mission and thus leave a regrettable vacuum in the Convention's system of human rights protection. Recalling the "essentially regional vocation of the Convention system", the Court pointed out that its comments in *Cyprus v Turkey* concerning the need to avoid such a vacuum had to be understood against the background that the territory in question, *but for the specific circumstances of the case*, would normally have been covered by the Convention.[41]

Needless to say, the ECHR is stating that cases which usually fall under its jurisdiction – both on the bases of the Convention and the ECHR's own case law – need to prove that they do not constitute specific or exceptional circumstances. For Human Rights to be protected relevant humans need to prove first that they are

40 Ibid., 169.
41 Ibid., 170.

not exceptional humans according to whatever definition of exception the Court may have decided to adopt in any particular case.

Rüth and Trilsch proceed to analyse and criticise each of the ECHR's claims regarding its lack of jurisdiction in turn:

> In its first decision related to NATO's military operation in Kosovo, the Court, seemingly in an effort to limit its rather broadly phrased findings in the Northern Cyprus cases, adopted a restrictive approach to the Convention's applicability in extraterritorial contexts. In so doing, the Court set what may well prove to be an important precedent for possible future complaints in connection with international military conflicts. In the Northern Cyprus cases, the Court had stressed that "under its established case-law the concept of jurisdiction under Article 1 of the Convention is not restricted to the national territory of the Contracting States", and had concluded that Turkey was bound by the Convention for acts relating to its occupation of Northern Cyprus. In the instant case, however, the Court *noticeably changed its use of terminology, thereby restricting its interpretation of earlier cases*. It claimed, in particular, *to have previously held that extraterritorial acts satisfy the requirement of state jurisdiction "only in exceptional cases", and that "equally exceptional circumstances" therefore had to be met in Bancovič*. Notably, the Court did not conduct its own, independent examination of whether a further exception was justified, but contented itself, instead, with the mere refutation of the applicants' submissions (dealing, in particular, with their proportionality argument).[42]

In other words, the Court itself created and defined new territory-based exceptional circumstances (which were not created in the *Cyprus v Turkey* case) and then, instead of conducting its own investigation on whether such circumstances applied, it decided that Bancovič and others did not do enough to prove *prima facie* that their cases did not constitute an exceptional circumstance as the Court defined it. Again, the point here is not that we should find the whole affair offensive or infuriating, rather, the point is that transcendental notions (Human Rights) utilise mechanisms to limit such transcendence and, therefore, become applicable at the level of immanence (through an analytic of finitude) through mechanisms that are fundamentally exclusive – *for exclusion comes logically with any effort to delimit a transcendental realm*.

Not surprisingly, Rüth and Trisch think that, "in sum, the Court's findings constitute a turnabout from its earlier decisions,"[43] further arguing that

42 Ibid., 171.

43 Ibid., 172. For a similar conclusion, consider Matthew Happold, "Bankovic v Belgium and the Territorial Scope of the European Convention on Human Rights". *Human Rights Law Review* Vol. 3, no. 1 (2003), 77–90.

> ...the Court's reasoning is not entirely persuasive. To start with, one may question the Court's principal assumption that the notion of "jurisdiction" under the Convention is necessarily identical with its ordinary meaning in public international law. Though correctly noting that the *travaux préparatoires* and state practice confirm, in principle, this essentially territorial conception, the Court avoided any substantive answer to the question of whether its methodological approach of interpreting the Convention according to "present-day conditions" could be applied to determine the meaning of "jurisdiction" in Article 1 – and therefore to determine, in effect, the very scope of the Convention itself. Rather than analyzing why, or even if, a dynamic interpretation was prohibited or inappropriate, however, the Court appeared merely to hold that any further analysis was dispensable since the Convention's *travaux préparatoires* confirmed the ordinary meaning of "jurisdiction" under public international law.[44]

It should be noted once again that the analytic of finitude (territoriality-based jurisdiction) deployed by the Court is enforced through a notion of historical finitude: thus, the insistence on 'present day conditions'. Indeed, the entire sentence "interpreting the Convention according to 'present-day conditions' in order to determine the meaning of 'jurisdiction' in Article 1 – and, therefore, determining, in effect, the very scope of the Convention itself" seems like a rather perfect crystallisation of the empirico-transcendental doublet and of its two axes of modernity (analytic of finitude meaning jurisdiction, and present day conditions meaning historical linearity) in the modern legal episteme. Are considerations over "modern day conditions", after all, nothing but an attempt to freeze temporality? Is this not strictly the same thing as Anderson's 'homogenous, empty time', which is a necessary pre-condition for the formulation of the idea of nationalism? Is this concept of nationalism embedded in a territory not, ultimately, what informs the reasoning of what was supposed to be a Court of (Universal) Human Rights?

Conclusion: Universal Exclusion and the Complexity Ethic

The chapter has sought to concretely show what, according to Žižek, the "usual notion of human rights as a universality only possible on the basis of a series of exclusions (women, children, the mad, the primitive), a universality from which ultimately everybody is excluded" looks like in practice.[45]

The links between a Complexity ethos and transcendental law may not be readily apparent. It would have been necessary to highlight how the legal discipline evolved according to the patterns of the modern episteme – in a way akin to the

44 Ibid., 171.

45 Butler, *Slavoj Žižek: Live Theory*, 8.

process through which this work outlined the evolution of the discipline of IR. It is hoped, however, that the previous chapters have provided a solid enough theoretical basis for the reader to discern the common threads, or parallelisms, occurring across the history and philosophy of science (in particular the events that followed the Vienna Circle), the history of 'scientific' IR theory and the contradictions evident within contemporary legal practice.

When considering these questions, one is tempted to ask what a "Complexity-based" legal practice would like, and how such practice would better address the issue of ethical responsibility. In a sense, the answer has already been partially provided by the presentation of the case for a jurisprudence-led approach to international law – whereas Complexity represents a drive towards anti-reductionism and Bergsonian 'superior empiricism', jurisprudence can be seen as a more holistic approach to the issue. It can be suggested that by keeping the criteria of analysis at the level of immanence a jurisprudence approach fails to repeat the Universal Exclusions that so often characterise contemporary legal thought and practice.

One is tempted to add that present approaches to knowledge are convenient precisely because they fail to enforce ethical relationships. In this sense, the modern episteme allows for a form of legal thought that portrays itself as Universal and, yet, excludes those particular components that happen to represent uncomfortable truths – and what is more, such inconsistencies are well embedded in the modern episteme, which means that they do not even appear to be inconsistencies at all, since it is precisely those that ground our possibility for knowledge. Another interesting paradox: it is this transcendental Universalist approach that creates an engine for Universal Relativism, and not post-structuralist thought which – understood strictly in a Deleuzian/Complexity way – demands rigour in what remains, admittedly, a probabilistic and holistic world.

Chapter 6
Ancient Ethnic Hatreds

L'Histoire est la science des choses qui ne se répètent pas – History is the science of things that do not repeat themselves.

Paul Valéry

I have tried to gather together a few facts which have come out of this conflict. It is taking place in an area which is and has been constitutionally unstable for 2,000 years. Had any of those in authority thought about it, an understanding of history might have helped.

Lord Belhaven and Stenton – Debates in the House of Lords[1]

"History", n. An account mostly false, of events mostly unimportant, which are brought about by rulers mostly knaves, and soldiers mostly fools.

Ambrose Bierce[2]

Introduction: Complexity and Six Hundred Years of Non-Linear History

Chapter 3 indicates that Žižek's reading of Deleuze – in particular of Deleuzian concepts of transcendental empiricism – conditions his views on the role of history in the Kosovo crisis. What are Žižek's views then? "There are no 'old myths' which we need to study if we are really to understand the complex situation, just the *present* outburst of racist nationalism which, according to its needs, opportunistically resuscitates old myths. To paraphrase the old Clintonian motto: no, it's not the old myths and ethnic hatreds, *it's the political power struggle*, stupid!"[3]

David Campbell has already identified how such proposition translated in the practice of settlement in Bosnia. With regard to Bosnia, Campbell maintains that, "the conflict is constituted in the *present*, and that 'history' is a resource in the contemporary struggle."[4] Ultimately, the Complexity paradigm also shows

1 UK Parliament, House of Lords, Hansard Debates, 6 May 1999, Column 857.

2 Ambrose Bierce, *The Unabridged Devil's Dictionary* (Athens GA: University of Georgia Press, 2002), 110.

3 Slavoj Žižek, *Against the Double Blackmail.*

4 Campbell, *National Deconstruction*, 84.

how the virtual is always ever being constructed (or actualised) in the present. Following Bergson, it is always quite impossible to exactly determine when the past becomes the present and/or when the present becomes the future: what needs to be studied is, in line with Foucault's arguments in the *Archaeology of Knowledge*, the immanent rules of formation of an argument (even a historical argument), in the immanent *present*.

The current chapter constitutes an attempt at placing the two insights above in a Complexity-epistemic context and to show how they apply to the case of Kosovo. First, it would be useful to remember that the Complexity ethic plays a crucial role in shaping a theory of 'immanent history', or to deconstruct, in tandem with post-structural philosophy, history as a meta-narrative.[5] Second, we should bear in mind that this brings up questions on the role that modernity plays in enforcing linear temporality – which, as it will be argued below, is an essential pre-condition for the formulation of any nationalist myth:

> One of the main aims of the instrumental rationality flowing from the enlightenment was to create conditions in which we are not controlled by contingency. To achieve these conditions, it is necessary to understand, and preferably *control*, the future. This demands a coordinated and goal-oriented action in the present. Modernism becomes a project that demands our total commitment against the forces of irrationality and chaos. The modernist project has two important effects on our understanding of time. In the first place, our actions need to be coordinated. This can only happen if time is universalised in such a way that we all live in the 'same' time…The second effect of instrumental rationality on our understanding of time is a result of the desire to control the future; for the future to be made knowable. This would only be possible if the future, in some essential way, resembles the past.…The actual result of this ideology is to extend the present into the future, causing us to live in a perpetual 'present'. The sacrifice made in order to achieve this, however, is nothing short of sacrificing the very notion of temporality. Nowotny calls it the "illusion of simultaneity."[6]

5 For arguments in favour of this hypothesis and on the Complexity-Post-structuralism consider Chapter 1 but also Cilliers, *Complexity and Postmodernism*, Matthew Abraham, "What is Complexity Science: Towards the end of Ethics and Law Parading as Justice", in *Thinking Complexity: Complexity and Philosophy*, ed. Paul Cilliers (Mansfield: ISCE Publishing, 2007), 121–22, Stephen Sheard, "Complexity Theory and Continental Philosophy Part 1: A Review of Letiche's Phenomenological Complexity Theory", in ibid., and Damian Popolo, "Complexity in a Complex Europe. Reflections on the Cultured Genesis of a New Science", in *Emergence: Complexity and Organisation* Vol. 8, no. 2 (2000), 65–76.

6 Paul Cilliers, "On the Importance of a Certain Slowness", in *Thinking Complexity: Complexity and Philosophy*, ed. Paul Cilliers (Mansfield: ISCE Publishing, 2007).

Thus, the scope of the current chapter is limited to outlining how this historical linearity – which has been thoroughly examined in the previous chapters – characterised both the emergence of the nationalist discourse in Serbia and in Kosovo and the reactions to such nationalisms in the 'West'. A first section of this chapter will deal with the former, whilst a second section will deal with the latter. The current chapter will also seek to demonstrate that such understandings inherent in the modern episteme conditioned the way in which the run-up to the conflict was perceived, and how the NATO intervention in itself was planned and implemented.

Living in the Past, in the Present: Apprehensions of Time in Nationalist Discourse

Benedict Anderson has addressed the role of linear temporality in the construction of nationalisms. One of the objectives of our case study will be to demonstrate that Anderson's arguments can not only be applied to the subjects experiencing the processes of identity formation, but that it also conditions how others, outsiders, frame and identify a particular group. In Anderson's classical study of nationalisms[7] an entire section (appropriately entitled *Apprehensions of Time*) is dedicated to the analysis of time as a fundamental component in the construction of national and ethnic identities.[8] Consider for example the following claim:

> Our own conception of simultaneity has been a long time in the making, and its emergence is certainly connected, in ways that have yet to be well studied, with the development of the secular sciences. But is it a conception of such fundamental importance that, without taking it fully into account, we will find it difficult to probe the obscure genesis of nationalism? What has come to take the place of the medieval conception of simultaneity-along-time is, to borrow again from Benjamin, an idea of 'homogenous, empty time', in which simultaneity is, as it were, transverse, cross-time, marked not by prefiguring and fulfilment, but by temporal coincidence, and measured by clock and calendar.[9]

The idea of nationalism cannot emerge without linear time, one of the two axes of modernity. According to Anderson, without an emerging concept of 'homogenous, empty time' it would be difficult, if not impossible, to imagine oneself as being part of a coherent community. Can we also say that without this notion it would be

7 Anderson, *Imagined Communities*.

8 Ibid., 22–36.

9 Ibid., 24. Contrast this notion of time as allowing simultaneity with Bergson's conception: "What is the role of time?...*Time prevents everything from being given at once*...Is it not the vehicle of creativity and choice? Is not the existence of time the proof of indeterminism in nature?"

equally difficult to imagine 'others' as being part of 'other' coherent communities? Is this the notion that characterised the conceptualisation of the 'Kosovars' and the 'Serbs', for example, from Rome to Washington via, Paris, Madrid and London? It is interesting that Anderson notes that the emergence of linear time is probably related to the creation of modern secular sciences, but that it is yet to be well studied, especially when one thinks that the emergence of such a concept in precisely those terms is identified by Foucault in a book subtitled *An Archaeology of the Human Sciences*, sciences which Foucault characterises as being strictly modern and secular. It remains unclear to what extent Anderson was aware of Foucault and to what extent the latter influenced the former. Although Anderson refers to a "Foucauldian sense of abrupt discontinuities of consciousness"[10] when comparing the notion of time in nationalistic and non-nationalistic works of literature, no explicit references to what would appear to be the most relevant work (i.e. *The Order of Things,* that is, where the notion of epistemic breaks and the rise of historical linearity is formulated) appears to be made in *Imagined Communities.* This is a theoretical vacuum we have hoped to fill in the presentation of Foucault's description of linear history as an enforcer of the empirico-transcendental doublet and, by extension, of the modern episteme.

The reproduction of the past into the present as a means of generating nationalist discourse is evident in the case of Kosovo. Whereas it is impossible to narrate the run up to the Kosovo crisis without outlining the broader context of Yugoslav politics in the 1990s, it would be a mistake to consider Kosovo simply as the latest chapter in the post-Cold War Balkan tragedy. Indeed, Kosovo provided the myth upon which the Yugoslav tragedy unfolded, and, as such, it ought to be regarded as the origin of the subsequent conflicts, including those that unfolded in Slovenia, Croatia and Bosnia. The fact that Kosovo was the last conflict to be 'actualised' does not mean that it was a consequence of the others – on the contrary, it means that, precisely because it represented the myth upon which all other myths were constructed, it was the myth which took the longest to conflagrate.[11] Thus, the following arguments will not only seek to elucidate how the axes of modernity conditioned the way in which knowledge was generated and deployed in the immediate run up to the war in Kosovo. Rather, it will be argued that a Complexity-informed epistemic approach calls for an understanding of how *the history of Kosovo that was constructed in order to support immanent political struggles which conditioned – in a very modern way – the entire Yugoslav crisis in the decade of the 1990s*. This is so because the Complexity paradigm calls for an understanding of how the constitution of linear histories shapes the way in which knowledge is generated and deployed in order to enforce contingency, and in our case the constitution of such linear histories – which is precisely what Complexity

10 Ibid., 28.

11 Indeed, Richard Holbrooke recognised that Kosovo represented, if anything, even a more difficult hurdle than Bosnia, and Kosovo was side-stepped at Dayton precisely because it was feared that its inclusion in the talks may have derailed the entire process.

identifies as the major rupture with other scientific paradigms and, thus, seeks to overcome – the linear history that enforced conceptual contingency on the entire Yugoslav crisis began in Kosovo, and found in Kosovo its point of origin.

Therefore, the 'Kosovo crisis', from a Complexity-epistemic point of view, does not begin in January 1998 (escalation of violence in the province), as policy-oriented, 'problem solving' approaches would indicate.[12] It also does not begin in June 1389 (battle of Kosovo Polje on the Field of the Blackbirds, which seals Ottoman rule on the area) as the nationalists on both sides and the adherents of a 'Clash of Civilizations' approach would have us believe.[13] Equally, it does not begin in March 1999 (NATO campaign), as military observers would put it. More importantly, it does not start in 1989 (collapse of the Soviet Union and of the related international system that prevented the conflict – which was always waiting to happen – from unfolding). The latter hypothesis is a standard in mainstream structural IR theory which, as it was presented in Chapter 3, needs to believe that the crisis was always waiting to happen – that is, it constantly lived in the present – and 'the international system' prevented it from happening: such commentators usually point out that Titoism successfully negotiated the Kosovo riots in 1981 precisely because of the very nature of Titoism, implying that once Titoism disappears such convulsions are allowed to degenerate into wider conflict.[14] Here, the influence of such thinking on the actual process of policy making is obvious.[15]

As discussed in the first part of this book, and as it will be further argued below, it is precisely the need to begin with such assumption that prevents this particular transcendental philosophy of the object to recognise the very immanent nature and origin of the crisis. This grand vision of events, which assumes that history, once unfrozen, would simply take its natural, pre-determined (by ancient ethnic hatreds…) course, fails to explain why the removal of the Cold War lid led to perfectly peaceful fragmentations (Czechoslovakia), a complete absence

---

12 House of Commons, Foreign Affairs Select Committee, "Fourth report: Kosovo, Vol. II, Minutes of evidence and appendices", 23 May 2000, p.97. Examination of witnesses: Judah, Sweeney and Roberts: 14.

13 Samuel Huntington, *The Clash of Civilizations and the Remaking of World Order* (New York: Simon and Shuster, 1998), 130 and 138.

14 Adams, "Structural Realism: the Consequences of Great Power Politics".

15 Consider for instance the official view of the UK Parliament: "The death of Tito in 1980, a growing desire for change in the constituent parts of Yugoslavia and the collapse of communism in central and eastern Europe led after 1990 to the implosion of the Yugoslav Federation. *With the restraints of the Cold War removed, a spasm of war convulsed the area over the 1990s*. A state simply disintegrated. Rioting in 1981 in Kosovo, and the removal in 1989 of previous Kosovan autonomy, had presaged the conflicts to come, and it was war in Kosovo, and NATO's bombing campaign against the residue of Yugoslavia, which ended the millennium." UK Parliament, House of Commons, Foreign Affairs Select Committee, "Fourth Report: Kosovo. Vol. 1, Report and Proceedings of the Committee", 23 May 2000: 9, emphasis added.

of fragmentation in countries with acute 'ethnic minorities' problems (Roma and Hungarians in Romania), or in countries where such problems were compounded by religious diversity (Albanian Islamic minorities in Macedonia, for example).

From a Complexity-epistemic perspective, the Kosovo crisis begins in the afternoon of 28 June 1987, when Slobodan Milošević, the then Chairman of the Serbian Communist Party, formally established the myth of Kosovo as the foundational myth for the entire political vision and programme of his party in a speech delivered in the town of Gazimestan, Kosovo. We are not referring to the events of 24 April 1987 – when Milošević pronounced the famous "No one should dare to beat you" speech to a crowd of angry Kosovo Serbs in the outskirts of Priština. At that point, the discourse was not yet a fully nationalist discourse: it had not yet engaged the process of generating the 'homogenous, empty time' Anderson asserts is necessary for the establishment of a fully-fledged nationalist agenda. It was on 28 June 1989 that Milošević consciously delivered a vision which linked the future of the nation to the past of Kosovo, thus grounding the discourse on firm nationalist bases by deploying a language and a symbolism designed to ensure that events that had occurred 600 years earlier were felt, sensed and internalised in the *present*.

The occasion was perfect. The 28 June 1989 marked the 600th anniversary of the battle of Kosovo. The first steps to bring the past back into the present were taken the previous winter, when "the bones of the medieval Serbian leader, Lazar, under the supervision of the church, toured the holy places in Serbian-populated territories before being returned to their resting place in the monastery Lazar founded at Ravanica. The arrivals of these relics in the months preceding the Kosovo anniversary were occasions for excitement and veneration."[16]

To re-inforce the relevance of Lazar's 'feats' in the context of the present political situation, "Portraits of Lazar and Milošević were held aloft by members of the audience, the medieval monarch alongside the Communist *apparatchik*."[17] The speech itself was delivered on a stage designed to suggest continuity: an enormous circle designed to encompass the dates 1389 and 1989 stood above the speaker's head.

But let's proceed to examine the documentary monument which is being credited with establishing the concept of 'empty time', thus elevating Kosovo as the foundational myth of all consequent Serbian nationalism. In the transcript of the speech the techniques used to bring the events that occurred 600 years earlier into the contemporary national consciousness are rather evident. Indeed, in commenting on the speech, Edit Petrović argues that Milošević sought to combine "history, memory and *continuity*", promoting "the illusion that the Serbs who fought against the Turks in Kosovo in 1389 are somehow the same as the Serbs

16 Thomas, *Serbia under Milošević*, 50.

17 Ibid., 50–51.

fighting for Serbian national survival today."[18] James Gow, on the other hand, asserts that the objective was to further Milošević's political campaign, which was "predicated on the notion of redressing this mood of victimisation and restoring the sense of Serbian pride and, most important of all, power."[19] Introducing the speech, Milošević mentions the battle of Kosovo and states that

> ...by the force of social circumstances this great 600th anniversary of the Battle of Kosovo is taking place in a year in which Serbia, after many years, after many decades, has regained its state, national, and spiritual integrity. Therefore, it is not difficult for us to answer today the old question: how are we going to face Milos [Milos Obilic, legendary hero of the Battle of Kosovo]. Through the play of history and life, it seems as if Serbia has, precisely in this year, in 1989, regained its state and its dignity and thus has celebrated an event of the distant past which has a great historical and symbolic significance for its future.[20]

Here, Milošević is referring to the constitutional changes which reduced autonomy of Serbia's provinces and strengthened the central rule. The first clear parallelism is thus presented: precisely in the year of the 600th anniversary of the battle of Kosovo Serbia is opening a new chapter in its history. He continues by stating:

> Today, it is difficult to say what is the historical truth about the Battle of Kosovo and what is legend. Today, this is no longer important. Oppressed by pain and filled with hope, the people used to remember and to forget, as, after all, all people in the world do, and it was ashamed of treachery and glorified heroism. Therefore it is difficult to say today whether the Battle of Kosovo was a defeat or a victory for the Serbian people, whether thanks to it we fell into slavery or we survived in this slavery. The answers to those questions will be constantly sought by science and the people. What has been certain through all the centuries until our time today is that disharmony struck Kosovo 600 years ago. If we lost the battle, then this was not only the result of social superiority and the armed advantage of the Ottoman Empire but also of the tragic disunity in the leadership of the Serbian state at that time. In that distant 1389, the Ottoman Empire was not only stronger than that of the Serbs but it was also more fortunate than the Serbian kingdom.

---

18 Edit Petrović, "Ethnonationalism and the Dissolution of Yugoslavia", in *Neighbors at War: Anthropological Perspectives on Yugoslav Ethnicity, Culture, and History*, eds, Joel Martin Halpern and David Kideckel (Penn: Penn State Press, 2000), 170, emphasis added.

19 James Gow, *The Serbian Project and Its Adversaries: A Strategy of War Crimes* (London: Hurst and Co. Publishers, 2003), 10.

20 All quotes from Milošević's Gazimestan speech are taken from Auerswald, *The Kosovo Conflict*, 30–34.

Milošević then seeks to place his speech in the context of the post-World War II history of Yugoslavia, in which Serbia's influence had been restricted through constitutional arrangements, thus diluting its power. This had been a long-running controversy in Serbian politics, particularly after Kosovo and the northern Serbian province of Vojvodina were granted influence over Serbia under Yugoslavia's 1974 constitution. Indeed, Sabrina Petra Ramet and Vjeran Pavlaković argue that Milošević sought to make "clear parallels between the Battle of Kosovo Polje and the Yugoslav constitution of 1974, both considered to be defeats in the Serbian national consciousness."[21] Milošević continues by stating that disunity has haunted Serbs throughout history. Such disunity among Serbian political leaders meant that they were "prone to compromise to the detriment of its own people", compromise which "could not be accepted historically and ethically by any nation in the world". However, "here we are now at the field of Kosovo to say that this is no longer the case".

Thus, the disunity the Serbian leadership allegedly showed in 1389 is inserted in the context of events in the second post world war period. The first case of disunity led to Ottoman conquest, the second to fascist aggression:

> Thanks to their leaders and politicians and their vassal mentality they felt guilty before themselves and others. This situation lasted for decades, it lasted for years and here we are now at the field of Kosovo to say that this is no longer the case…Serbia of today is united and equal to other republics and prepared to do everything to improve its financial and social position and that of all its citizens. If there is unity, cooperation, and seriousness, it will succeed in doing so.

In an elaboration of another of the major motifs of the Kosovo myth, that of the purity of Serbian motives, Milošević asserts that

> …Serbs have never in the whole of their history conquered and exploited others. Their national and historical being has been liberational throughout the whole of history and through two world wars, as it is today. They liberated themselves and when they could they also helped others to liberate themselves.

The middle section of the speech took a markedly different line from the nationalist expressions which characterised the beginning of it, to the point that Louis Sell describes it as sounding "as if it was written by his wife"[22] (Mirjana Marković, who was known for her hard-line communist views). Indeed, Milošević goes on praising the virtues of ethnic tolerance and socialism, describing how "the world is more and more marked by national tolerance, national cooperation and even

21 Sabrina Petra Ramet and Vjeran Pavlaković, *Serbia Since 1989: Politics and Society Under Milošević and After* (Washington: University of Washington Press, 2005), 13.

22 Louis Sell, *Slobodan Milošević and the Destruction of Yugoslavia* (Durham: Duke University Press, 2003), 88.

national equality" and calling for equal and harmonious relations among the peoples of Yugoslavia.

Milošević then went on to portray medieval Serbia as not just the defender of its own territory, but of all Europe in the fight against the Ottoman Turks. He declared that "Six centuries ago, Serbia heroically defended itself in the field of Kosovo, but it also defended Europe. Serbia was at that time the bastion that defended the European culture, religion, and European society in general". According to Arne Johan Vetlesen, this was an appeal "to the values of Europe, meaning to Christianity, to *modernity*, to Civilization with a capital C, exploit[ing] Orientalist sentiments and help[ing] to amplify the Balkanism widespread in Western governments."[23]

Finally, the most obvious example of continuous time in the speech:

> Six centuries later, now, we are being again engaged in battles and are facing battles. They are not armed battles, although such things cannot be excluded yet. However, regardless of what kind of battles they are, they cannot be won without resolve, bravery, and sacrifice, without the noble qualities that were present here in the field of Kosovo in the days past. Our chief battle now concerns implementing the economic, political, cultural, and general social prosperity, finding a quicker and more successful approach to a civilization in which people will live in the 21st century.

MacDonald also notes the visual analogies with the past, "Orthodox priests held aloft icons of Milošević and Lazar, while thousands of men and women crowded around the podium. Arguably, this was Milošević's finest hour."[24] Thomas agrees, "in Milošević the man and the moment were well met…while Milošević himself may not have been a Serbian nationalist by nature his background, coming from the small provincial town of Pozarevac in eastern Serbia with a father who studied Orthodox theology, would have meant that he understood the habits and thought patterns of that creed."[25] Nonetheless, according to MacDonald, "secretly, however, he admitted that most of this was nothing more than 'bullshit'."[26]

But what was the reason behind this nationalist appeal, and why did it have to be delivered through a mystification of Kosovo?

According to Thomas:

> …while the inability of democracy to put down firm roots can be attributed in part to weaknesses and fault-lines within Serbian society, the decisions of individuals and personalities have also played a critical role both in the failure to bring about, or *in actively seeking to thwart*, the process of democratic

23 Arne Johan Vetlesen, *Evil and Human Agency: Understanding Collective Evildoing* (Cambridge: Cambridge University Press, 2005), 153, emphasis added.

24 MacDonald, *Balkan Holocaust?*, 71.

25 Thomas, *Serbia under Milošević*, 47.

26 MacDonald, *Balkan Holocaust?*, 71.

> consolidation. It follows that if contingent factors played a role in the failure of democratic development in Serbia during the 1990s then there was no cultural *inevitability to the triumph of authoritarianism.*[27]

In other words, it was individuals and personalities who were responsible for the triumph of authoritarianism, and not the end of the Cold War, nor the presence of ancient ethnic hatreds. Authoritarianism, on the other hand, necessitated a nationalist discourse to survive: "Milošević and his supporters from within the regime apparatus were not only able to use nationalism to cling to power at the end of the 1980s, but would continue throughout the 1990s to use 'nationalist mobilisation' as a means by which Serbian society could be kept in a state of 'permanent revolution'."[28]

The Kosovo battle of 1389 provided perfect materials for the creation of nationalist myths, especially myths designed to polarise public opinion, portray the values of 'unity' and parade Milošević as the great unifier (see the content of the Gazimestan speech). However, as Thomas outlines, "Of perhaps greater influence was the way in which the events of the battle of Kosovo were incorporated into, and elaborated in, a body of folk poetry which developed amongst the Serbian communities within the Ottoman empire."[29]

These are myths that recurred thanks to the immobilisation of history throughout the 1990s, serving the political purposes of the Serbian leadership. The first myth (the acquisition of redemption through defeat) was very much present on the eve of the NATO strikes. The other myth (absolute need to avoid Serbian disunity) played an important role in justifying policies directed towards the abolition of Albanian autonomy and the bringing of the province under the direct control of Belgrade. The Kosovo myth also played a role in determining Serbian views and policies throughout the Yugoslav crisis, and especially in Bosnia. The particular significance

27 Thomas, *Serbia under Milošević*, 4, emphasis added.

28 Ibid., 5.

29 Thomas continues, "In these poems historical personages were transformed into mythic archetypes of virtue and villainy. The Serbian leader, Lazar, became the embodiment of saintly self-sacrifice. According to legend, on the eve of the battle of Kosovo, Lazar had been offered the choice between 'earthly' victory in the battle against the Ottomans, or to suffer defeat and death thereby securing spiritual victory and the 'heavenly kingdom'. By choosing the latter course he sacrificed himself so that his people could attain future redemption. The poem also celebrated the exemplary heroism of Miloš Obilić. Before the battle Obilić had been accused of treason, and during the next day's fighting he had sought to redeem his own personal honour and avenge the defeat of the Serbian army by infiltrating the Ottoman camp and killing Sultan Murat before being slain himself…While Obilić's conduct was celebrated that of Vuk Branković was deplored. Branković, a Serbian noble and Lazar's son-in law, had betrayed his leader and his people by refusing during the battle of Kosovo to commit his fighters to the struggle. Vuk Branković would remain an enduring symbol of the dangers posed to the Serbian people by internal strife and disunity." Ibid., 13.

of Kosovo was outlined in 1983 by the Orthodox ecclesiastical establishment. It is difficult to find a more suitable description of the myth's construction as a modern nationalist ideology reliant on empty time and metaphysical approaches:

> Kosovo is not simply a physical dwelling place rather it is a metaphysical creation. This Serbian homeland situated between the land and the sky translates a spiritual phenomenon into one of time and space. That is the greatest demonstration that ownership of a land cannot simply be reckoned in terms of numbers, or the composition of the mass of its inhabitants, but rather it is a spiritual concept which has come into being in an existential way. The process of ideogenesis is in this case the most important from ethnogenesis.[30]

The Banality of Ethnic Conflict and Immanent Power Struggles

At this point, the likes of Cviic ask: "In 1991 Milošević converted to the concept of the Greater Serbia that had previously been the preserve of nationalists like Vuk Draskovic and Vojislav Seselj. This was a political master-stroke because it completed the process of Milošević's transformation into a national icon. *But what made this possible? Why did the Serbs respond to him so well?*"

The point is that they did not. In fact,

> ...in early elections in Serbia, Slobodan Milošević controlled the media and essentially bought the vote by illegally using public funds – hardly a sign of enormous public appeal, and an act that was foolhardy as well because it greatly accelerated the breakup of the country. Moreover, like Tudjman's party, Milošević's party was comparatively well organized and widely based and had an enormous advantage under the election rules. Although it garnered less than half the vote, it gained 78 percent of the seats. Milošević's fortunes were further enhanced because Kosovo Albanians boycotted the election, allowing his party to win that area.[31]

In this context, the idea according to which Milošević used the Kosovo-Serbian unity myth in order to deprive Kosovo from its autonomy[32] precisely to ensure that

---

30 Ibid., 38.

31 John Mueller, "The Banality of 'Ethnic War'", *International Security* Vol. 25, no. 1 (2000), 45–46.

32 Two months before the Gazimestan speech, "Kosovo was finally brought under Milošević's control on 23 March 1989 when the Kosovo assembly voted itself out of existence following heavy deployments of Serbian police and troops of the Yugoslav National Army (JNA) and the arrest of the deposed Albanian provincial leader, Azem Vllasi". Thomas, *Serbia under Milošević,* 46. Albanian abstention in the 1990 elections came as a result of this development.

Kosovo Albanians – who were unlikely to fall for such nationalist agenda – did not participate in the vote, is not entirely implausible. The fact remains that had they voted in the election there was every chance that Milošević would have lost it.[33]

Further evidence that nationalism was not rampant in Yugoslavia is presented by Mueller:

> A poll conducted throughout Yugoslavia in the summer and autumn of 1990, even as the nationalists were apparently triumphing in elections, more accurately indicates the state of opinion after centuries of supposed ethnic hatreds and after years of nationalist propaganda. The question, "Do you agree that every (Yugoslav) nation should have a national state of its own"? elicited the following responses: completely agree, 16 percent; agree to some extent, 7 percent; undecided, 10 percent; do not agree in part, 6 percent; and do not agree at all, 61 percent.[34]

A Complexity-informed epistemic approach demands that we look at the immanent political struggle which generated the nationalist discourse which then characterised the conflict. Whilst it has been possible to answer Cviic's first question (what made it possible?) by outlining how the nationalist discourse followed strictly modern epistemic rules, which were further refined by Anderson's critique of 'homogeneous and empty time', an answer to the second question (Why did they respond to it so well? – the answer being, they did not) allows us to further understand why the conflicts were fought in the way they were, and how the construction of the Kosovo historically linear myth characterised all clashes in the former Yugoslavia throughout the 1990s.

For example, it is precisely because there was a nearly absolute absence of nationalist rhetoric that the war in Bosnia had to be fought by paramilitary forces. On the absence of ancient ethnic hatreds in Bosnia, consider: "…the casual notion that each ethnic or national group in Yugoslavia (or indeed anywhere else) is united by deep bonds of affection is substantially flawed. Serbs in Serbia have expressed little affection for the desperate and often rough rural Serbs who have fled to their country from war-torn Croatia and Bosnia."[35] And: "The great divide within Yugoslav society was increasingly that between rural and urban communities, not that between peoples".[36]

33 On this point, see Susan Woodward, *Balkan Tragedy: Chaos and Dissolution after the Cold War* (Washington: Brookings, 1995), 121.

34 Mueller, "The Banality of 'Ethnic War'", 46. On this point see also Laslo Sekelj, *Yugoslavia: The Process of Disintegration* (Highland Lakes: Atlantic Research and Publications 1992), 277.

35 Mueller, "The Banality of 'Ethnic War'", 97.

36 Christopher Bennett, *Yugoslavia's Bloody Collapse* (New York: New York University Press, 1995), 63.

In support of this latter argument, Peter Maas observes that "to a surprising extent, this was a war of poor rural Serbs against wealthier urban Muslims, a *Deliverance* scenario."[37] Donia and Fine conclude that it was the "relatively uneducated armed hillsmen, with an hostility toward urban culture and the state institutions (including taxes) that go with it...*who proved susceptible to Serbian chauvinist propaganda*...allowing themselves to be recruited into Serb paramilitary units and formed a significant portion of those shelling Bosnia's cities."[38] Thus, the reliance on paramilitaries. Indeed, the Yugoslav army fell apart very quickly – 'Yugoslav' soldiers did not really know what they were fighting for, and refused to be drafted. Mass desertion did not really leave many options for those willing to pay any price to cause havoc, and the use of (criminal) paramilitaries became not only very attractive, but the only viable solution. Mueller provides comprehensive evidence of this:

> Significantly, the Serbian (or Yugoslav) army substantially disintegrated early in the hostilities. There may well have been hatreds, and there surely was propaganda. But when ordinary Serb soldiers were given an opportunity to express these presumed proclivities or to act in response to the ingenious televised imprecations in government-sanctioned violence, they professed they did not know why they were fighting and often mutinied or deserted en masse. Meanwhile, back in Serbia young men reacted mainly by determined draft-dodging. Some 150,000 or more quickly emigrated or went underground. In one city, only two of the 2,000–3,000 "volunteers" expected in a call-up showed up, and in several towns there were virtual mutinies against conscription. Overall, only 50 percent of Serbian reservists and only 15 percent in Belgrade obeyed orders to report for duty. Because Serbs from Serbia proper were unwilling to fight outside their own republic, Belgrade had to reshape its approach to the wars in Croatia and Bosnia in major ways. As a Serbian general put it, modification of Belgrade's military plans was made necessary by the "lack of success in mobilisation and the desertion rate". Part of the solution involved arming the locals, particularly in Serb areas of Croatia and Bosnia. But in general the fighting quality of the militaries, especially initially, was very poor: There was a lack of discipline, ineffective command and control, and, especially in the case of the Serbs, a reluctance to take casualties. Such deficiencies, as Steven Burg and Paul Shoup observe, "led all sides to rely on irregulars and special units."[39]

A quick analysis of the situation in Bosnia is important because: 1) the Kosovo myth was utilised to justify actions that otherwise may have been regarded as lacking legitimacy, 2) the situation largely conditioned the way in which developments in Kosovo were interpreted, and in particular, 3) by the end of the war in Bosnia

37 Peter Maas, *Love Thy Neighbor: A Story of War* (New York: Knopf, 1995), 159.

38 Robert Donia and John Fine, *Bosnia and Hercegovina: A Tradition Betrayed* (New York: Columbia University Press, 1994), 28, emphasis added.

39 Mueller, "The Banality of 'Ethnic War'", 48–49.

the conflict had already been framed along 'ancient ethnic hatreds' lines: this very much conditioned NATO's decision to initiate the bombing campaign.

For the first point above, it is important to consider the reality of combatants who operated largely outside established military frameworks and who suffered from a particularly bad reputation.[40] Not surprisingly, the appeal to myths – allowed for by the original delineation of such myths as a matter of national policy – became very attractive for legitimising what constituted, otherwise, actions that were broadly regarded as being criminal.[41]

For the second point above (the situation in Bosnia largely conditioned the way in which developments in Kosovo were interpreted), it may be interesting to take official stances at face value. The UK Parliament's Foreign Affairs Select Committee identified the primary reason behind intervention in Kosovo: "Guilt over past inaction regarding Bosnia (the then Defence Secretary, George Robertson, said on 12 June 1998: 'the world has learned its lessons from Bosnia. The international community now knows it must be united, firm and determined from the earliest possible moment in dealing with the Balkans'".[42]

It has been established that the absence of nationalist fervour is precisely what led to the strategy of relying primarily on paramilitaries. Thus, if it can be reasonably argued that those paramilitaries committed most of the actions over which past inaction generated a sense of guilt, it would be possible to argue that, by extension, it was precisely the absence of nationalist fervour that led to the atrocities in Bosnia, which in turn led to the intervention in Kosovo. Indeed, the link between paramilitary action and serious war crimes is well documented.[43]

40 As Mueller explains, "The most dynamic (and murderous) Serbian units were notably composed not of committed nationalists or ideologues, nor of locals out to get their neighbours, nor of ordinary people whipped into a frenzy by demagogues and the media, but rather of common criminals recruited for the task. Specifically, the politicians urged underworld and hooligan groups to get into the action, and it appears that thousands of prison inmates, promised shortened sentences and enticed by the prospect that they could 'take whatever booty you can', were released for the war effort". Ibid.

41 For example, "On 28 June [1995], shortly after his troops had repelled the Bosnian government assault, Mladić celebrated in the town of Bijeljina. Speaking to his fighters, he recalled the circumstances of the battle of Kosovo and affirmed his continuing sense of personal mission. He said that on the day of the battle "Prince Lazar took communion with his army and submitted himself to the heavenly kingdom, defending his fatherland, faith, freedom and the honour of the Serbian nation. We must understand the essence of that sacrifice so that we can draw from it a historical lesson. The fact that we have today created a victorious army has ensured that Lazar's sacrifice has passed beyond the realms of simple myth". Thomas, *Serbia under Milošević*, 237.

42 House of Commons, Foreign Affairs Select Committee, "Fourth Report: Kosovo. Volume 1, Report and Proceedings of the Committee", 23 May 2000, 27.

43 "As Susan Woodward notes, paramilitary gangs, foreign mercenaries, and convicted criminals roamed the territory under ever less civil control. And 'war crimes', observes Norman Cigar, were their 'primary military mission'. Vladan Vasilijević, an expert on

A United Nations (UN) commission notes a "strong correlation between paramilitary activity and reports of killing of civilians, rape, torture, destruction of property, looting, detention facilities, and mass graves."[44]

Then, of course, we have Srebrenica. What probably remains the most comprehensive enquiry on the matter was the report commissioned by the Dutch Government to the Netherlands Institute for War Documentation.[45] As the BBC reported, "former Yugoslav President Slobodan Milošević – on trial at The Hague on a genocide charge citing Srebrenica – is not linked to the killings by the researchers. 'No evidence had been found that suggests the involvement of the Serbian authorities in Belgrade,' the report says."[46]

Commenting on the report, Noam Chomsky contends that

> …the worst crime, the one that they were really going to charge him [Milošević] for that genocide was Srebrenica. Now, there is a little problem with that: namely there was an extensive, detailed inquiry into it by the Dutch Government, which was the responsible government, there were Dutch forces there, that's a big, you know, hundreds of pages of inquiry, and their conclusion is that Milošević did not know anything about that, and that when it was discovered in Belgrade, they were horrified.[47]

---

organized crime, says that most of the well-documented atrocities in Bosnia were committed by men with long criminal records." Mueller, "The Banality of 'Ethnic War'", 52.

44 Ibid. Please note that stating that irregular forces committed the majority of the crimes in Bosnia (Kosovo being a different case) does not mean that official forces did not commit any, nor does it diminish the burden of guilt of either regular or irregular forces. There is something paradoxical, however, in having the ICTY trying to prove Milošević's direct involvement in massacres such as Srebrenica: arguably his biggest crime was the absence of direct involvement, and the fact that such a lack led to a situation of virtual anarchy in Serb-controlled areas. Although that is the law and there is not much the ICTY could have done about it, the current situation seems to send a message according to which genocide committed by proxy may go unpunished, because it generates situations in which it is very difficult to assign direct responsibility, precisely because it was done by proxy (and vice-versa – serious crimes may be committed by proxy precisely because such crimes are likely to go unpunished). The issue of the differential level of analysis that has been applied in the legal discourse (aggregate for NATO, individual for the former Yugoslavia) is addressed in the next chapter. Perhaps it would have been better to adopt an aggregate level of responsibility for the likes of Milošević, for that is where their responsibilities mainly rest.

45 Peter Romijn and JCH Blom, *Srebrenica: A Safe Area. Reconstruction, Background, Consequences and Analyses of the Fall of the Safe Area* (Amsterdam: Netherlands Institute for War Documentation, 2002). Available online at: http://www.niod.nl/default.asp (accessed 15 April 2008).

46 BBC, "Srebrenica blame 'must be shared'", 10 April 2002, http://news.bbc.co.uk/2/hi/europe/1920357.stm (accessed 15 April 2008).

47 Noam Chomsky, "On the NATO Bombing of Yugoslavia: Noam Chomsky interviewed by Danilo Mandic", RTS Online, 25 April 2006. Interview available online at: http://www.chomsky.info/interviews/20060425.htm (accessed 15 April 2008).

The Dutch report has not remained unchallenged,[48] and claims that point to the local nature of the massacre should not be necessarily interpreted as attempts at removing responsibility at the central level.[49] The point here is that the absence of nationalist feeling led to the very formation of paramilitaries who, acting under varying degrees of central control, committed the bulk of the atrocities in the former Yugoslavia. This is not being argued in order to discuss responsibility, but in order to demonstrate the argument according to which it was the absence of 'ancient ethnic hatreds' that determined how the conflict developed in the first instance, and how it was interpreted (precisely as the opposite of what it was, that is, a case of ancient hatreds) in the second instance. As Mueller concisely put it, "Ethnicity proved essentially to be simply the characteristic around which the perpetrators and the politicians who recruited and encouraged them happened to array themselves. It was important as an ordering device or principle, not as a crucial motivating force."[50]

The rest of this chapter will be largely about defending the third point above (interpretation of the Kosovo crisis as an issue of ancient ethnic hatreds). The next section will also look at how the absence of nationalistic feelings in Serbia shaped Serbian strategy towards the Kosovo issue, exploiting such issue in the context of immanent political struggles.

Clashes of Modernities: Apprehensions of Time in Reaction to Nationalist Discourse

At this point, an observation could be reasonably made: the fact that ethnic hatreds were absent in Bosnia does not necessarily mean that they were absent in Kosovo. This final section will counter such hypothetical observation by seeking to argue two related points:

1. The conflict in Kosovo had a priori been construed on the basis of historical linearity by key players and shapers of public opinion following the flawed understanding of the Bosnian tragedy. However, historical linearity characterised responses to Bosnia and to Kosovo differently: whereas

48 Consider, for example, an article published by Karen Meirik, "Controversial Srebrenica Report Back on Table", the Institute for Peace and War Reporting, 6 February 2004: http://www.iwpr.net/?p=tri&s=f&o=166497&apc_state=henitri2004 (accessed 15 April 2008).

49 On the contrary, Belgrade has enormous responsibilities for forming and arming the paramilitaries in the first instance, and letting them run loose in the second instance. An important contribution here is provided by Bob de Graaff, "The Difference Between Legal Proof and Historical Evidence: The Trial of Slobodan Milošević and the Case of Srebrenica", *European Review* Vol. 14 (2006), 499–512.

50 Mueller, "The Banality of 'Ethnic War", 62.

Bosnia was a matter of "letting the violence run its course" (Mueller, below), Kosovo was the opposite, and it was so precisely because of a notion of guilt, which was caused by an excess of violence in Bosnia, which was itself caused by reliance on paramilitaries because of the *absence* of ancient ethnic hatreds. Chapters 5 and 6 will demonstrate how a mixture of historical linearity and analytical finitude conditioned NATO's campaign.
2. The modus operandi of the Kosovo conflict proper was not entirely dissimilar from the Bosnian experience. It was mainly characterised – contrary to the perceptions of many – by immanent political struggles implemented by proxy due to the overwhelming absence of intense ancient ethnic hatreds.

Michael Brown produced a timely reminder of the way in which 'ethnic' conflicts are perceived by outlining a short compendium of relevant statements:

> Many policymakers and journalists believe that the causes of internal conflicts are simple and straightforward. The driving forces behind these violent conflicts, it is said, are the 'ancient hatreds' that many ethnic and religious groups have for each other. In Eastern Europe, the former Soviet Union, and elsewhere, these deep-seated animosities were held in check for years by authoritarian rule. The collapse of authoritarian rule, it is argued, has taken the 'lid' off these ancient rivalries, allowing long-suppressed grievances to come to the surface and escalate into armed conflict. US President George Bush, for example, maintained that the war in Bosnia between Serbs, Croats and Muslims grew out of 'age-old animosities'. His successor, Bill Clinton, argued that the end of the Cold War "lifted a lid from a cauldron of long-simmering hatreds. Now, the entire global terrain is bloody with such conflicts". Writing about the Balkans, the American political commentator Richard Cohen declared that "Bosnia is a formidable, scary place of high mountains, brutish people, and tribal grievances rooted in history and myth born of boozy nights by the fire. It's the place where World War I began and where the wars of Europe persist, an ember of hate still glowing for reasons that defy reason itself". Serious scholars reject this explanation of internal conflict.[51]

It would appear that the creation of 'vacuous, empty time' is not only present in the formulation of nationalist myths, but that it is equally present in the understanding of other issues as nationalist problems proper. Furthermore, the intellectual apparatus in question works in ways that are strikingly similar to the way in which academic IR – that modern empirical science based on transcendental philosophies of the object – argues that "the enduring anarchic character of international politics accounts for the striking sameness in the quality of international life through the

51 Michael Brown, "The Causes of Internal Conflict", in *Nationalism and Ethnic Conflict*, Revised Edition, eds, Michael Brown, Owen Coté, Sean Lynn-Jones and Steven Miller (Cambridge: MIT Press, 2001), 3.

millennia."[52] Note that in both cases the organising principle is anarchy – anarchy thus provides the objective transcendental on the bases of which the subjects will be studied. In one case, anarchy is the result of the collapse of order (the removal of the Communist lid), in the other case it is an enduring characteristic of international politics. Again, the formation of theories of IR are not studied in virtue of what they *say* or claim to explain, rather, they are studied in virtue of what they (epistemically) *represent*.

The presence of this empty, linear time is evident in the images that the discourse deploys to offer explanations for the conflict. As such, the construction of the nationalist myth on the one hand, and the interpretation of a conflict as having nationalist causes on the other hand, correspond to an enforcement of the historical linearity and empty time Anderson and Foucault identify as a primary component of the modern episteme. These are essentially modern understandings of conflicts which, in the end, generate and deploy similar understandings of conflicts. Under this perspective, Žižek is not entirely wrong when he argues:

> Recently, one of the American negotiators said that Milosevic is not only part of the problem, but rather the problem itself. However, was this not clear from the very beginning? Why, then, the interminable procrastination of the Western powers, playing for years into Milošević's hands, acknowledging him as a key factor of stability in the region, misreading clear cases of Serb aggression as civil or even tribal warfare, initially putting the blame on those who immediately saw what Milošević stands for and, for that reason, desperately wanted to escape his grasp (see James Baker's public endorsement of a "limited military intervention" against Slovene secession), supporting the last Yugoslav prime minister Ante Markovic, whose program was, in an incredible case of political blindness, seriously considered as the last chance for a democratic market-oriented unified Yugoslavia, etc.? When the West fights Milošević, it is not fighting its enemy, one of the last points of resistance against the liberal-democratic New World Order; it is rather fighting its own creature, a monster that grew as the result of the compromises and inconsistencies of the Western politics itself.[53]

We would add that such inconsistencies are generated precisely by the nature of modernity: the fact that the West fights 'its own creature' is epitomised by the fact that the West understood the conflict precisely in the same way as the perpetrators of such conflict understood it and wanted it to be understood: in other words, such understandings all belong to the same modern way of generating and deploying knowledge.

In this context, it is interesting to see how the recurring images and discursive techniques (for example, reliance on the notion of memory) can be found in Milošević's Gazimestan speech, in the presidential statements above, and in any

52 Waltz, "Laws and Theories", 53.

53 Žižek, *Against the Double Blackmail*, strong emphasis in the original.

attempt to validate the 'ancient ethnic hatred' hypothesis. For example, Robert Kaplan made extensive use of relevant discursive techniques as he systematically "described the Balkans as 'a region of pure memory' where 'each individual sensation and memory affects the grand movement of clashing peoples', and where the processes of history and memory were 'kept on hold' by communism for forty-five years, 'thereby creating a kind of multiplier effect for violence'."[54]

These arguments are not inconsequential: in this context, it is not surprising to learn that Clinton was fond of Kaplan's Balkan doomsday books, and that such books significantly influenced Clinton's policy in the Balkans.[55] In any case, assumptions of historical linearity can be found throughout relevant biographical accounts of the key people who shaped policy towards Kosovo from the mid 1990s onwards. Clinton's views on Bosnia are outlined above, but just to confirm that those very same views persisted in the case of Kosovo: consider what the then President announced to his nation on 24 March 1999: "Take a look at this map. Kosovo is a small place, but sits on a major fault line between Europe, Asia and the Middle East, at the meeting place of Islam and both the Western and Orthodox branches of Christianity…all the ingredients for a major war are there: ancient grievances…"[56]

It is interesting that Clinton adopted this view, which – to his credit – he later publicly regretted on 14 May 1999, stating:

> There are those who say Europe and its North American allies have no business intervening in the ethnic conflicts of the Balkans. They are the inevitable results, these conflicts, according to some, of centuries-old animosities which were unleashed by the end of the Cold War restraints in Yugoslavia and elsewhere. *I, myself, have been guilty of saying that on an occasion or two, and I regret it now more than I can say.* For I have spent a great deal of time in these last six years reading the real history of the Balkans, and the truth is that a lot of what passes for common wisdom in this area is a gross oversimplification and misreading of history. The truth is that for centuries these people have lived together in the Balkans and southeastern Europe with greater or lesser degree of tensions, but often without anything approaching the intolerable conditions and conflicts that exist today.[57]

54 Mueller, "The Banality of 'Ethnic War'", 44.

55 Michael Kaufman. "The Dangers of Letting a President Read", *The New York Times*, 22 May 1999, http://query.nytimes.com/gst/fullpage.html?res=9E00E6D61631F931A15756C0A96F958260&partner=rssnyt&emc=rss (last accessed 7 July 2008). http://query.nytimes.com/gst/fullpage.html?res=9E00E6D61631F931A15756C0A96F958260&sec=&spon=&pagewanted=all (accessed 15 April 2008).

56 Auerswald, *The Kosovo Conflict*, 730.

57 CNN, "Transcript: Clinton Justifies U.S. Involvement in Kosovo", 19 May 1999, http://www.cnn.com/ALLPOLITICS/stories/1999/05/13/clinton.kosovo/transcript.html (accessed 15 April 2008), emphasis added.

Yet, why is it that the 'common wisdom' Clinton refers to is based on a "gross oversimplification and misreading of history"? Could we be dealing here with some sort of 'modern epistemic reflex'? Because such 'common wisdom', as the next chapters will also outline, was certainly present in the minds of most key policy makers (including Clinton) as key decisions regarding the various Balkan conflicts (including Kosovo's) were being made.[58] If this was the case, Complexity could be an ideal remedy for this reflexive disorder, as it is argued in the conclusion of this chapter. Chris O'Sullivan has explored at length the nature of this reflex in the major formers of public opinion – and considering the role that public opinion increasingly plays in determining geopolitical goals, as Kolossov and O'Loughlin argue,[59] this is a matter of extreme importance:

> These conflicts are often described as 'ancient ethnic conflicts' pitting 'neighbor against neighbor' which are rooted in, and conditioned by *an abstract and seemingly unknowable 'history'*. While generally acknowledged as tragic, these events often persist because 'that's just the way those people are'. Such statements have tremendous consequences for shaping public opinion, as well as for influencing the views of public officials…When the news media do focus on world conflicts, it frequently emphasises one particular causation at the expense of other possible explanations. Media concentration on 'ethnic identity' *and 'history' with its stress on inevitability and determinism*, can often overlook the critical political and economic factors that contribute to violence. Such approaches can contribute to popular misconceptions of wars being fought solely for 'historical' and 'ethnic' reasons which are beyond the comprehension of everyday media users. *Increasingly, historical context is offered, if at all, as a 'final verdict'. In many cases, historical analogies and precedents are used, not to lend context or substance to a particular conflict, but to support an all-encompassing theory to explain a specific conflict.*[60]

If any concrete example of how Anderson's continuous time is necessary in order to understand any conflict as a modern, nationalist conflict, consider the quotes of many prominent journalists:

> "The Battle of Kosovo", wrote *Time Magazine*'s Lance Morrow, "when the Turks, advancing west toward Vienna in 1389, defeated the Serbs and left their bodies to the crows – *might have been the day before yesterday*". "Is it better to remember or to forget?" wrote *Time Magazine*'s Lance Morrow in the midst of

58 John Norris, *Collision Course*, 19.

59 O'Loughlin and Kolossov. "Still Not Worth the Bones of a Single Pomeranian Grenadier: the Geopolitics of the Kosovo War 1999".

60 Chris O'Sullivan, "The News Media and the Resolution of Ethnic Conflict: Ready for the Next Steps?", *The Global Review of Ethnopolitics* Vol. 1, no. 2 (2001), 55 and 57, emphasis added.

> the Balkan conflict. "Forgetting – even without its sainted better half, forgiveness – is sometimes the only route to sanity. If only the Balkans, for example, could be enfogged by a massive forgetting. As it is, every generation of Serbs remembers, *as if it were last Saturday*, their defeat by the Turks at the Battle of Kosovo in the year 1389. The result has been centuries of self-renewing reciprocal atrocity between Serbs and Muslims. Massacre is the Balkan national flower." When violence in *Kosovo* began to grab world attention, the media had already been reporting warnings that NATO might need to occupy the Balkans for years to come. It thus seemed to many that a durable peace anywhere in the Balkans was an unattainable goal. The conflicts by and large stemmed *from ancient hatreds, many in the media asserted, and while such tensions might be buried for years or decades, they would ultimately surface*.[61]

In reality, the Kosovo conflict proper was characterised by many of the features that characterised Bosnia, namely, a pronounced reliance on paramilitaries due to a distinct absence of nationalist feeling, the whole framed in the context of immanent political struggles. As Muller puts it:

> Although there are differences, the Serb rampages in Kosovo in 1999 often resembled those seen earlier in Bosnia and Croatia. The army provided a sort of generalised support, it participated directly in some areas, and it hardly escapes blame for the results in any case. But, as one report puts it, "in hundreds of interviews" Kosovo Albanians "have said that nearly all the killings of civilians were committed by Serbian paramilitary forces and not by the regular army"... whilst released criminals formed an important component of Serb forces.[62]

The comprehensive UK Parliamentary report reaches similar conclusions:

> The fact that elements of the campaign against the Kosovo Albanians were planned does not mean that, overall, the campaign was smoothly directed and well organised. Different elements of the Serb security apparatus appear to have had different agendas. One source quoted by Tim Judah states that "there were differences between the police and the army. The police were in favour of the expulsions because they could steal money from people. The intelligence guys were against it...*the worst were the paramilitaries and the locals*". The OSCE also records that "*paramilitaries appear to have meted out particularly savage treatment*" and, by way of contrast, reports an incident where a young Serb soldier helped a wheelchair-bound Kosovo Albanian woman, returning her documents after paramilitaries had seized them, and subsequently organising food, water and medicine for a mosque where villagers were sheltering. *The picture is one of generalised violence against the Kosovo Albanians, with some*

61 Ibid., 58–60, emphasis added.

62 Mueller, "The Banality of 'Ethnic War'", 58, footnote 57.

> *elements organised from Belgrade, but much of the violence was not carefully orchestrated. This picture is consistent with a confidential memorandum provided to us by the FCO.*[63]

And the evidence suggests that this situation is largely the consequence of a distinct unwillingness on the part of the Serbian population to fight and die for Kosovo. Indeed,

> ...public opinion in Serbia was by the spring of 1998 characterised by political apathy, and social and economic exhaustion. A poll published in the *Nedeljni telegraf* showed that more than 70 per cent of those asked would be against having their close relations sent to fight in Kosovo. Even Ljubomir Tadić, the veteran *Praxis* activist who ten years earlier had played a key role in opposing the 1974 constitution, said: "I feel personally apathetic even though I understand the issue intellectually...People don't have pensions. The Americans have frozen our money. It is hard to get passionate about it".[64]

In order to reinforce this point, it would be important to elucidate some detail on the emergence of the warring parties before examining some of the detail of the run up to the crisis outlined in the table opposite.

The emergence of Albanian armed resistance in Kosovo broadly obeyed the same patterns that applied to the formation of Serb paramilitaries in Croatia and Bosnia. The first known incident involving the Kosovo Liberation Army occurred on 22 April 1996 when three Serbian refugees from Krajina were killed whilst drinking in a café. On the same night, two policemen were killed in the towns of Peć and Štimlje. To most people's mind, the idea that a genuine provincial guerrilla movement could have committed such acts was not even worth contemplating. Indeed,

> ...when a group called the Kosovo Liberation Army claimed responsibility for the attacks...the mainstream Albanian political leadership in Kosovo sought to cast doubt on the idea that these killings were the work of Albanians using 'terrorist' methods. According to Ibrahim Rugova they were more likely to be a "provocation whose origins can be found in Serbian extremist circles". It came to be widely believed that the UCK [KLA] was in fact a creation of the Serbian state and its agencies. While it was perhaps not surprising that such a belief should take root among the Albanian population, who were fundamentally alienated from the Serbian state and its institutions, it was more remarkable, and indicative, that *such ideas should find an echo with key Serbian 'opinion*

63 House of Commons, Foreign Affairs Select Committee, "Fourth Report: Kosovo. Volume 1, Report and Proceedings of the Committee", 23 May 2000: paragraphs 97–98, strong emphasis added.

64 Thomas, *Serbia under Milošević,* 410.

Table 6.1 Chronology of the crisis

1997	
September	Contact Group discusses Kosovo
September–November	European pressure on Belgrade for dialogue
November	KLA attack Serb patrol
1998	
February–March	Escalating violence in Kosovo
March	North Atlantic Council expresses concern and calls for all sides to reduce tension Contact Group's 10 point action plan United Nations Security Council Resolution (UNSCR) 1160
May	Hopeful signs from Milošević/Rugova meeting dashed
June	EU Sanctions imposed NATO begins initial military planning – Cardiff European Council threatens Milošević if repression does not cease
July	KLA controls large areas of Kosovo
August	Serb counter-offensive, 250,000 internally displaced by end of month
September	UNSCR 1199 Serbian forces commit serious human rights violations in the Drenica valley. Activation warning to NATO forces
October	Holbrooke to Belgrade – Activation Orders by NATO – Milošević agrees to verification – UNSCR 1203 – Activation Orders put on "soft trigger"
November	OSCE verifiers arrive, but violence continues
November–December	Christopher Hill shuttle diplomacy
1999	
January	Raçak massacre – Hill draws up package as basis for Rambouillet – NATO's solemn warning
February	Rambouillet begins
March	Holbrooke in Belgrade – Talks reconvene at Kleber Centre, and are adjourned – Holbrooke again in Belgrade – Bombing begins

formers' in Kosovo. In January 1997, for instance, when the Serb rector of Priština University, Radovoje Papović, was injured in a bomb attack, for which the UCK [KLA] reportedly claimed responsibility, the Serbian Orthodox bishop of Raška-Prozen, Artemije, publicly emphasised that it remained 'unclear' who was behind the bombing and he suggested that the 'regime' could have been the true initiator of the attacks.[65]

65 Ibid., 400, strong emphasis added.

And, yet, the KLA really existed: but it was more the product of the generalised permissiveness allowed for by the collapse of state authority – itself caused by the incapability of the Serbian military apparatus to control the situation – than by a widespread popular sentiment. Indeed, few question the fact that the movement was financed by organised crime.[66] Also, there is every chance that the movement started as a means of providing territorial safe-heavens for organised criminal activity: "Observers noted that in the area of both sides of the border between Kosovo and Albania the UCK [KLA] insurrection was being used as a cover for the activities of various criminal gangs."[67]

By early 1998, the KLA had managed to effectively control the Drenica valley. Whilst this did not constitute a major security threat, such development was disastrous in the context of the very difficult political situation Milošević was facing at home. Indeed, the escalation of violence in Kosovo was rendering intense political negotiations between Milošević's Socialist Party of Serbia (SPS) and the Serbia Renewal Movement (SPO) very difficult for Milošević, "as the commencement of hostilities in Kosovo facilitated a fundamental change in the Serbian political landscape…as the negotiations progressed the SPO had significantly raised the level of their demands."[68] In a sense, this was unsurprising: after all, Milošević was coming under attack for failing to fulfil expectations precisely in the context of the myth upon which much of his political career was constructed. As such, accusations of betrayal had a certain multiplier effect, especially when these were pronounced – with a certain degree of perceived plausibility – by the likes of Momčilo Trajkovič, the president of the Serbian Resistance Movement (the main movement of Serbs in Kosovo): "Kosovo and Metohija helped Milošević and the Socialist Party of Serbia to achieve and preserve power, now the regime wants to turn the people against Kosovo and is seeking to create a situation in which the public will find it easy to accept some future act which will free Serbia from the burden which is called Kosovo."[69]

This is the political background of one of the most violent episodes in the conflict, that is, the Serb assault on the Drenica valley. Indeed, "Milošević seemed to believe that decisive police/military action in the Drenica region would allow him once again to present himself as the defender of the Kosovo Serbs. He calculated that, as on previous occasions in his career, the rhetoric and symbolism

66 Roger Boyes and Eske Wright, "Drugs Money Linked to the Kosovo Rebels," *The Times* (London), 24 March 1999. Also consider the recent serious allegations made by Carla del Ponte, former prosecutor at the ICTY and Ian Traynor, "Former war crimes prosecutor alleges Kosovan army harvested organs from Serb prisoners", *The Guardian* (Manchester) Saturday, 12 April 2008. http://www.guardian.co.uk/world/2008/apr/12/warcrimes.kosovo (accessed 16 April 2008).

67 Thomas, *Serbia under Milošević,* 412.

68 Ibid., 414.

69 Ibid., 401.

of nationalism could be used to rally popular support behind him."[70] Nonetheless, Milošević was well aware that war in Kosovo would have jeopardised the excellent links he had been cultivating with the international community. In this context, the events of 23 February 1998 are significant, as

> ...Robert Gelbard, the US envoy in the Balkans, gave a press conference in Priština in which he praised Milošević in lavish terms and described the UCK [KLA] as a terrorist organisation. These comments were made shortly after Milorad Dodik had been appointed, with Milošević's backing, as Prime Minister in the Republika Srpska and Gelbard was apparently trying in these statements to highlight the 'positive' role played by Milošević in these events. Milošević, however, chose to interpret Gelbard's gesture as a 'green light' for a security crackdown in Kosovo.[71]

Thus began the planning for the assault on the Drenica valley. Yet, with very few Serbs willing to fight – precisely because of a manifest lack of nationalist fervour[72] – and with the army in a state of disarray, Milošević had to rely on paramilitaries and special units. As such, "the operations were reportedly spearheaded by members of the Special Anti-terrorist Unit (SAJ)."[73] Just to confirm that the SAJ conform with the notion of a special unit populated by thugs and petty criminals presented by Mueller in the context of Bosnia,

> ...the SAJ effectively acted as Milošević's personal praetorian guard within the state security apparatus. During the war in Bosnia the SAJ had organised the arming and training of paramilitaries, and had even co-operated with them in the field. During the opposition winter protests of 1996/7 members of the SAJ were reported to be roaming the streets of Belgrade looking for demonstrators to beat up. In the autumn of 1997 Simatović's men were back in Bosnia attempting, unsuccessfully, to engineer the overthrow of Biljana Plavšić. In Kosovo in early 1998 the SAJ were once again in the front rank acting as the trusted executors of Milošević's policies.[74]

It is, thus, not surprising that the first major military operation – which had to be conducted, by the force of necessity, by infra-military means – coincided with gross human rights violations. As Human Rights Watch observed:

70 Ibid., 405.

71 Ibid., 406.

72 This lack of fervour is also what characterised Milošević's political problems at home, and Kosovo was precisely an attempt at revitalising the nationalist discourse. See Thomas, *Serbia under Milošević,* Chapter 29.

73 Ibid., 407.

74 Ibid.

> The Yugoslav Army, Serbian police, and paramilitaries were all responsible for war crimes in Kosovo. In general, however, *paramilitaries appear to have been more extensively involved in the most violent abuses, specifically the executions and rapes*. While police and army units are by no means exempt from responsibility in this regard, *the paramilitaries were more commonly engaged in arbitrary killings and sexual violence*. But paramilitary forces were not operating on their own. On the contrary, paramilitary units were operating in close concert with the police, army, and secret police (known as the state security service). There may have been specific incidents when paramilitary units or individuals got out of control, but the general deployment of paramilitary units and their coordination with other sectors of the security apparatus were planned components of the Kosovo campaign.[75]

The fact that SAJ reported directly to Milošević means that it is more likely that they were under Milošević's direct control. Nonetheless, as stated above, "There may have been specific incidents when paramilitary units or individuals got out of control".

Whether the primary driving force behind NATO's intervention – the Raçak massacre, which brought Holocaust-like memories back via Srebrenica – was characterised by paramilitaries "getting out of control" or by direct central orders, is a matter of considerable controversy. What is for sure, is that there was a substantial paramilitary presence in the assault.[76] British journalist Julius Strauss conducted extensive research into the matter. According to the survivors that he interviewed:

> …a small group of men dressed all in black and wearing gloves and balaclavas… co-ordinated the attack on the village and the subsequent executions. Men had been separated from women and children before being led away to be executed. Some of the Serbs were in blue, some in black. The men in black appeared to be in control and wore balaclavas over their heads. Some had uniforms with insignia which included a Serbian flag; some had none. They carried automatic guns and, as we were led up the hill, both units started shooting us.[77]

In a slight modification of Cviic's question, we could ask, "there is ample evidence that the conflict was not generated by ancient ethnic hatreds, yet public opinion and key policy makers understood it as if it was. Why?". Our Complexity-inspired epistemic approach can begin to provide an answer. Facing a situation that it

75 Human Rights Watch. *Under Orders: War Crimes in Kosovo – 3, Forces in the Conflict*, http://www.hrw.org/reports/2001/kosovo/undword-02.htm (accessed 16 April 2008), emphasis added.

76 As outlined in Ignatieff, *Virtual War: Kosovo and Beyond*, 59.

77 Julius Strauss. "Military 'death squads' behind Kosovo massacre". *Daily Telegraph*, 27 January 1999.

struggled to understand, the "West" sought to make sense of the circumstances. Naturally, in trying to understand the situation, the crisis was objectified, analysed and studied according to the fundamental rules of the modern episteme, which quickly proceeded to fully enforce historical linearity in order to make the situation understandable and knowable on the basis of a classical transcendental philosophy of the object (anarchy). Whilst Mueller argues that in the case of Bosnia "*a misguided assumption that the conflicts stemmed from immutable ethnic hatreds made international military intervention essentially impossible until the violence appeared to have run its course*",[78] we can argue that in the case of Kosovo exactly the opposite became true: the absence of ancient ethnic hatreds caused the particularly vicious violence in Bosnia, which culminated in Holocaust-like images which, in turn, made a similar strategy in relation to Kosovo impossible to contemplate. *An immanent Complexity approach – which refuses to acknowledge any time reversible argument – reveals that the line was crossed precisely because such ancient ethnic hatreds were mostly absent: this absence characterised the way in which the war was conducted (reliance on paramilitaries), which, in turn, determined its brutality and its crossing of ethical-analytical lines. Finally, it was precisely because the conflict was framed along the axes of the modern episteme that those lines were crossed: First, because historical linearity, as Mueller suggests above, encouraged inaction, second, because parallelisms between the massacres in Srebrenica and Raçak can only be compared to the Holocaust in the context of 'empty, homogeneous time'.*

Conclusion: Historical Linearity at Work

Paul Cilliers has noted that Complex systems share a number of characteristics with postmodern societies as Lyotard has described them:

1. Complex systems are comprised of a large number of elements;
2. The elements in a complex system interact dynamically;
3. The level of interaction is fairly rich;
4. Interactions are non-linear;
5. The interactions have a fairly short range;
6. There are loops in the interconnections;
7. *Complex systems are open systems*;
8. Complex systems operate under conditions far from equilibrium;
9. *Complex systems have histories*;
10. Individual elements are ignorant of the behaviour of the whole system in which they are embedded.

---

78 Mueller, "The Banality of 'Ethnic War'", 44, strong emphasis added. Mueller substantiates this assertion through extensive quotations and numerous references to a number of works in the article.

By analogy:

1. Postmodern societies have millions of agents operating within them at any one time;
2. The agents fulfil roles in a number of dynamic and multiple roles (teacher, consumer, parent, child, etc.);
3. In a postmodern society, the level of interaction between agents and between agents and mechanisms at the societal level are extremely rich and diverse. Examples include economic transactions and market consumption;
4. Societal relationships in postmodern society are nonlinear. It is within these asymmetrical power relationships that people operate as teachers, students, consumers, and citizens…;
5. Individuals interact on local levels. Although local levels influence other local levels, there is no "metalevel controlling the flow of information";
6. All interpretations are local, contingent and provisional. In this situation, paralogy and dissensus rather than homology prevail;
7. *Open systems such as the social interact with other open systems such as the ecological*;
8. Social disequilibrium characterizes the postmodern condition;
9. *Although the concept of history is dismissed as a grand narrative in the postmodern, local narratives tell the histories of individuals and groups*;
10. It is impossible for an individual to have a complete understanding of the operations of the entire social system in which they live and interact.[79]

These 10 features characterised the Kosovo conflict too. As such, the current research could have focussed on any of these 10, or on all of them. We would then have proceeded to define how the Kosovo crisis stood in relation to this Complex-postmodern 'checklist'. Indeed, Kosovo represented, in many respects, an incredibly 'complex' operation. The NATO machinery had to face the test of the reality of war for the very first time, a test which – according to the Supreme Allied Commander – NATO failed.[80] Reading Clark's account, the first feature of Complex systems (the large number of relevant actors) is immediately obvious: "we have 19 countries who all think they can be boss", Clark famously complained.[81]

---

79 Abraham, "Towards the End of Ethics and Law Parading as Justice", 121–22, strong emphasis added. The meaning of the term paralogy in this context relates to the use of the word in biology: paralogy is the contrary of homology, homology being the term used to describe similarities between species with common ancestors in evolutionary biology. Jean-François Lyotard uses the term paralogy to describe any movement that is opposed to established ways of reasoning. See Jean-François Lyotard, *The Postmodern Condition: A Report on Knowledge* (Minneapolis: University of Minnesota Press, 1984), 60.

80 Clark, *Waging Modern War.*

81 Alastair Campbell, *The Blair Years: Extracts from the Alastair Campbell Diaries* (London: Hutchinson, 2007), 384.

Indeed, as John O'Loughlin and Vladimir Kolossov outlined, the very geopolitical objectives of the 19 countries were being simultaneously defined by 19 – some times very different – bodies of public opinion.[82] Also, all agents involved in the crisis fulfilled "a number of dynamic and multiple roles." For example, Clark, as a four star general, was asked to transcend his military expertise and fulfil a role usually reserved for public relations experts. Much to his surprise, many in Washington were not pleased about his perceived incompetence in such area:

> "Wes, at the White House meeting today there was a lot of discussion about your press conference", Shelton began. "The Secretary of Defense asked me to give you some verbatim guidance, so here it is: 'Get your fucking face off the TV. No more briefings, period'. That's it. I just wanted to give it to you like he said it. Do you have any questions?". Unfortunately, the speaker phone was on, and several members of the staff probably heard the call.[83]

Since Clark was seen to be insufficiently savvy, NATO asked Alistair Campbell to spend some time in Brussels and coordinate NATO's public relations effort.[84]

Instead of ticking all 'Complexity criteria', or attempting to focus on a number of these characteristics enumerated above at random, the research has focussed on the two specific features that have been emphasised in the list above: Complex systems are open systems and Complex systems have histories. The epistemic approach adopted allowed for – and demanded – a discrimination of criteria precisely on the bases of a detailed understanding of the nature of the modern episteme, and a related understanding of what the requirements for transcending such modern episteme are. This epistemic approach has allowed the current research to focus on the two crucial issues of historical linearity and analytical finitude, thus allowing for the identification of clear linkages between Complexity and postmodernity, in a strictly Foucauldian sense (that is, anything that is seen as transcending the modern episteme). And those linkages are to be found precisely at the level of historical linearity – consider Prigogine's assertions on the arrow of time and his acknowledged debt to Bergson who, according to Foucault, is the first philosopher to transcend the modern episteme precisely by virtue of his thought on temporality.[85]

It is for this reason, that this chapter has focussed so much on the issue of how temporalities are constructed and deployed, and how this fundamentally determines how the conflict is framed and acted upon. A Complexity approach allows for the following statement to be made whilst an epistemic approach allows for such statement to be understood in the context of all of the implications that it entails:

82 O'Loughlin and Kolossov. "Still Not Worth the Bones of a Single Pomeranian Grenadier".

83 Clark, *Waging Modern War*, 273.

84 For an informative account see Campbell, *The Blair Years*, 362–89.

85 See Chapter 1.

the arrow of time is irreversible. If we could go back in time and see the Kosovo conflict unfolding again there is a probability of zero that it would have unfolded in the way it has. The number of emerging variables is too high, and countless butterfly effects interact: what if, for example, Clinton had never read Kaplan's books? An epistemic understanding demands that two conclusions are made from this apparently innocuous claim: *First, the absence of reversibility undermines all knowledge constructions on the Kosovo crisis and second, this is so because historical linearity is at the heart of the modern episteme's machinery. Following Foucault's insights on the empirico-transcendental doublet, without reversibility subjects of enquiry cannot be isolated and studied, that is, an analytic of finitude could not be enforced; which, in turn, means that no transcendental philosophy of the object – which in this case based on the notion of Anarchy – is possible. In this modern epistemic vicious circle, an imperative to render a particular subject knowable demands that historical linearity is constructed and analytical finitude enforced.*

This does not mean that a Complexity-ethic advocates the idea that nothing is determined and therefore that nothing can be studied. Indeed,

> …Cilliers uses his analogy between complex systems and postmodern societies to dismiss the notion that postmodernism sanctions an "anything goes mentality" in which relativism reigns supreme. Instead, he asserts, postmodernism leads us to new ethical horizons and commitments. He draws on Lyotard to emphasize this point: "the breaking up of the grand Narratives…leads to what some authors analyze in terms of the dissolution of the social bond and the disintegration of social aggregates into a mass of individual atoms thrown into the absurdity of Brownian motion. Nothing of this kind is happening: this point of view, it seems to me, is haunted by the paradisaic representation of a lost 'organic society'."[86]

The same argument is to be applied to knowledge, and to those who regret the loss of an organic knowledge. Interestingly, Foucault described the results of the modern episteme precisely as organic constructs of knowledge.

86 Abraham, "Towards the End of Ethics and Law Parading as Justice", 122.

Chapter 7
Conclusion: International Relations, Complexity and the Kosovo Crisis

"All truth is simple" – Is that not a compound lie?

Friedrich Nietzsche[1]

On 17 February 2008, Kosovo's Parliament unilaterally declared independence from Serbia and established the Republic of Kosovo.[2] This brought to an end nearly a decade of negotiations regarding Kosovo's final status and – despite the fact that the Republic of Kosovo is likely to remain dependent on international support for the foreseeable future – independence brought an end to the formal United Nations administration mandate in the province.

More importantly, it brought to an end Western hopes for the states of the former Yugoslavia, and for Kosovo in particular, as these were outlined by the Contact Group's foreign ministers on 3 April 1999: "we want a peaceful, *multiethnic Kosovo in which all its people live in security*."[3] In 2004, reputable organisations such as the International Crisis Group used once again the expression "ethnic cleansing" following the riots in March that year, but this time the sentence referred to the cleansing of Serbs:

> On 17 March 2004, the unstable foundations of four and a half years of gradual progress in Kosovo buckled and gave way. Within hours the province was immersed in anti-Serb and anti-UN rioting and had regressed to levels of violence not seen since 1999. By 18 March the violence mutated into the ethnic cleansing of entire minority villages and neighbourhoods. The mobs of Albanian youths, extremists and criminals exposed the UN Mission in Kosovo (UNMIK) and the NATO-led peacekeeping force (KFOR) as very weak. Kosovo's provisional institutions of self-government (PISG), media and civil society afforded the rioters licence for mayhem. The international community urgently needs new policies – on final status and socio-economic development alike – or Kosovo instability may infect the entire region. The rampage left nineteen dead, nearly 900 injured, over 700 Serb, Ashkali and Roma homes, up to ten public

1 Friedrich Nietzsche, *Twilight of the Idols, Or How to Philosophise with a Hammer* (Oxford: Oxford University Press, 1998), 5.

2 As of 21 April 2008, 37 out of 192 sovereign United Nations members recognised the new Republic.

3 Norris, *Collision Course*, 23, strong emphasis added.

> buildings and 30 Serbian churches and two monasteries damaged or destroyed, and roughly 4,500 people displaced. The riots were more spontaneous than organised, with extremist and criminal gangs taking advantage, particularly on day two. Frustration and fear over the international community's intentions for Kosovo, UNMIK's inability to kick-start the economy and its suspension of privatisation, and Belgrade's success over recent months in shredding Kosovo Albanian nerves all built the tension that was released with explosive force by the inciting incidents of 16 March.[4]

Paradoxically, it was the fear that such riots may occur again that led to accelerated negotiations on the final status, which, by now, were inevitably geared towards independence. Such independence constituted the very partition exercise the West wanted to avoid, and the irreducible paradox that the West nevertheless had to face: this was either about supporting formal partition (independence) so as to encourage the new sovereign entity to respect whatever was left of its minority groups, or to risk having a completely cleansed province on the ground. In a version of the principle of Universal Exclusion, it seems that "ethnic minorities" can indeed be protected in principle as long as they populate sovereign entities in which they constitute, precisely, a minority (that is, as long as they have been conceptually excluded by the 'majority').[5]

It is not as if the main actors were not aware of the dangers – on the contrary, such dangers were so entrenched in the minds of key actors that independence was not even considered as an option. As John Norris narrates:

> While NATO had clear preferences for the peacekeeping operation, its vision of Kosovo's status was carefully hedged. NATO wanted to keep Yugoslavia intact, and many of the Allies were firmly opposed to independence for Kosovo. NATO feared an independent Kosovo would trigger instability in Greece, Macedonia, Albania, Bulgaria, while encouraging other secessionist movements to drag the Alliance into their violent liberation struggles."[6]

These words come from the very top in the US administration (John Norris served Strobe Talbott – Deputy State Secretary at the time and main negotiator on Kosovo. Talbott endorsed Norris' account in the foreword he wrote for his colleague's book), and, as such, they do carry some weight. The principle of Yugoslav territorial integrity was also unequivocally enshrined in UN Resolution 1244, which insisted on "reaffirming the commitment of all Member States to the

4 International Crisis Group, "Collapse in Kosovo", Europe Report Number 155, 22 April 2004, http://www.crisisgroup.org/home/index.cfm?id=2627&l=1 (accessed 21 April 2008).

5 It is estimated that only around 120,000 "Serbs" remain in Kosovo.

6 Norris, *Collision Course*, 135.

sovereignty and territorial integrity of the Federal Republic of Yugoslavia and the other states in the region, as set out in the Helsinki Final Act."[7]

On the other hand, it is difficult to imagine how these players could have possibly foreseen an outcome different from independence as the consequence of the bombing campaign. The difficult job of having to implement precisely what he had always been against fell to the brave former Finnish President Ahtisaari. Ahtisaari played a key role in negotiating the ceasefire whose main sticking point was the composition of the NATO peacekeeping force and the presence of Yugoslav forces in the province.[8] Whilst NATO's line was that absolutely no Yugoslav forces should be allowed to remain, Ahtisaari was well aware that such forces may have constituted the last (weak) defence against a possible future secession:

> President Ahtisaari continued to defend his position that a limited number of Yugoslav 'stay-behinds' should have been allowed in the peace agreement with Milošević. "If there was an understanding that less than 1,000 Serbs would be allowed to stay, they should have been allowed to stay. The mere fact that they had to go out and then return was not practical." Ahtisaari argued that it became impossible for any of these Serbs to return and that an alternative approach may have eased the transformation process, "Now, I don't think we have any choice but to give Kosovo independence. It leaves a bit of a bad aftertaste that so many Serbs had to leave. Whether we can have a multiethnic society is unclear. *It is dangerous to have monoethnic societies such as the way Kosovo is developing*".[9]

This is, in many ways, an unusual book. It is hoped, however, that the few paragraphs above convey some additional paradoxes that characterised the Kosovo conflict, which make it so difficult to understand. For instance, the considerations above lead to the conclusion that in order to safeguard a "multi-ethnic Kosovo" NATO embarked on the creation of a "mono-ethnic Kosovo", a development which was recognised as being "dangerous". Furthermore, these were the very principles that NATO vehemently defended in order to avoid partition (refusal to grant Russia an independent sector and refusal to allow Yugoslav forces to participate in the

7 "United Nations Security Council Resolution 1244, June 10 1999" in Auerswald, *The Kosovo Conflict*, 1127.

8 The failure to reach an agreement with the Russians (who refused to serve under a NATO commander who insisted on being allocated a specific sector – conditions which were regarded as inadmissible by NATO precisely because of fear that these would lead to partition) led to Russia's unilateral deployment towards the Pristina airfield and to Clark's (disobeyed) orders to engage Russian troops. See ibid.

9 Ibid., 298, strong emphasis added. Despite being opposed to independence it was precisely Ahtisaari who, after nearly 10 years of failed negotiations, had to propose "supervised independence" as the only remaining solution under the Ahtisaari Plan. For Ahtisaari's strong opposition to independence see Martti Ahtisaari, *Mission to Belgrade* (Helsinki: WSOY Press, 2000).

policing of the province) which, at least according to Ahtisaari, led to partition on a bigger scale (independence) and to the formation of what he considered to be a dangerous mono-ethnic society. Kosovo thus represents, in many ways, an unusual conflict. There is something intrinsically ironic (or tragic, depending on the point of view) in fighting a war in order to safeguard a "multi-ethnic" Kosovo whilst assuming that the conflict was generated by ancient ethnic hatreds. It is like offering as a solution what one believes is the cause of the problem.

This work was emphatically not about 'explaining' the 'strategic reasons' or the 'bureaucratic processes' that ultimately pushed NATO to intervene militarily in the region. It was not about explaining how the conflict emerged on the bases of underlying (hidden) ethnic, historical, social or economic forces, which a science based on transcendental philosophy of objects could unveil. It was, rather, an attempt at elucidating what epistemic constraints conditioned the way in which Yugoslav actors had to deploy a particular discourse in order to survive immanent political struggles, and in outlining how such constraints led NATO and other relevant stakeholders to conceptualise the conflict in the way they did. In exploring Complexity epistemology, the study sought to present alternative frameworks for the production and deployment of knowledge related to the conflict.

There are a number of relevant variables that characterised the decision-making process, and the exploration of such variables falls within the remit of history, or rather, historiography. Unfortunately, it seems that what information is available in the public domain at the moment is not sufficient to initiate such a critical historiographical project. Moreover, the retrieval of information that would shed light on such variables appears to be a task that is beyond our possibilities at the moment, although this is not for lack of trying.[10] However, this study shares the intuition of Eric Hobsbawm regarding the nature of NATO's motivations (or lack thereof), as the historian declared that the war had no specific purposes and brought no advantages to Western powers. In other words, it was just a mistake (or 'pasticcio', in Italian).[11] As more information becomes available, it will be interesting to analyse it with a Complexity approach in mind: it may just be that NATO powers found themselves in a complex, *emergent* situation that, due to various institutional processes and evolving contexts, seems to have acquired a life of its own. This is a view that 'social science' may not be well equipped to accept.

---

10 Throughout 2004/5 the Foreign and Commonwealth Office (FCO) has refused to disclose information requested by this author under the Freedom of Information Act. The legal exemptions that have been invoked to back this refusal are most revealing: they include clauses regarding information that "may harm the diplomatic relations of the United Kingdom with other States", and the 'State' that was cited in official FCO correspondence is 'Kosovo'. This is intriguing given the legal limbo in which the province found itself prior to a final status settlement, which is when the request was made.

11 Hobsbawm, "Guerra Umanitaria? No, e solo un pasticcio", 58–67.

More than anything, this study was about *elucidating what made specific discourses and understandings possible, and explaining the way in which such discourses could be challenged.* As the title of the study suggests, two instruments were used: an epistemic approach was deployed to outline what made relevant (and modern) discourse formation processes possible, whilst an epistemic understanding of Complexity described the way in which such processes constitute outdated techniques for the generation of knowledge and understanding. Those two instruments led to the three concise research questions presented at the beginning of the study:

1. In what way can the emergence of what we loosely refer to as 'Complexity Theory' enhance our understanding of social affairs generally, and of IR in particular?
2. Why is the Kosovo conflict a particularly good example to illustrate the role that Complexity can have in enhancing such understanding? To what extent can we speak of a new Complexity-based *episteme* as a break from the current configuration of knowledge?
3. What epistemic constraints led to a particular understanding of the Kosovo conflict which resulted in a particular response? And how would a Complexity-based approach produce different understandings, and different solutions?

Before attempting a conclusive and comprehensive answer it may be useful to summarise the findings.

First, Complexity was introduced from an epistemic perspective. In order to answer our three questions, the study began by outlining how Foucault provided a 'falsification test' for the modern episteme which, due to its reliance on historical linearity, was considered by Foucault as having inaugurated the 'Age of History'. The test relies on the notion that knowledge would move beyond the modern episteme once it ceased to regard history as that which enforces the contingency demanded by the empirico-transcendental doublet and regarded history as precisely the opposite: that is, the primary source of novelty and uncertainty. Thus, Foucault identified in Henri Bergson the first philosopher who moved beyond the modern episteme, precisely by virtue of his understanding of time. The chapter continued to note how Ilya Prigogine – one of the main Complexity theorists and founder of the Complexity strand in the biological sciences – used precisely Bergson's conceptualisation of time as a point of departure for his Complexity approach. On these bases the chapter sought to offer a solid, epistemic-based definition of Complexity science as a knowledge framework that relies on time irreversibility (thus undermining one of the axes of modernity, that is, linear time) and on a notion of open systems (thus undermining the other axis, that is, analytical finitude) in order to produce 'uncertain knowledge', where uncertainty is regarded and accepted as an intrinsic quality of nature and not as a result of imperfect knowledge. Complexity's focus on the realm of immanence, coupled with its anti reductionism (which was presented through a detailed explanation of Prigogine's understanding of the collapse of wave functions) provided bases for the formulation of parallelisms between Complexity and post-structural philosophy in general, and Deleuze's thought (which, incidentally, also takes Bergson's conceptualisation of time as a point of departure) in particular. Failing to resist the temptation of digging deeper, the research revealed that a number of Complexity's precursors were influenced by German Romanticism and Natural Philosophy, especially by the likes of Goethe. Considering Hobsbawm's account of Europe's 'epistemic civil war' it was argued that Complexity brings back to light an old, quintessentially European debate about the role of Reason after the Enlightenment, suggesting that whereas modern metaphysical knowledge assigns to Reason the task of providing certainty, Complexity-based, postmodern knowledge (in a strictly Foucauldian sense) tasks Reason with the role of enabling humans to cope with uncertainty and the fundamental element of randomness that is inherent in nature. The main finding can be summarised as such: Complexity is a clear case of postmodern science (strictly in the Foucauldian-epistemic sense) which presents striking similarities with philosophers such as Deleuze. Such similarities are rooted in different understanding of temporality and contingency.

Chapter 2 proceeded to present the modern episteme and to explain how such episteme conditioned the formation of knowledge frameworks in the disciplines of economics and biology. The main findings of the chapter relate to the unveiling of modernity as a knowledge practice which allows for a number of approaches to knowledge. Within this modern framework, however, the modern empirical sciences were shown to be based on transcendental philosophies of the object, which, in turn, are based on an empirico-transcendental doublet (the mechanism whereby the relationship between the metaphysical and the immanent is negotiated). Such empirico-transcendental doublet is, in turn, based on the notions of analytical finitude and historical linearity which, in virtue of the roles these fulfil within the modern episteme, have been referred to throughout the book as the 'axes of modernity'. Economics and biology represent but two disciplines which have been constituted on the bases of such axes. The chapter concluded by outlining how the scientific method proper had – following the conclusions of the Vienna Circle – shifted towards the transcendental philosophy of objects extreme in the modern configuration of knowledge and was therefore governed by the requirements of the axes of modernity. It was argued that such shift is significant because this is precisely what led the academic discipline for IR – which is responsible for producing knowledge related to international conflicts – in the same direction.

Chapter 3, as a whole, sought to build the link between meta-theory and theory by carefully analysing how the empirico-transcendental doublet characterised the formation of knowledge in the fields of IR and Law/Ethics. Chapter 3 picked up the argument where Chapter 2 left it and proceeded to prove that the academic discipline of IR explicitly sought to emulate those developments in the epistemology of science (the formulation of metaphysical, or paradigmatic, science following the Vienna Circle) which were responsible for the introduction of the empirico-transcendental doublet in the scientific method. Drawing parallelisms with the disciplines Foucault himself had analysed (Economics and Biology), the chapter proceeded to demonstrate that an understanding and emulation of metaphysical science led academic IR to formulate knowledge on the nature of crisis based on the principles of the modern episteme. Thus, an analysis of the subject 'Man' (or States) that proceeded through the prism of the transcendental philosophy of the object (in this case Anarchy) led to a vision that entailed historical immobility (historical linearity) and the isolation of international problems to state interactions (analytical finitude). It was argued that this was of crucial importance as it formed the (conscious and subconscious) intellectual grounds upon which the formation of knowledge on the Kosovo crisis, based on immutable 'ancient ethnic hatreds', could be constructed.

The Intermezzo sought to distil the theoretical arguments in order to outline how such arguments are concretely used to generate an understanding of the Kosovo crisis. As such, the Intermezzo sought to initiate the transition between the theoretical and empirical parts of the study by outlining how the empirical parts elucidate the ways in which the theoretical notion of historical linearity was deployed in relation to Kosovo by elaborating arguments on the 'ancient ethnic hatreds' (that allegedly were at the roots of the conflict), whilst an analytic of finitude was enforced through Universal Exclusion in legal and ethical discourse. Thus, the rest of the study proceeded to examine how the two axes of modernity conditioned the generation and deployment of knowledge on the Kosovo conflict, and to explain how an episteme-based Complexity approach allows for the identification and dismissal of such discourse formation techniques.

Chapter 4 sought to present the most salient debates surrounding the Kosovo crisis. The objective was to synthesise all such debates from an epistemic perspective, in order to demonstrate that these debates had common roots and represented different ways in which the modern episteme was deployed in order to formulate related questions. In particular, it was shown that all debates/questions related to the inevitable paradoxes that must be faced whenever transcendental or metaphysical concepts (which are allowed for by the modern episteme) have to be applied in the realm of immanence.

Chapter 5, on the other hand, examined how the formulation of knowledge in the areas of law and ethics also followed the rules inherent in the modern episteme. It was argued that with the implementation of the empirico-transcendental doublet, ethics and law imported the paradoxes that came with it, and that these paradoxes generally arise whenever the relationship between the metaphysical (or Universal, such as, for example, a notion of Human Rights) has to be reconciled with the immanent through the mechanisms provided by the empirico-transcendental doublet. Chapter 5 deployed the readings of Slavoj Žižek and of Niklas Luhmann to argue that a metaphysical approach to law and ethics engenders, in the first instance, situations in which 'Universal Exclusions' have to be built at the level of immanence for a transcendental principle to be implemented and that, in the second instance, Luhmann's Complexity approach leads him to formulate a division between ethics and morality whereby "ethics is charged with minimizing the devastation morality is capable of unleashing".

Chapter 6 proceeded to analyse how, following Benedict Anderson's insights on the rise of nationalisms, a concept of linear finitude mutates into a notion of 'homogeneous, empty time' which in turn allows the nationalist discourse to be thought. According to Anderson, linear time is needed to provide an otherwise absent feeling of simultaneity without which it would be difficult for a multitude of individuals to feel part of a single imagined community. The chapter applies these insights to an analysis of how such linear temporality was used by Yugoslav improvised nationalists in the formation of the Kosovo myth and in the deployment of such myth throughout the1990s. The chapter also elucidates how such notion of empty time needs to be present in the minds of interpreting outsiders in order to accept that the crisis is, as the nationalists allege, indeed, based on immutable ethnic hatreds. Here, there are striking similarities between the way in which academic IR understands the nature of international conflict and the way in which key policy-makers and the media understood the Kosovo crisis in a temporally linear fashion – giving a whole new emphasis on Walker's thought according to which, IR theory is constitutive of IR practice. Chapter 6 also proceeds to examine how a Complexity-informed analysis of the conflict would have focussed on the immanent political struggles within the former Yugoslavia and the way in which such struggles determined the way in which the past was constructed in the present. The chapter shows that, whereas the standard historically linear account attributed the brutality of developments in Bosnia and in Kosovo to the presence of incomprehensible ancient ethnic hatreds, such brutality was caused precisely by the opposite: the absence of such visceral hatreds and, in the case of Kosovo, the progressive collapse of the nationalist discourse. Kosovo is, thus, presented as a consequence of the failed understanding of Bosnia – and of such failed understanding's consequent guilt – and as a case of renewed misunderstanding of the conflicts' causes (historical linearity metamorphosed into ancient ethnic hatreds) coupled with related feelings of guilt (memories of the Holocaust, courtesy of Srebrenica and Raçak).

On the bases of these findings, it is possible to elaborate an overall conclusion on the merits of engaging Complexity thinking for the purposes of analysing conflict and the way in which conflict is often (erroneously) framed by mainstream IR approaches. Answering the first research question of this study, we can argue that Complexity – understood in an epistemic context – has the potential to enhance our understanding of social reality in general and of conflict in particular, because it provides an alternative framework for the framing of such realities. In a nutshell, whilst the study has demonstrated that traditional modern approaches to knowledge (epitomised by Neorealist theories of IR) fundamentally rely on the twin epistemic axes of analytical finitude and historical linearity, Complexity's most salient differences in this context – as outlined in the conclusion of Chapter 6 – consist of its insistence to consider all systems as open systems (denying the contingency that analytical finitude enforces in the modern episteme), whilst emphasising the fact that all such open systems have a non-reversible history (thus eliminating the contingency that historical linearity plays in the modern context). Thus, *by systematically undermining what Foucault described as the twin engines of modern understanding – the mutually dependent notions of historical and analytical (anthropological) finitude – Complexity forces us to look beyond certainty-based, contingent frameworks of knowledge as we seek to interpret and understand conflict*. Crucially, Complexity re-opens the question of what exactly should be the role of Reason after the Enlightenment, suggesting that Reason should be that which enables us to cope with uncertainty (which is a fundamental and objective property of nature, in both the natural and social worlds), rather than that which encourages us – as if by automatic reflex – to look for certainty-based explanatory models.

So, what does Complexity deliver in relation to the Kosovo conflict (which is the focus of our second research question)? An epistemic-Complexity approach enabled this study to reveal how modern assumptions on the production and deployment of knowledge conditioned the way in which the Kosovo conflict was framed and acted upon. In particular, it allowed us to identify the very real impact that legal and ethical reasoning based on an analytic of finitude – which, by virtue of its function (the provision of contingency), must necessarily exclude some elements in order to analyse others – has on the way in which ethics and the law were deployed in the context of the conflict. Whilst the 'anthropological finitude' axis of modernity could be discerned in ethic-legal understandings of the Kosovo conflict, the related 'historical finitude' element was clearly discernible in the way in which historically linear arguments (the 'ancient ethnic hatreds' approach) came to play such a dominant role in the collective symbolic imagery – and therefore in collective understandings – of the causes of the Kosovo conflict. Do we need Complexity to argue that the war had little to do with such imagined ethnic hatreds? No. However, *by placing concepts which are diametrically opposed to the axes of modernity at the heart of its methodology, Complexity forces us to systemically look for modernity-caused reflexes in the ways the Kosovo conflict was understood and acted upon*. Such systematic and comprehensive undermining of the modern episteme is, thus, necessary if we are to go beyond refuting specific aspects of modern understanding (ethnic hatreds) and into linking and seeing such various aspects as being part of an internally coherent (modern) whole. Through Complexity we can see why an argument based on the 'ethnic hatreds' approach finds in legal 'universal exclusionary' principles its logical counterpart in the field of ethics and in the law. Furthermore, Complexity allows us to go beyond simple rebuttals of modernity-based approaches and into secondary lines of questioning. For example, it allows us to ask why the 'ethnic hatred' approach gained such popularity in public opinion despite its evident lack of validity. By concentrating on the two elements that set Complexity apart from the modern episteme (open systems and time irreversibility) Complexity understands that modern approaches will have conditioned answers to questions regardless of any evidence that may be available. In other words, Complexity delivers a roadmap of counter-questions to be asked, of counter-arguments to be explored, and of counter 'modern-intuitive' attitudes to adopt. *Complexity, thus, does a lot more than provide an alternative theory for the cause of conflicts – it provides an alternative ethos with which we can embark on the discovery of evidence no-one had sought to unveil, or of evidence no-one sought to relate to other elements in the (open) system* (evidence that lies outside the Kuhnian paradigmatic black box, for example). In our case, Complexity provided clear guidance towards the way in which contradictory events and statements (the pursuit of multi-ethnicity through partition, the implementation of Universal principles through institutions characterised by jurisdiction based on very Particular criteria, and so on) could be understood and contested. For the common thread is a particular ethos characterised by a restless pursuit of certainty, whose various forms and facets are only clearly identifiable as pertaining to a single phenomenon (modernity) once such phenomenon has been fully understood in Complex, postmodern terms.[12]

Thus, after having identified the very modern constraints that characterised a modern formation of knowledge (the nature of our third research question), our Complexity-inspired approach led us to thoroughly examine questions that are strictly related to the two axes of modernity – for it allowed us to discriminate by pointing to the fundamental importance of these two axes. It led us to look at ethical and legal theory, without worrying too much about formal academic-disciplinary boundaries. It encouraged us to look at what Foucault would have called historical-epistemic 'monuments', where we could find traces of the two axes of modernity, and such traces took the most varied forms: a speech, a photograph, a legal statement, a biography, a memory, an academic study, an interview with a taxi driver…

At this point, the reader may complain that the study has not offered any Complexity-inspired 'solutions' for the crisis. A response to this hypothetical critic would consist in outlining how an epistemic approach has allowed a critique and understanding of the way in which the conflict was understood and acted upon to take place, whilst the presentation of Complexity's ethos indicated how alternative understandings are both more accurate and, crucially, more consonant with the way in which knowledge is currently being generated in the sciences. What this means in practice is, as it were, detail. Accepting that history is not that which causes things to be the way they are, but that it is, rather, that which allows a number of infinite virtual alternatives to be actualised, entails innumerable consequences for those wishing to produce 'practical' advice for policy-makers. For example, understanding that generalised violence in the former Yugoslavia was caused more by the ambition of individuals competing in a transformed political environment than by the alleged presence of historical hatreds, may have warranted a more concerted and focussed action, based perhaps on incentives (membership of the

12 Again, I am taking the freedom to use concepts such as 'postmodernity' on the understanding that such concepts have been fully defined throughout the study. In all cases, we are referring to modernity as understood by Foucault, and postmodernity as defined by Foucault as something that takes us beyond the "Age of History".

European Union, international support, and so on) and disincentives (lack of the aforementioned incentives for policy-makers that did not comply), at the relevant specific (political) level. Understanding that the lack of ancient hatreds (rather than the opposite), coupled with the immanent need to formulate nationalistic discourses, is what caused such extreme levels of violence may have led to the conclusion that it may have been relatively easy to extinguish the nationalist fires through political action aimed at maintaining the status-quo (for example, through a commitment not to recognise any of the former republics which did not achieve independence legally, and therefore by consensus, Czechoslovakia-style) and that doing the opposite (German unilateral recognition of Croatia, for example) may lead to the augmentation of such fires. Understanding that Bosnia and Kosovo were, to a certain extent, also vulgar *criminal* problems rather than ethnical quagmires may have led to an approach more focussed on international policing solutions rather than on international military solutions. And so on.

Finally, it is hoped that this study has opened up new, Complexity-inspired research agendas for the disciplines of IR and Critical Geopolitics. The introduction of Critical Geopolitics – with its analysis on the social construction of *space* – and an accurate study of 'ethnic nationalisms' – which implies an analysis of the social construction of *time* – correspond to the Complexity agenda insofar as they relate to Prigogine's maxim on the nature of 'truth' and the related objectives of scientific enquiry. In particular, an epistemic-based and Complexity-inspired analysis of the modern episteme has revealed how modern identity formation processes rely on a *spacialisation of time* (linear time) and on a *temporal immobilisation of social space* (consider, for example, the European Court of Human Right's decision to link jurisdiction to previously existent territory). By deconstructing the processes that led to these two outcomes, a Critical Geopolitical stance (responsible for analysing the socio-political construction of space) and a 'Critical Diplomatic History'[13] approach (responsible for analysing how sovereign political actors have created their past in the present, and how other actors have interpreted such histories…in other words, a discipline charged with analysing the socio-political construction of time) could move our understanding of social realities beyond the modern episteme and into Complexity-based, postmodern frameworks. They would constitute Complex Geotemporal critiques, capable of establishing the intellectual grounds for the creation of what we can hope will be more adroit political solutions. Or political solutions that are more in tune with genuine complex realities at the level of immanence. More importantly, solutions which accept the fundamental principle of uncertainty whilst moving away from the very modern idea according to which the role of reason after the Enlightenment (and therefore, of knowledge) should be that of providing certainty for decisions on human action. Solutions which fundamentally embrace the insight:

> "All truth is simple" – Is that not a compound lie?

13 For lack of a better term.

Bibliography

Abraham, Matthew. "What is Complexity Science: Towards the End of Ethics and Law Parading as Justice". In *Thinking Complexity: Complexity and Philosophy,* edited by Paul Cilliers. Mansfield: ISCE Publishing, 2007.

Abu Lughod, Janet. *Before European Hegemony: The World System A.D. 1250–1350*. Oxford: Oxford University Press, 1989.

Adams, Karen Ruth. "Structural Realism: The Consequences of Great Power Politics". In *Making Sense of International Relations Theory*, edited by Jennifer Sterling-Folker. Boulder: Lynne Rienner, 2006.

Ahtisaari, Martti. *Mission to Belgrade*. Helsinki: WSOY Press, 2000.

Alberts, David and Thomas Czerwinski, eds, *Complexity, Global Politics and National Security*. Washington DC: National Defense University Press, 2003.

Ali, Tariq, ed. *Masters of the Universe? NATO's Balkan Crusade*. London: Verso, 2000.

Allison, Graham. *The Essence of Decision: Explaining the Cuban Missile Crisis*. Boston: Little Brown, 1971.

Anderson, Benedict. *Imagined Communities*. London: Verso, 1991.

Anzulovic, Branimir. *Heavenly Serbia: From Myth to Genocide*. London: Hurst, 1999.

Aron, Raymond. *Peace and War: A Theory of International Relations*. New York: Praeger, 1966.

——"Qu'est-ce qu'une Théorie des Relations Internationales?" *Revue Française de Science Politique*, October 1967.

Ashley, Richard. "The Poverty of Neorealism". In *Neorealism and its Critics*, edited by Robert Keohane. New York: Columbia University Press, 1986.

Auerswald, David. "Explaining Wars of Choice: An Integrated Decision Model of NATO Policy in Kosovo". *International Studies Quarterly* no. 48 (2004).

Auerswald, Philip and David Auerswald. *The Kosovo Conflict, a Diplomatic History through Documents*. The Hague: Kluwer Law International, 2000.

Babich, Babette. *Nietzsche's Philosophy of Science: Reflecting Science on the Ground of Art and Life*. New York: State University of New York Press, 1994.

Balzacq, Thierry. "Interview with Robert Jervis". *Review of International Studies* Vol. 30, no. 4 (October 2004).

Banac, Ivo. *The National Question in Yugoslavia: Origins, History, Politics*. Ithaca, London: Cornell University Press, 1984.

Barberousse, Anouk, Max Kistler and Pascal Ludwig. *La Philosophie Des Sciences Au Xxe Siècle*. Manchecourt: Flammarion, 2000.

BBC. "Strebenica Blame 'Must be Shared'", 10 April 2002. http://news.bbc.co.uk/2/hi/Europe/1920357.stm.

Benedikter, Thomas. *Il Dramma del Kosovo: dall'Origine fra Serbi e Albanesi agli Scontri di Oggi*. Rome: Datanews Publications, 1998.

Bennett, Christopher. *Yugoslavia's Bloody Collapse*. New York: New York University Press, 1995.

Bennett, Max and Peter Hacker. *Philosophical Foundations of Neuroscience*. London: Blackwells, 2003.

Benvenuti, Paolo. "The ICTY Prosecutor and the Review of the NATO Bombing Campaign against the Federal Republic of Yugoslavia". *European Journal of International Law* Vol. 12, no. 3 (2001).

Bergson, Henri. *Matter and Memory*. New York: Cosimo Classics, 2007.

——*The Creative Mind*. Littlefield: Rowman Publishers, 1979.

——*Oeuvres*. Paris: Presses Universitaires de France, 1959.

——*Creative Evolution*. Mineola, New York: Courier Dover Publications, 1998.

Beyerchen, Alan. "Clausewitz, Nonlinearity and the Unpredictability of War". *International Security* Vol. 17, no. 3 (Winter 1992).

Bierce, Ambrose. *The Unabridged Devil's Dictionary*. Athens GA: University of Georgia Press, 2002.

Bildt, Carl. *Peace Journey*. London: Weidenfeld and Nicolson, 1998.

Blair, Brian. "Knowledge, Power, and the Modern State: Towards a Geneaology of Universal Productionist Order, 1500–1815". Phd thesis, University of Newcastle, 1997.

Boundas, Constantin. "Deleuze – Bergson: An Ontology of the Virtual". *In Deleuze: A Critical Reader*, edited by Paul Patton. Oxford: Blackwell Publishers, 1996.

Boyes, Roger and Eske Wright. "Drugs Money Linked to the Kosovo Rebels", *The Times* (London) 24 March 1999.

Boyle, Francis. *Foundations of World Order: The Legalist Approach to International Relations (1898–1922)*. London and Durham: Duke University Press, 1999.

Branham, Robert Bracht. "Defacing the Currency: Diogenes' Rhetoric and the Invention of Cynicism." In *The Cynics: The Cynic Movement in Antiquity and its Legacy*, edited by Robert Bracht Branham and Marie-Odile Goulet-Cazé. Berkeley: University of California Press, 1997.

Brown, Michael. "The Causes of Internal Conflict". In *Nationalism and Ethnic Conflict*, Revised Edition, edited by Michael Brown, Owen Coté, Sean Lynn-Jones and Steven Miller. Cambridge: MIT Press, 2001.

Butler, Rex. *Slavoj Žižek: Live Theory*. New York: Continuum, 2005.

Buzan, Barry and Richard Little. *International Systems in World History: Remaking the Study of International Relations*. Oxford: Oxford University Press, 2000.

Byrne, David. *Complexity Theory and the Social Sciences: An Introduction*. London: Routledge, 1998.

Campbell, Alastair. *The Blair Years: Extracts from the Alastair Campbell Diaries*. London: Hutchinson, 2007.

Campbell, David. *National Deconstruction: Violence, Identity and Justice in Bosnia*. Minneapolis: University of Minnesota Press, 1998.

——"Justice and the International Order: the Case of Bosnia and Kosovo". In *Ethics and International Affairs: Extents and Limits*, edited by Jean Marc Coicaud and Daniel Warner. Tokyo: The United Nations University Press, 2001.

Chesterman, Simon. *Just War or Just Peace? Humanitarian Intervention and International Law*. Oxford, New York: Oxford University Press, 2001.

Chomsky, Noam. *The New Military Humanism: Lessons from Kosovo*. London, Pluto Press, 1999.

—— "On the NATO Bombing of Yugoslavia: Noam Chomsky interviewed by Daniel Mandic", RTS Online, 25 April 2006. Interview available online: http://www.chomsky.info/interviews/20060425.htm.

Cilliers, Paul. *Complexity and Postmodernism*. London: Routledge, 1998.

——"On the Importance of a Certain Slowness". In *Thinking Complexity: Complexity and Philosophy*, edited by Paul Cilliers. Mansfield: ISCE Publishing, 2007.

Clark, Wesley. *Waging Modern War*. New York: Public Affairs, 2002.

Clemens, Walter, ed. In *The Baltic Transformed: Complexity Theory and European Security*. New York: Rowman and Littlefield Publishers, 2001.

CNN. "Transcript: Clinton Justifies US Involvement in Kosovo", 19 May 1999: http://www.cnn.com/ALLPOLITICS/stories/1999/05/13/clinton.kosovo/transcript.htm.

Cochrane, Kathryn. "Kosovo Targeting: A Bureaucratic and Legal Nightmare: The Implications for US/Australian Interoperability." In *Australian Aerospace Center*, June 2001. http://www.defence.gov.au/raaf/airpower/html/publications/papers/apdc/apdc_03_kos ovo_targeting.pdf.

Coicaud, Jean-Marc and Daniel Warner, eds. *Ethics and International Affairs: Extents and Limits.* Tokyo: The United Nations University Press, 2001.

Corson, Mark and Clemson Turregano. "Spaces of unintended consequences: The Ground Safety Zone in Kosovo," *GeoJournal* Vol. 57, no. 4 (2002).

Cosic, Dobrica. *Kosovo*. Belgrade: Novosti, 2004.

Cox, Robert. *Approaches to World Order*. Cambridge: Cambridge University Press, 1996.

Cviic, Christopher. "The Serbian Exception". *International Affairs* Vol. 75, no. 3 (1999).

Daalder, Ivo and Michael O'Hanlon. *Winning Ugly: NATO's War to Save Kosovo*. Washington DC: Brookings Institution Press, 2000.

De Graaff, Bob. "The Difference Between Legal Proof and Historical Evidence: The Trial of Slobodan Milošević and the Case of Srebrenica". *European Review* Vol. 14 (2006).

De Landa, Manuel. *A Thousand Years of Nonlinear History*. New York: Zone Books, 1997.

——*Intensive Science and Virtual Philosophy*. London: Continuum, 2002.

Deleuze, Gilles. *Bergsonism*. New York: Zone Books, 1988.

Dillon, Michael. "Poststructuralism, Complexity and Poetics". *Theory, Culture and Society* Vol. 17, no. 5 (2000).

Donia, Robert and John Fine. *Bosnia and Hercegovina: A Tradition Betrayed*. New York: Columbia University Press, 1994.

Douglass, Paul. "Deleuze and the Endurance of Bergson". *Thought* Vol. 67, no. 264 (1992).

——"Deleuze's Bergson: Bergson Redux". In *The Crisis in Modernism: Bergson and the Vitalist Controversy*, edited by Frederick Burwick and Paul Douglass. Cambridge: Cambridge University Press, 1996.

Dreyfus, Hubert and Paul Rabinow. *Michel Foucault: Beyond Structuralism and Hermeneutics*. Chicago: University of Chicago Press, 1983.

Dupré, John. *The Disorder of Things: Metaphysical Foundations of the Disunity of Science*. London: Harvard University Press, 1995.

Eve, Raymond, Sara Horsefall and Mary Lee, eds. *Complexity and Sociology: Myths, Models and Theories*. London: Sage Publications, 1997.

Fine, Robert. "Hannah Arendt: Politics and Understanding after the Holocaust". In *Social Theory after the Holocaust*, edited by Robert Fine and Charles Turner. Liverpool: Liverpool University Press, 2000.

Fisk, Robert. "Once you kill people because you don't like what they say, you change the rules of war". *The Independent* (London), 24 April 1999.

Foucault, Michel. *The Order of Things: An Archaeology of the Human Sciences*. London: Routledge, 1989.

——*Surveiller et Punir*. Saint-Amand: Editions Gallimard, 1993.

——*L'Archeologie du Savoir*. Mayenne: Gallimard, 2001.

——*Les Mots et les Choses*. Saint Amand, Cher: Gallimard, 2001.

Gaddis, John Lewis. *We Now Know: Rethinking Cold War History*. Oxford: Oxford University Press, 1997: Chapter 1, Section II.

George, Jim. *Discourses of Global Politics: Critical (Re)Introduction to International Relations*, London: Palgrave Macmillan, 1994.

Gheciu, Alexandra. "International Norms, Power and the Politics of International Administration: The Kosovo Case". *Geopolitics* Vol. 10, no. 1 (2005).

Girgus, Sam. "The new Covenant and the Dilemma of Dissensus: Bercovitch, Roth and Doctorow". In *Summoning: Ideas of the Covenant and Interpretative Theory*, edited by Ellen Spolsky. New York: State University of New York Press, 1993.

Gleick, James. *Chaos: Making a New Science*. New York: Viking Penguin, 1987.

Glennon, Michael. *Limits of Law, Prerogatives of Power: Intervention After Kosovo*. New York: Palgrave, 2001.

Gordon, Michael. "Crisis in the Balkans: The Overview". *The New York Times* 13 May 1999.

Gorman, Anthony. "Whither the Broken Middle? Rose and Fackenheim on Mourning, Modernity and the Holocaust". In *Social Theory after the Holocaust*, edited by Robert Fine and Charles Turner. Liverpool: Liverpool University Press, 2000.

Gow, James. *The Serbian Project and Its Adversaries: A Strategy of War Crimes*. London: Hurst and Co. Publishers, 2003.

Gray, Christine. *International Law and the Use of Force*. Oxford, New York: Oxford University Press, 2000.

Guattari, Felix. *Chaosmosis: An Ethico-Aesthetic Paradigm*. Bloomington: University of Indiana Press, 1995.

Gutting, Gary. *Michel Foucault's Archaeology of Scientific Reason, Modern European Philosophy*. New York: Cambridge University Press, 1989.

——*French Philosophy in the Twentieth Century*. Cambridge: Cambridge University Press, 2001.

Guzzini, Stefano. *Realism in International Relations and International Political Economy: The Continuing Story of a Death Foretold*. Florence: European University Institute Press, 1992.

Hacking, Ian. *The Emergence of Probability: A Philosophical Study of Early Ideas about Probability, Induction and Statistical Inference*. Cambridge: Cambridge University Press, 2006.

Han, Béatrice. *Foucault's Critical Project: Between the Transcendental and the Historical*. Stanford: Stanford University Press, 2002.

Happold, Matthew. "Bankovic v Belgium and the Territorial Scope of the European Convention on Human Rights". *Human Rights Law Review* Vol. 3, no. 1 (2003).

Hardt, Michael. and Antonio Negri. *Empire*. Cambridge MA: Harvard University Press, 2000.

Harrison, Ewan. "Waltz, Kant and Systemic Approaches to International Relations". *Review of International Studies* Vol. 28, no. 1 (2002).

Hobsbawm, Eric. *L'Age des Extremes*. Brussels: Editions Complexes, 1999.

——"Guerra Umanitaria? No, e solo un pasticcio" In *L'Ultima Crociata? Ragioni e Torti di una Guerra Giusta*, edited by Ulrich Beck and Norberto Bobbio. Rome: Libri di Reset, 1999.

——*The Age of Revolutions*. London: Abacus, 2003.

Hoffmann, Stanley. "Théories et Relations Internationales". *Revue Française de Science Politique* (March 1961).

Holbrooke, Richard. *To End a War*. New York: The Modern Library Editions, 1998.

Holzgrefe, J.L. "The Humanitarian Intervention Debate". In *Humanitarian Intervention: Ethical, Legal and Political Dilemmas*, edited by Robert Keohane and J.L. Holzgrefe. Cambridge: Cambridge University Press, 2003.

House of Commons, Defence Select Committee, "Fourteenth Report", 24 October 2000.

House of Commons, Foreign Affairs Committee, "Fourth Report, Kosovo, Vol. II Minutes of Evidence and Appendices", 24 May 2000, p. 97. Examination of witnesses: Judah, Sweeney and Roberts.

House of Commons, Foreign Affairs Select Committee: "Fourth Report:Kosovo. Vol. 1, Report and Proceedings of the Committee", 23 May 2000.

House of Lords, Hansard Debates 6 May 1999.
Human Rights Watch. Under Orders: War Crimes in Kosovo-3, Forces in the Conflict. http://www.hrw.org/reports/2001/Kosovo/undword-02.htm.
Huntington, Samuel. *The Clash of Civilizations and the Remaking of World Order*. New York: Simon and Shuster, 1998.
Ignatieff, Michael. *Virtual War: Kosovo and Beyond*. London: Chatto and Windus, 2000.
Independent International Commission on Kosovo. *The Kosovo Report: Conflict, International Response, Lessons Learned*. Oxford: Oxford University Press, 2000.
International Court of Justice. "Decision by the International Court of Justice on the Case Concerning the Legality of Use of Force (*Yugoslavia v United States of America*), 2 June 1999." In *The Kosovo Conflict, a Diplomatic History through Documents*, edited by Philip Auerswald and David Auerswald. The Hague: Kluwer Law International, 2000.
International Court of Justice. "Dissenting opinion of Judge Kreca". The Hague. http://www.icj-cij.org/docket/index.php?pr=371&code=yus&p1=3&p3=6&case=114&k=25.
International Criminal Tribunal for the Former Yugoslavia (ICTY). "Final Report to the Prosecutor by the Committee Established to Review the NATO Bombing Campaign Against the Federal Republic of Yugoslavia". http://www.un.org/icty/pressreal/nato061300.htm.
International Crisis Group. "Collapse in Kosovo," Europe Report Number 155, 22 April 2004. http://www.crisisgroup.org/home/index.cfm?id=2627x1=1.
JASS book review. http//jasss.soc.surrey.ac.uk/2/2/review1.html.
Jervis, Robert. *System Effects: Complexity in Political and Social Life*. New Jersey Princeton University Press, 1999.
Joffe, Natasha. "At War with NATO". *The Guardian* (Manchester), 23 October 2001.
Judah, Tim. *Kosovo: War and Revenge*. London, New Haven: Yale University Press, 2000.
Kant, Immanuel. *Critique of Pure Reason*. Indianapolis: Hackett Publishing, 1999.
Kaufman, Michael. "The Dangers of Letting a President Read." *The New York Times*, 22 May 1999. http://query.nytimes.com/gst/fullpage.html?res=9E00E6D61631F931A15756COA96F958260&partner=rssnyt&emc=rss. http://query.nytimes.com/gst/fullpage.html?res=9E00E6D61631F931A15756COA96F958260&sec=&spon=&pagewanted=all.
Keeley, James. "Towards a Foucauldian Analysis of International Regimes". *International Organization* Vol. 44, no. 1 (1999).
Kissinger, Henry. *Diplomacy*. New York: Simon and Schuster Paperbacks, 1994.
——"New World Disorder: The ill-considered war in Kosovo has undermined relations with China and Russia and put NATO at risk". *Newsweek* (31 May 1999).

Kola, Paulin. *The Search for the Greater Albania*. London: Hurst, 2003.

Kolossov, Vladimir. "Border Studies: Changing Perspectives and Theoretical Approaches". *Geopolitics* Vol. 10, no. 4 (2005).

Kratochwil, Friedrich. "International law as an approach to international ethics: A plea for a jurisprudential diagnostics". In *Ethics and International Affairs: Extents and Limits*, edited by Jean Marc Coicaud and Daniel Warner. Tokyo: The United Nations University Press, 2001.

Krisch, Nico. "Legality, Morality and the Dilemma of Humanitarian Intervention After Kosovo". *European Journal of International Law* Vol. 13, no. 1 (2002).

Kuhn, Thomas. *The Structure of Scientific Revolutions*. Chicago: University of Chicago Press, 1970.

Kustermans, Jorg. "Walker, R.B.J. (1993), Inside/outside: International Relations as Political Theory, Cambridge/New York: Cambridge University Press" IPIS Book Review http://www.ipisresearch.be/download.php?id=125.

Lapid, Yosef. "Through Dialogue to Engaged Pluralism: The Unfinished Business of the Third Debate". *International Studies Review* Vol. 5, no. 1 (2003).

Lecourt, Dominique. *Marxism and Epistemology: Bachelard, Canguilhem, Foucault*. London: New Left Books, 1975.

Lewin, Roger. *Complexity: Life at the Edge of Chaos*. Chicago: University of Chicago Press, 2000.

Linklater, Andrew. "Neoralism in Theory and Practice". In *International Relations Theory Today*, edited by Steve Smith and Ken Booth. Oxford: Polity Press, 1995.

Littman, Mark. *Kosovo: Law and Diplomacy*. Paper published by Chamaleon Press: Centre for Policy Studies, November 1999.

Lyotard, Jean-François. *The Postmodern Condition: A Report on Knowledge*. Minneapolis: University of Minnesota Press, 1984.

Maas, Peter. *Love Thy Neighbor: A Story of War*. New York: Knopf, 1995.

MacDonald, David Bruce. *Balkan Holocaust? Serbian and Croatian Victim-centred Propaganda and the War in Yugoslavia*. Manchester: Manchester University Press, 2002.

Malcom, Noel. *Kosovo: A Short History*. Basingstoke: Macmillan, 1998.

Mamadouh, Virginie and Gertjan Dijkink. "Geopolitics, International Relations and Political Geography: The Politics of Geopolitical Discourse". *Geopolitics* Vol. 11, no. 3 (2006).

Manzer, Karl. *Thinking in Complexity: The Complex Dynamics of Matter, Mind, and Mankind*. Berlin: Springer-Verlag, 2004.

Martin, Pierre and Mark Brawley. *Alliance Politics, Kosovo and NATO's War: Alliance or Forced Allies*? London: Palgrave, 2001.

MccgWire, Michael. "Why did we bomb Belgrade?" *International Affairs* Vol. 76, no. 1 (2000).

Meirik, Karen. "Controversial Srebenica Report Back on Table", the Institute for Peace and War Reporting, 6 February 2004: http://www.iwpr.net/?p=tri&cs=f&o=166497&apc_state=henitri2004.

Mertus, Julie. *Kosovo: How Myths and Truths Started a War*. London, Berkeley: University of California Press, 1999.
Morçol, Goktug. "What Is Complexity Science? Postmodernist or Postpositivist?" *Emergence* Vol. 3, no. 1 (2002).
Mueller, John. "The Banality of 'Ethnic War'". *International Security* Vol. 25, no. 1 (2000).
Nietzsche, Friedrich. *The Gay Science: With a Prelude of Rhymes and an Appendix of Songs*. New York: Vintage Books Edition, 1974.
——*Twilight of the Idols, Or How to Philosophise with a Hammer.* Oxford: Oxford University Press, 1998.
Norris, John. *Collision Course*. London: Praeger, 2005.
Norton-Taylor, Richard. "Serb TV Station was Legitimate Target, says Blair". *The Guardian* (Manchester), 24 April 1999.
O'Loughlin, John and Vladimir Kolossov. "Still Not Worth the Bones of a Single Pomeranian Grenadier: The Geopolitics of the Kosovo War 1999". *Political Geography* Vol. 21 (2002).
Orend, Brian. "Michael Walzer on Resorting to Force". *Canadian Journal of Political Science* Vol. 33, no. 3 (2000).
O'Sullivan, Chris. "The News Media and the Resolution of Ethnic Conflict: Ready for the Next Steps?". *The Global Review of Ethnopolitics* Vol. 1, no. 2 (2001).
Ó Tuathail, Gearóid. *Critical Geopolitics*. London: Routledge, 1996.
Ó Tuathail, Gearóid and Carl Dahlman. "The Clash of Governmentalities: Displacement and Return in Bosnia Herzegovina". In *Global Governmentality: Governing International Spaces* edited by Wendy Larner and William Walters. London: Routledge, 2004.
Owen, David. *Balkan Odyssey*. New York: Harcourt Brace, 1995.
Pearson, Keith Ansell. *An Introduction to Nietzsche as a Political Thinker*. Cambridge: Cambridge University Press, 1994.
——*Philosophy and the Adventure of the Virtual. Bergson and the Time of Life*. London: Routledge, 2002.
Petrović, Edit. "Ethnonationalism and the Dissolution of Yugoslavia". In *Neighbors at War: Anthropological Perspectives on Yugoslav Ethnicity, Culture, and History*, edited by Joel Martin Halpern and David Kideckel. Penn: Penn State Press, 2000.
Popolo, Damian. "French Philosophy, Complexity, and Scientific Epistemology: Moving beyond the Modern Episteme". *Emergence* Vol. 5, no. 1 (2003).
——"Complexity in a Complex Europe: Reflections on the Cultural Genesis of a New Science". *Emergence: Complexity and Organisation* Vol. 8, no. 2 (2006).
——"Complexity in a Complex Europe: Reflections on the Cultural Genesis of a New Science". In *Thinking Complexity: Complexity and Philosophy*, edited by Paul Cilliers. Mansfield, MA: ISCE Publishing, 2007.
——"Complexity as an Epistemic Revolution: Considerations on the New Science in the Context of Western Intellectual History". In *Philosophy and Complexity – Worldviews, Science and Us*, edited by Carlos Gershenson. London: World Scientific, 2007.

Popov, Nebojša. *The Road to War in Serbia: Trauma and Catharsis*. Budapest: Central University Press, 2000.

Popper, Karl. *Conjectures and Refutations: The Growth of Scientific Knowledge*. London, Routledge, 2002.

Prigogine, Ilya. *From Being to Becoming: Time and Complexity in the Physical Sciences*. San Francisco: W.H. Freeman, 1980.

Prigogine, Ilya and Isabelle Stengers. *The End of Certainty: Time, Chaos, and the New Laws of Nature*. New York: Free Press, 1997.

Protevi, John. *Political Physics: Deleuze, Derrida and the Body Politic*. London: Continuum, Athlone, 2001.

Proust, M. *Remembrance of Things Past (In Search of Lost Time)*. France, Grasset and Gallimard, 1913–1927.

Quine, Willard Van Orman. "Two Dogmas of Empiricism". In *From a Logical Point of View*, edited by Willard Van Orman Quine. Cambridge MA: Harvard University Press, 1951.

Ramet, Sabrina Petra and Vjeran Pavlaković. *Serbia Since 1989: Politics and Society under Milošević and After*. Washington: University of Washington Press, 2005.

Rasch, William and Cary Wolfe, eds. *Observing Complexity: Systems Theory and the Postmodern Episteme*. Minneapolis: University of Minnesota Press, 2000.

——"Immanent Systems, Transcendental Temptations, and the Limits of Ethics". In *Observing Complexity: Systems Theory and the Postmodern Episteme*, edited by William Rasch and Cary Wolfe. Minneapolis: University of Minnesota Press, 2000.

Restuccia, Maria Rosario. "Deleuze E Bergson". *Cannochiale* Vol. 1, no. 2 (1983).

Robbins, Stephen. "Semantics, Experience and Time". *Cognitive Systems Research* Vol. 3, no. 3 (2002).

Roche, Jean Jacques. *Théories des Relations Internationales*. Paris: Montchrestien, 1999.

Romijn, Peter and JCH Blom. *Srebrenica: A Safe Area. Reconstruction, Background, Consequences and Analyses of the Fall of the Safe Area*. Amsterdam: Netherlands Institute for War Documentation, 2002. Available online at: http://www.niod.ni/default.asp.

Rosenau, James. *Turbulence in World Politics, a Theory of Change and Continuity*. New Jersey: Princeton University Press, 1992.

Ruggie, John Gerard. "Continuity and Transformation in the World Polity: Toward a Neorealist Synthesis". In *Neorealism and its Critics*, edited by Robert Keohane. New York: Columbia University Press, 1985.

——"Territoriality and Beyond: Problematizing Modernity in International Relations". *International Organization* Vol. 47, no. 1 (1993).

Rüth, Alexandra and Mirja Trilsch. "Bancovič v Belgium, Admissibility, Application No. 52207/99". *The American Journal of International Law* Vol. 97, no. 1 (2003).

Schmitt, Carl. *The Concept of the Political.* Chicago: Chicago University Press, 1996.

Schnabel, Albrecht and Ramesh Thakur, eds. *Kosovo and the Challenge of Humanitarian Intervention: Selective Indignation, Collective Action, and International Citizenship.* Tokyo: United Nations Press, 2000.

Sekelj, Laslo. *Yugoslavia: The Process of Disintegration.* Highland Lakes: Atlantic Research and Publications, 1992.

Selby, Jan. "Engaging Foucault: Discourse, Liberal Governance and the Limits of Foucauldian IR". *International Relations* Vol. 21, no. 3 (2007).

Sell, Louis. *Slobodan Milošević and the Destruction of Yugoslavia.* Durham: Duke University Press, 2003.

Sheard, Stephen. "Complexity Theory and Continental Philosophy Part 1: A Review of Letiche's Phenomenological Complexity Theory". In *Thinking Complexity: Complexity and Philosophy*, edited Paul Cilliers. Mansfield: ISCE Publishing, 2007.

Sloterdijk, Peter. *Critique of Cynical Reason.* Minneapolis: University of Minnesota Press, 1987.

Smith, Martin. *The Kosovo Crisis and the Evolution of Post Cold War European Security.* Manchester: Manchester University Press, 2003.

Smith, Martin and Graham Timmins. *Uncertain Europe: Building a New Security Order?* London: Routledge, 2001.

Smith, Steve. "Positivism and Beyond". In *International Theory: Positivism and Beyond*, edited by Ken Booth, Steve Smith and Marysia Zalewski. Cambridge: Cambridge University Press, 1996.

——"The Discipline of International Relations: Still an American Social Science?". *The British Journal of Politics and International Relations* Vol. 2, no. 3 (2000).

Smith, Steve and Ken Booth, eds. *International Relations Theory Today.* London: Polity Press, 1995.

Smith, Steve and Martin Hollis. *Explaining and Understanding International Relations.* Cambridge: Cambridge University Press, 1996.

Smouts, Marie-Claude. *Les Nouvelles Relations Internationales.* Paris: Presses de Science Politique, 1998.

Sokal, Alan and Jean Bricmont. *Fashionable Nonsense: Postmodern Intellectual's Abuse of Science.* New York: Picador, 1999.

Sterling-Folker, Jennifer. *Making Sense of International Relations Theory.* Boulder: Lynne Rienner, 2006.

Strange, Susan. "International Relations and Political Economy, a Case of Mutual Neglect". *International Affairs* Vol. 46, no. 2 (1970).

Strauss, Julian. "Military 'Death Squads' Behind Kosovo Massacre." *Daily Telegraph*, 27 January 1999.

Thomas, Robert. *Serbia under Milošević.* London: Hurst and Co. Publishers, 1999.

Tomasello, Michael. *The Cultural Origins of Human Cognition*. Cambridge: Harvard University Press, 2003.

Tsagourias, Nikolaos. *Jurisprudence of International Law: The Humanitarian Dimension*. Manchester: Manchester University Press, 2000.

Turner, Frederick. "Foreword". In *Chaos, Complexity, and Sociology: Myths, Models, and Theories*, edited by Raymond Eve, Sara Horsfall and Mary E. Lee. Thousand Oaks, California: Sage Publications, 1997.

United Nations Security Council. Press Release, SC/6870, 2 June 2000. www.un.org.

Urry, John. *Global Complexity*. Polity Press, 2002.

Van Ham, Peter and Sergei Medvedev. *Mapping European Security After Kosovo*. Manchester: Manchester University Press, 2002.

Veremis, Thanos and Evangelos Kofos. *Kosovo: Avoiding another Balkan War*. Athens: Hellenic Foundation for European Foreign Policy and University of Athens, 1998.

Vetlesen, Arne Johan. *Evil and Human Agency: Understanding Collective Evildoing*. Cambridge: Cambridge University Press, 2005.

Vickers, Miranda. *Between Serbs and Albanians: A History of Kosovo*. London: Hurst, 1998.

Waller, Michael; Kyril Drezov and Bulent Gokay. *Kosovo: The Politics of Delusion*. London, Portland: Frank Cass, 2001.

Wallerstein, Immanuel. *Open the Social Sciences: Report of the Gulbenkian Commission on the Restructuring of the Social Sciences*. Stanford: Stanford University Press, 1996.

Waltz, Kenneth. *Theory of International Politics*. New York: McGraw-Hill, 1979.

——"Laws and Theories". In *Neorialism and its Critics*, edited by Robert Keohane. New York: Columbia University Press, 1986.

——"Political Structures". In *Neorialism and its Critics*, edited by Robert Keohane. New York: Columbia University Press, 1986.

——"A Response to my Critics". In *Neorialism and its Critics*, edited by Robert Keohane. New York: Columbia University Press, 1986.

—— "Realist Thought and Neorealist Theory". *Journal of International Affairs* Vol. 44, no. 1 (1990).

——"Structural Realism after the Cold War". *International Security* Vol. 25, no. 1 (2000).

——*Man, the State, and War: A Theoretical Analysis*. New York: Columbia University Press, 2001.

Weller, Marc. *The Crisis in Kosovo 1989–1999: from the Dissolution of Yugoslavia to Rambouillet and the Outbreak of Hostilities*. Cambridge: Documents and Analysis Publishing, 1999.

Wendt, Arendt. *Social Theory of International Politics*. Cambridge: Cambridge University Press, 1999.

Wheeler, Nicholas. *Saving Strangers: Humanitarian Intervention in International Society*. Oxford, New York: Oxford University Press, 2000.

Winnifrith, Tom. *Shattered Eagles, Balkan Fragments*. London: Duckworth, 1995.

Woodward, Susan. *Balkan Tragedy: Chaos and Dissolution after the Cold War*. Washington: Brookings, 1995.

Žižek, Slavoj. *Organs without Bodies: On Deleuze and Consequences*. London: Routledge, 2004.

——*The Universal Exception*. London: Continuum International Publishing Group, 2005.

——*Against the Double Blackmail*, http://www.lacan.com/kosovo.htm.

Index

For Product Safety Concerns and Information please contact our EU representative GPSR@taylorandfrancis.com
Taylor & Francis Verlag GmbH, Kaufingerstraße 24, 80331 München, Germany

www.ingramcontent.com/pod-product-compliance
Ingram Content Group UK Ltd.
Pitfield, Milton Keynes, MK11 3LW, UK
UKHW011003180926
475701UK00004B/533

* 9 7 8 1 1 3 8 3 7 9 6 9 5 *